PRAISE FOR *THINKING WITH YOUR HANDS*

"Gesture is all around us, but we often fail to understand its importance. In this book, Susan Goldin-Meadow shows how gesture forms an essential parallel to language, one that provides a unique window into our thoughts. *Thinking with Your Hands* reveals a hidden dimension of human communication."

—CAROL DWECK, author of *Mindset*

"Goldin-Meadow has expanded our understanding of language with her fascinating research on gesturing, and in this book, she illuminates the nature of gesture and its intimate relationship to language and communication. *Thinking With Your Hands* is rich with information and insight."

—STEVEN PINKER, author of *The Language Instinct*

"Goldin-Meadow has astonished the scientific community time and again with her pathbreaking discoveries. Now she has written a tour de force for the rest of the world to benefit from. *Thinking with Your Hands* is one of those rare books that doesn't just entertain and inform but changes the way you think about yourself and the people around you. It should be required reading for anyone who has ever used their hands to convey an idea or witnessed someone else do the same, which is to say, all of us."

—ETHAN KROSS, bestselling author of *Chatter*

"We modern humans swim in a sea of words, both written and spoken. Goldin-Meadow reveals a deeper current of communication: the gestures we make with our hands. Her book is a fascinating exploration of the way gesture shapes how we learn, how we interact, even how we imagine and create. *Thinking with Your Hands* is an accessible and enjoyable book by the researcher who remade the field."

—ANNIE MURPHY PAUL, author of *The Extended Mind*

"This fascinating book will make you watch others' hands—and be aware of your own. You will think differently about the nature of language, the nature of communication, and about the many ways gestures can change your own thought and that of others."

—BARBARA TVERSKY, author of *Mind in Motion*

"*Thinking with Your Hands* gives us an inspirational overview of a lifetime of work on an aspect of human behavior that is fundamental to who we are as a species. With humor and humility, Goldin-Meadow introduces us to the inner workings of gesture and the tireless efforts of those scientists trying to understand it. Richly illustrating her explanations with a huge array of thought-provoking examples, she reveals how our hands help us think and convey information about our unspoken inner world; what gesture can tell us about the evolution of language; and how understanding gesture could help us become better parents, doctors, and teachers. This is an accessible, eye-opening, and endlessly fascinating account from the undisputed authority in the field."

—SIMON KIRBY, head of linguistics, University of Edinburgh

"*Thinking with Your Hands* provides a fascinating look into the universal human phenomenon of gesturing in both children and adults. Gesture is a critically important component of human communication, and this book is a wonderful and enjoyable contribution to its understanding. I highly recommend it."

—HENRY L. ROEDIGER III, James S. McDonnell Distinguished University Professor, Washington University in St. Louis

"Young children communicate in rich ways with gestures before language. With the acquisition of language, their gestures take on new functions—not just for communication but for supporting thinking. Goldin-Meadow's new book tells this story, much of it based on her own research, with both wisdom and wit."

—MICHAEL TOMASELLO, Duke University

THINKING WITH YOUR HANDS

THE SURPRISING SCIENCE BEHIND HOW GESTURES SHAPE OUR THOUGHTS

SUSAN GOLDIN-MEADOW

BASIC BOOKS
New York

Basic Books
Hachette Book Group
1290 Avenue of the Americas, New York, NY 10104
www.basicbooks.com

Printed in the United States of America

First Edition: June 2023

Published by Basic Books, an imprint of Perseus Books, LLC, a subsidiary of Hachette Book Group, Inc. The Basic Books name and logo is a trademark of the Hachette Book Group.

The Hachette Speakers Bureau provides a wide range of authors for speaking events. To find out more, go to hachettespeakersbureau.com or email HachetteSpeakers@hbgusa.com.

Basic books may be purchased in bulk for business, educational, or promotional use. For information, please contact your local bookseller or Hachette Book Group Special Markets Department at special.markets@hbgusa.com.

The publisher is not responsible for websites (or their content) that are not owned by the publisher.

Illustrations © Linda K. Huff

Print book interior design by Jeff Williams.

Library of Congress Cataloging-in-Publication Data

Names: Goldin-Meadow, Susan, author.
Title: Thinking with your hands : the surprising science behind how gestures shape our
    thoughts / Susan Goldin-Meadow.
Description: First edition. | New York : Basic Books, 2023. | Includes bibliographical
    references and index.
Identifiers: LCCN 2022041572 | ISBN 9781541600805 (hardcover) | ISBN
    9781541600652 (ebook)
Subjects: LCSH: Body language. | Gesture—Psychological aspects. | Thought and
    thinking. | Cognition.
Classification: LCC BF637.N66 G647 2023 | DDC 153.6/9—dc23/eng/20230201
LC record available at https://lccn.loc.gov/2022041572

ISBNs: 9781541600805 (hardcover), 9781541600652 (ebook)

LSC-C

Printing 1, 2023

*This book is dedicated with profound love
and respect to my late husband Bill,*

*the best gesturer and most caring husband, father, friend,
coach, teacher, mentor, and doctor that I have ever
known, for being half of an everlasting team*

ALSO BY SUSAN GOLDIN-MEADOW

Hearing Gesture:
How Our Hands Help Us Think

The Resilience of Language:
What Gesture Creation in Deaf Children Can Tell Us
About How All Children Learn Language

Language in Mind:
Advances in the Study of Language and Thought

Gesture in Language:
Development Across the Lifespan

CONTENTS

INTRODUCTION

My Journey into Gesture

DURING SEASON 4 OF *THE CROWN*, LADY DIANA, SOON TO BECOME Princess Diana, gets a quick lesson on how to behave in royal society, including how to use—or not use—her hands when she speaks. Her teacher actually ties up her hands with string, saying, "Gestures reveal us, whether we are anxious, or agitated, or cross. It's best not to give that away. One should never try to show one's emotions." Diana's teacher believes, as most people do, that your gestures reveal your feelings.[1]

I agree with Diana's teacher. There is a vast body of work on nonverbal behavior showing that your gestures can reveal your emotions. But that's not all gestures can do. They can also reveal your thoughts. They can tell the world not only that you're angry but also what you might be angry about and why. And the thoughts you express in gesture don't always appear in your speech, as this example illustrates.

A native speaker of Guugu Yimithirr in Queensland, Australia, was out fishing one day when his boat overturned, rolling to the west. After he got back to shore, he recounted the harrowing experience to a group of onlookers. He talked about the boat

1

overturning, and as he did, he produced a rolling motion away from his body. He happened to be facing west, so his gesture rolled from east to west. On another occasion two years later, he was asked to tell the story again, but this time he was, by chance, facing north rather than west. He produced the rolling-over gesture again, but now his hands rolled from right to left. In other words, despite the awkwardness of the movement, his gesture again moved from east to west. He never explicitly *said* that the boat rolled from east to west. But he didn't have to—his hands said it for him.[2]

This book is about the movements we make with our hands when we speak—our gestures—and what they can tell us about our thinking. Etiquette expert Emily Post tells us that to be good conversationalists, we may use our hands to punctuate a point, but excessive gesturing is distracting. In her view, a proper amount of gesture should accompany speech, dictated by etiquette and not by what you want to say. I think Emily Post is wrong about gesturing: the thoughts you have and want to communicate, not your manners, should dictate your gestures.[3]

One way to make your thoughts known is to talk about them. Another is to write about them. In fact, most people consider language to be the fundamental substance of thought. Some go so far as to say that language is required to have thoughts in the first place—that prelinguistic children don't really think; nor do language-less animals. We see language as the medium through which we understand, or misunderstand, one another. If you have ever wondered whether your child is developing apace, whether a student understands what you're trying to teach them, or whether your coworker really agrees with your proposal, chances are you're looking for answers in what is *said*. But, as we will see, children's gestures can tell you whether they are on track; your student's gestures can tell you whether you are getting through; and your coworkers' gestures can reveal thoughts they don't want to say or don't even know they have. Language is only one window—and maybe not always the best one—into your thoughts. Languages, both spoken and signed, are rule-governed systems that package information into categories. Gesture assumes a less discrete and more pictorial form and, as such, provides a complementary and, I argue, essential vantage point onto the mind.

I focus here on thoughts that are hidden in your hands. You may not be consciously aware of them, but you're thinking them. It may surprise (and dismay) you to know that, because they are displayed in your hands, these thoughts are visible to others; everyone is able to read the thoughts your hands express. This means an undercurrent of conversation is taking place when we speak, one that is often unacknowledged. If we want to fully communicate with others, and maybe even with ourselves, we need to understand what's happening with our hands.

I also argue that focusing exclusively on language as the foundation of communication is wrong. It relies on an incomplete understanding of how the mind works, interfering with our ability to fully understand each other and ourselves. For fifty years, I have been studying how and why people gesture, and I have come to believe that gesture not only reveals our attitudes and feelings about ourselves, our listeners, and the conversation between us, but also contributes to the conversation itself. When Diana's teacher ties up her hands, she keeps Diana not only from betraying her emotions but also from expressing her ideas.

Let's take an example from March Madness, the annual basketball tournament of the National Collegiate Athletic Association. On March 20, 2022, Gonzaga was playing Memphis and was behind at the end of the first half when the referees called a shooting foul on Drew Timme, a Gonzaga player. His coach, Mark Few, made his displeasure known by furrowing his brow, a facial gesture that revealed his emotions. But it was his hand gesture—an extended point at the screen on the scoreboard where the presumed foul was being replayed—that got him into trouble. The point connected the coach's emotion with the foul—it may have been obvious that he felt angry, but the gesture made clear that he thought the call was wrong—and now everyone in the stadium knew it. That gesture also earned him a technical foul, which gave Memphis additional free throws and put Gonzaga further behind. As Gene Steratore, a rules analyst and retired referee himself, put it, "You expect some verbal . . . but when you start pointing, when you start gesturing, physically, that optic is not good for the game." Hand gestures say what's on your mind—even when keeping it to yourself would be wiser.

But why do we gesture at all when we already have language? To answer that question, we need to know a little something about how our minds work. Imagine a world in which all forms of language (spoken, signed, written) have been wiped out, along with everyone's knowledge of these forms, but everything else stays the same. If you were living in this world, you would continue to think, but obviously not in your language. How would you communicate your thoughts?

It may sound like an impossible test to carry out, but my research explores an even more extreme scenario. Would you communicate if you had never been exposed to language and, if so, what would that communication look like? Of course, we cannot ethically deprive a child of linguistic input. We can, however, take advantage of what we might call an *experiment of nature*—a situation in which a child, often for complex reasons, is *not* exposed to linguistic input. Consider, for example, a child whose hearing losses are so profound that he cannot hear, and therefore cannot learn, the spoken language that his hearing parents use to communicate. If this child is also not exposed to a sign language, he will lack usable linguistic input. Will the child communicate?

This question followed me through my early years as an undergraduate at Smith College. Smith is in Northampton, Massachusetts, down the street from the Clark School for the Deaf, which was, and still is, a premier school that focuses on training deaf children to produce and understand spoken language. Over time, the field of deaf education has come to realize that not every deaf child can develop this ability, and the school now tries to identify the students who are likely to succeed at learning spoken language. But when I was an undergraduate nearby, many deaf children who went to the Clark School failed in this effort. The rumor, which I confirmed when watching children out of the teacher's view, was that even children who were having trouble using spoken language in their classes were able to communicate with one another—using their hands. Children who are not exposed to usable linguistic input can communicate, and they use their hands to do so. The next question is whether this communication shares enough properties with the languages used around the world to be considered a language in its own right.

Propelled by what I'd witnessed as an undergraduate, I decided to focus my graduate studies at the University of Pennsylvania on language and how it is developed. At Penn, I met Professor Lila Gleitman and fellow graduate student Heidi Feldman. Lila and Heidi were interested in the same questions I was, so we began by meeting the deaf community and learning sign language ourselves—until we realized that the children we wanted to study were *not* part of the deaf community. We wanted to study children born to hearing parents who didn't know sign language and may never have even met a deaf person before their child was born. The parents wanted their children to learn to speak and did not seek out the deaf community.

We began visiting local oral schools for deaf children (like the Clark School), asking if we could observe some of their students. The hearing parents of six deaf children gave us permission to videotape their children as they interacted naturally at home with them and with us. The parents spoke to their children—language that the children could not hear and therefore could not learn. The parents also did not know a sign language—language that their children could have learned but were not exposed to. Like the hypothetical adults in the far-fetched scenario I asked you to imagine who find themselves suddenly language-less, these children are surrounded by the modern world but lack a way to communicate their thoughts. However, the children in our studies never had a language—the adults I asked you to imagine would have had a language before all language disappeared.

We found that each of these deaf children communicated with the hearing people in their worlds and used their hands to do so. The hand movements are called *homesigns* (because they were created in the home) and the children *homesigners*. All animal species communicate in some way—bees, ants, and dolphins use sights, smells, and sounds to communicate with each other—so it's hardly surprising that a human child will communicate even under challenging circumstances.[4]

The crucial question is whether the hand movements that the deaf children make to communicate resemble human language. To address this question, we compared the deaf children to other children in the early stages of acquiring a conventional language. At the time, there was relatively little research on deaf children learning sign language from their deaf parents, so we focused on hearing children learning spoken language from their hearing parents. We found striking similarities not only in the topics that the deaf children and the hearing children communicated about but also in how the two groups structured their communications. The deaf children's homesigns were simple—they were children, after all—but they had many of the features found in human language, signed or spoken. In an important sense, homesign looks and acts more like sign language than like the gestures that accompany speech.

One possibility may be nagging at you, as it nagged at me— maybe the deaf children's *hearing parents* fashioned the homesigns to overcome the language barrier, and their children copied the signs from their parents. If so, the parents, not the children, would have invented homesign. The only model the deaf children had for their homesigns was the gestures their hearing family members used as they talked to them—known as *co-speech gestures*. But, importantly, the deaf children's homesigns did not look like their parents' gestures. My collaborators and I have studied deaf children from many countries, including the United States, China, Turkey, and Nicaragua, none of whom know one another. Yet they all do the same thing: they build a language from scratch with their hands, without learning the language from their hearing parents. The disparity between the deaf children's homesigns and their hearing parents' gestures underscores two important points. First, the deaf children, not their hearing parents, are inventing their homesign systems. Second, homesign looks different from co-speech gesture.

What does homesign look like? Perhaps it looks like mime. Homesigners could communicate information by enacting events as a mime would. As the example below illustrates, world-famous mime Marcel Marceau's fluid and continuous movements as he mimes eating an apple capture the experience. Mimes attempt to replicate (and maybe even exaggerate) the actual movements made when grabbing an apple and eating it.

  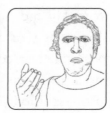 

But homesigners don't mime. They don't replicate the actual movements of an event. Instead, they break a scene into parts and then combine gestures for each part into a structured string. Their gestures look like a string of discrete movements rather than one unbroken movement. Homesign highlights the aspects of eating that are most informative, leaving out subtle details of the act—a point at an apple, followed by an EAT gesture (fingers touching the thumb while jabbing at the mouth). The picture below depicts a real homesigner who happened to be holding a toy hammer while gesturing and, as a result, produced his gestures with the hammer in hand, making those gestures look even less like the act of eating: point with the hammer at the apple; EAT performed with the hammer in hand; point with the hammer at me to invite me to eat an apple. Homesign looks like beads on a string rather than a picture painted in the air and, in this sense, resembles sign language more closely than mime.

Homesign is created by individual children who aren't exposed to a conventional language. As a result, it reveals the structures that children impose on their communications when they don't have a language to learn from. Studying homesign strips away the effect of linguistic traditions, the buildup of language changes that accumulate over generations, which allows us to better see how the mind structures language. Some deaf educators in the past assumed that profoundly deaf children who could not learn a spoken language were not able to think (at the time these educators did not consider sign language a legitimate language). The homesigns that deaf children create make clear that this assumption is wrong. Homesigners do think, and they communicate their thoughts. Homesign provides the best evidence we have for properties of mind that humans bring to language.

But most people use their mouths for language. What do they do with their hands when they're talking? They gesture. Homesigners use their gestures to take on the full burden of communication—*as a language*. In contrast, speakers use their gestures along with language and as a supplement to it—*as co-speech gesture*. It's easy to understand the need for gesture when you don't have a language, but that doesn't explain why you gesture when you do have a language.

As we've already established, co-speech gestures are a frequent part of communication—even in speakers who have never seen anyone gesture. Individuals who were born blind move their hands just like sighted people do when they talk. You don't need to have seen anyone gesture in order to gesture yourself. And gesturing happens all over the world, not only in all speaking cultures but also in signing cultures. Signers use their hands for language, and those sign languages share structural properties with spoken language. Like speakers, signers produce gestures along with their language. These co-sign gestures are distinct in form and function from sign language and share many qualities with co-speech gestures. Facts like this convince us that gesture is a pervasive, although often overlooked, human behavior. The facts also hint that language, on its own, may not be capable of expressing the full range of human thought.

The categories involved in language's rule-governed systems make it easy, even necessary, to express certain types of information. For example, English requires that you choose a verb that agrees with the number of objects you're talking about. If you say, "The fish *is* swimming," you're clearly talking about one fish. If you say, "The fish *are* swimming," you're talking about more than one fish. The number of fish that are swimming may not be relevant to your conversation, but that doesn't matter—English requires you to specify whether it's one fish or more than one.

Singular versus plural verbs make it easy to convey information like quantity, but they don't help you convey other types of information. That's where gesture comes in. If you outline a tight circle with your index finger as you say, "The fish are swimming," you suggest to your listener that the fish are swimming in a bowl. A more expansive gesture might indicate that the fish are swimming in an outdoor environment, like a pond or lake. Gesture can help you convey thoughts that do not fit neatly into the prepackaged units provided by your language.

The ideas that you embed in your gestures clearly reflect your thinking, but those thoughts are rarely explicitly recognized as such—their communicative power is subtle to both speakers and listeners. Ideas that you don't want to express in speech, that you don't yet know how to express in speech, or that you generally don't want to focus on will often appear in your hands. And you won't necessarily be held accountable for having expressed those ideas in your hands because we consider language, not gesture, to be our primary vehicle of communication.

Imagine a friend who earnestly tells you that he thinks men and women are equally good leaders. But when he talks about men's leadership skills, he gestures at eye level, and when he talks about women's leadership skills, he gestures a bit lower, at mouth level. He may think that he believes in the equality of male and female leadership, but his hands have given him away. This isn't necessarily an instance of trying to conceal his views. Your friend may really believe that he has an egalitarian view of men and women as leaders. The nonegalitarian view displayed in his hands is an implicit, internalized belief, one that he doesn't realize he holds. Yet his unspoken and unacknowledged belief was expressed and can be read by all, including his listener, who challenges him on his nonegalitarian views. He is offended because he *said* he believed men and women are equally good leaders. But his listener swears he heard him say otherwise, not fully realizing why.

In the Watergate hearings, witnesses who testified were convinced that Richard Nixon had said incriminating things. But the incriminating words didn't always show up on the tapes, raising doubts about the witnesses' testimony. Anything incriminating that was "said" in gesture would have shown up on a video but *not* on an audio recording of the conversation. Perceptions of what was or wasn't said, and therefore what is or isn't the "truth," were based on speech and gesture for those present in the room but only on speech for those listening to a recording—and those perceptions were likely to differ. You may have heard that when Nixon ran against John F. Kennedy for the presidency for the first time (and lost), people who saw their debates on television thought Kennedy had won, but those who heard the debates over the radio thought Nixon had won. The nonverbal realm, including gesture, influences what observers take from a speech or conversation.[5]

Gesture does seem to have a special hold on the truth. One of my former graduate students, Amy Franklin, in her dissertation, told adults to describe a series of vignettes from a Tweety Bird cartoon. In half of the descriptions, they were supposed to describe what they saw. In half, they were supposed to mis-describe the event by, for example, saying the cat jumped to the pole when he actually ran to the pole. The adults did as they were told and mis-described the events—at least in speech. But the truth came out—through their hands. They produced a running gesture while saying that the cat jumped.[6]

Sometimes the stakes regarding what is said or unsaid can be particularly high. Even if you are a trained lawyer, you may not appreciate the power that gestures give you to read your witnesses' minds. Imagine a child witness describing the person who allegedly abused him. While talking, he makes a GLASSES gesture—he makes a circle with his right index finger and thumb and another with his left and holds the circles up at his eyes. He doesn't mention glasses when he speaks, which means that glasses are not part of the transcript. When the lawyer next asks, "Was he wearing glasses?" it reads like he's asking a leading question. But he isn't—glasses were introduced into the conversation not by the lawyer but by the child, through his gestures. The child hadn't even realized he had noticed the glasses; he had unconsciously registered them and depicted them later only with his hands. The lawyer didn't realize that the child *had not actually said* the word *glasses*—if he had recognized that the glasses idea came from the child's gestures, he would have mentioned the gestures explicitly since only the transcript of what is said counts as legal evidence. The lawyer brought up glasses because he *thought* he heard the child say *glasses*, but the child had merely gestured.

Communication goes both ways, and lawyers use gesture not only to see into their witnesses' minds but, more ominously, to influence those minds. Generally, lawyers are supposed to ask open-ended rather than leading questions: "What else was he wearing?" rather than "What color was the hat he was wearing?" But if you ask an open-ended question ("What else was he wearing?") while making a HAT gesture (tipping your fist toward your head), witnesses are very likely to mention a hat even if there wasn't one—just as likely as if the lawyer had asked a leading question in speech ("What color was the hat he was wearing?"). Gesture can cue objects or events and, in so doing, bring them to mind. Gesture is already a powerful tool, but in contexts where speech is highly regulated, it can become even more influential.

Of course, gestures don't exist simply to give your thoughts away. Gestures help you express ideas that are on the cusp of your understanding—ideas that you are in the process of learning. Imagine two identical tall, thin glasses, each containing the same amount of water, which the child looks at and verifies. The water is poured from one of the tall, thin glasses into a short, wide glass, and the child is asked whether the amount of water in the still-full tall glass is the same as the amount of water in the short glass. You or I would say, "Of course." But at a certain stage, children are convinced that the amount is different. When asked to justify her misguided belief, the child in the drawing below says that the amount is different "cause that's down lower than that one." She focuses on the height of the liquid in her speech. But, at the same time, she tells us with her gestures, and only her gestures, that she has noticed the width—she uses two C-shaped hands to indicate the fat width of the shorter glass (illustration on the left) and a single C-shaped hand to indicate the thin width of the taller glass (illustration on the right).

"Cause that's down lower"   "than that one"

In order to truly understand that the amount of water does not change when it's poured from a tall, thin glass into a short, wide one, you have to recognize that the larger width in the short glass compensates for its height. We know that the child in the example is not far from comprehending this concept, because when we later give her a lesson in conservation of quantity, she succeeds on the task. Her gestures tell us that she is ready to learn the principle.

Let's look at a more challenging example with adults. What would you do if you were asked to prove that two molecules are mirror images of one another and cannot be superimposed? These molecules are called stereoisomers, but you wouldn't know that if you hadn't studied organic chemistry. So you might not recognize that to check your solution, you would need to rotate one of the molecules around an axis. Think right and left hands, which are not superimposable—you can only cover your left hand with your right hand and have your thumbs align by rotating your right hand. As a result, you don't *say* anything about rotating the molecules when you're asked to explain your solution. However, you produce a rotation gesture with your hands along with your spoken explanation: you do know rotation is required; you just don't know that you know it! The student pictured below illustrates this point. He says, "You can't superimpose *this*" (while pointing at the drawing of the molecule hidden by his body on his left; the middle panel) "on top of *that*" (while pointing at the drawing of the molecule on his right; the last panel). He shows that he knows about rotation by circling his pointing finger in the air as he begins speaking (the first panel).

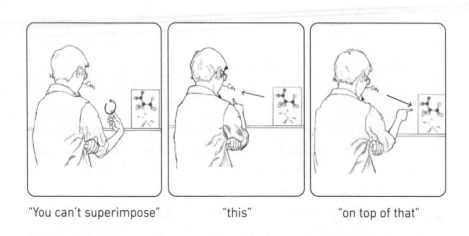

"You can't superimpose"   "this"   "on top of that"

If, after your explanation, you are taught more about stereoisomers, you are likely to improve your understanding of the concept and recognize the importance of rotation—more likely than if you had *not* produced the rotation gesture before the instruction. The rotation gesture you produced also lets your teacher know that you are thinking about rotation and that this is a perfect moment to explicitly introduce the notion into the lesson. Expressing that knowledge with your hands can help you develop, extend, and retain what you know.

Our word *idea* comes from a Greek word meaning *to see*. Gesture plays an important role in thinking and learning in part because it's so well suited to capturing ideas visually—to outlining shapes, recreating movements, and displaying transformations. Many of these ideas, thoughts, or beliefs can be expressed in language—it's just often more difficult to put them into words. If, for example, you want to describe the East Coast of the United States, you could describe in words what Maine looks like, moving down the coast to Florida. But a gesture outlining the coast would do the job much more efficiently and reliably and would include details that are awkward to express verbally—for example, the way in which Maine extends to the east beyond Florida. We use gesture to tailor an imperfect language to the needs of both speaker and listener. Unlike with language, we use gesture without recognizing its benefits—or its pitfalls. In fact, we undervalue gesture so much that we rarely realize that we're gesturing.

You probably think people gesture a lot less than they actually do. Take one of my studies designed to look at the gestures college students produce. At the end of the study, we debriefed the students and told them that we had been watching their gestures. They all apologized profusely for not having gestured. In fact, all of them had gestured quite a lot. They knew they had been talking—we all are aware when we talk—but they hadn't realized they were also moving their hands while they talked. One question I will address later in the book is what happens when we make people aware of their gestures. Does that awareness alter whether their gestures express their implicit, unspoken thoughts? If so, we should be careful about telling people to watch and produce gesture. But if not, consciously watching and producing certain gestures could be just what we need to make communication richer, deeper, and more connected.

This book will show you not only how your thoughts, beliefs, and ideas translate into your gestures but how gesture forces you to rethink the way you understand others. Knowing how gestures work could lead to fewer misunderstandings and deeper connections. It could also make you more aware of how communication technologies are inadvertently stymieing gesture and interfering with your ability to connect with and understand others. How can gesture be part of the conversation when you're holding your iPhone and its camera is trained to follow your face? And what about conversations via Zoom: the boxes on Zoom make it difficult to see the gestures of the person who is speaking, a limitation that makes education on Zoom a challenge at best. How can students learn from the gestures their teachers produce if the students' webcams can't pick up those gestures? And how can a teacher learn about students' minds from their gestures if those gestures aren't visible to them? Gesture is produced in all contexts—parenting, teaching, lawyering, doctoring, just hanging out. You can recognize and take advantage of the insights it offers and fundamentally change how deeply you communicate—or you can ignore it and miss half the conversation.

Before we go any further, I want to mention two caveats up front. When people hear that I work on gesture, they immediately assume I'm studying gestures like *thumbs-up*, *okay*, and *shhhh*—conventional gestures, called *emblems*, that everyone in a particular culture knows. These gestures always take the same form within those specific cultures. You form *thumbs-up* by pointing your thumb up in the air. Pointing your pinky up would not have the same effect. In fact, pointing the pinky up in Taiwan means *bad*, not *good*. Emblems fall outside my scope precisely because they do not change form to reflect a speaker's current thoughts— they are like words in a dictionary, with fixed forms and fixed meanings. I'm interested in what fluid gesture can tell us that fixed gestures and words can't.

The second caveat is that most of the studies described in this book involve children—that's because I'm a developmental psychologist who looks at change over childhood. However, I believe that the findings from studies of co-speech gesture in children will generalize to adults. The few studies that we have done with adults confirm this theory. By contrast, the studies of language creation in homesigning deaf children are more difficult to generalize to adults. Language creation, like language learning, may be something that comes more naturally to children than adults. But (thankfully) it's not easy to find someone who hasn't been exposed to language and is creating a language de novo *as an adult*, so we don't really know whether the homesign findings generalize from children to adults.

I have organized the book into three sections that explore the landscape of gesture studies and how understanding gesture can help us better understand each other. In Part I, I start with a behavior that we all do and can therefore relate to: gesturing while talking. But I don't just want to draw on your intuitions about gesturing; I want to show you how the science of gesture either confirms those intuitions or explains why they are wrong. My intuitions have been wrong many times, which is why we need science. As we go along, I'll point out where my intuitions were wrong and how our studies have informed and corrected them. In Part II, I consider situations where gesture is produced without speech—silent gesture—in order to understand how it differs from co-speech gesture. Silent gesture offers us insight into how the mind structures communication when there's no spoken language to constrain it. Part III takes what we've learned about gesture, with and without simultaneous speech, and shows what you can do with it.

Part I begins by exploring *why* you gesture: What makes you move your hands when you speak, and do these hand movements help you in any way? I then analyze the gestures that speakers produce when learning a new concept and offer evidence that learners can express ideas about concepts in their gestures that *cannot* be found in their speech. These gestures consequently offer a unique window into our minds. But gesture can do much more. It can go beyond reflecting our thoughts to changing those thoughts.

Gesture—the gestures others produce and the gestures you your-self produce—have the potential to help you learn. Part I illus-trates how gesture can reveal and shape thought and describes concrete scenarios where paying attention to gesture can help us all become more effective and thoughtful communicators.

Part II takes a closer look at the phenomenon I began studying in graduate school: deaf children who are *not* exposed to usable linguistic input and, as a result, are not learning language from their elders. Like hearing children, they use their hands to com-municate, but their gestures don't look like hearing children's gestures. This is surprising because, as previously mentioned, the only gestures that the deaf children see are their hearing parents' co-speech gestures. If the children's parents are providing a model for their children's gestures, homesigns ought to look like the ges-tures described in Part I: mimetic pictures drawn in the air. But they don't. Here's a guess as to why: the gestures that accom-pany speech work together with that speech; they can't commu-nicate fully without it. If homesigners are going to use gesture as their primary language, they are going to have to alter co-speech gesture to make it capable of standing on its own. And they do. The gestures homesigners create take on forms that character-ize language: discrete categories that combine with each other to express longer and longer thoughts. Homesigners create gestures that label objects, actions, and attributes, and combine them into strings that are structured and follow a consistent ordering—in other words, sentences.

Gesture in homesigners serves the function of a primary lan-guage and takes on the form of language. In contrast, gesture in speakers serves as an essential adjunct to language and takes on the form of mimetic *pictures in the air*. To crystallize these differ-ences, Part II also contrasts the homesign gestures that deaf chil-dren create with the co-speech gestures that their hearing parents produce. Homesign tells us what's special about co-speech gesture by showing us that its forms are not inevitable: they are not the gestures children use when they need to create a primary communication system.

In the last chapter of Part II, I explore how far a homesigner can go toward inventing human language. Although it's possible that homesigners are able to develop all of the properties found in natural human language on their own, it's not likely. If they are not able to recreate language entirely, what conditions are required to develop the languages we have today? This section helps us understand the pressures that have led to language as we know it.

Part III makes the case that knowing how the hands communicate can help you better understand people. Parents, clinicians, and educators do not necessarily realize that gesture cues us when people are ready to change—babies learning to speak, middle schoolers learning math, college students learning chemistry, and men grappling with the leadership qualities of women, to take a few examples. I look first at how hands can help us parent. I then explore how hands can help us identify children who have diverged, or are about to diverge, from typical developmental tracks, and how hands can help us intervene to get children back on course. Finally, I look at how hands can help us educate. Gesture is powerful for all learners, but it is particularly key for students with disabilities such as autism or Down syndrome and for students from less privileged backgrounds. If used well, gesture may help us level the playing field for learners with different skills and from different backgrounds.

Our hands are always with us. They are part of our humanity. Why would we not listen to what they have to say?

Part I
THINKING WITH OUR HANDS

1

WHY DO WE USE OUR HANDS WHEN WE TALK?

I F YOU'VE EVER THOUGHT ABOUT YOUR GESTURES, YOU MAY HAVE wondered why you do them. Gesturing doesn't feel as if it serves any purpose. But maybe that intuition is wrong. If, as I've argued in the introduction, gesture conveys meaningful information, it could be useful to your listener. And if gesturing helps you stay focused and think, it could help you in your role as speaker. Understanding why we gesture could give us techniques to use gesture more effectively, as both listeners and speakers. We'll turn to this topic in Part III. For now, we delve into the science behind your intuitions about why we gesture. But first a few words about what we mean by *why*.

Why questions in English are interesting. There are actually two questions hidden in the English *why*: *why* and *how*. To illustrate, let's take an example from a distant species—the Mississippi alligator. In the evening, the alligators go down into the Mississippi River. Because the alligator is cold-blooded, and because the night air becomes quite cold, often much colder than the water, the evening trip into the river has an important purpose for the alligator: maintaining its body temperature during the night, preventing it from freezing. Remember, alligators aren't like us: they can't regulate their own temperature and instead take on the temperature of the environment around them. Given this purpose, we might guess that the process leading to the evening river trips would also involve the alligator's temperature-regulation system in some way. But it doesn't. The process underlying the evening river trips involves sensitivity to light: the fading afternoon light is the cue that sends the alligator into the water. We know this from laboratory studies where light and temperature can be artificially separated. If the temperature drops but the light does not dim, the alligator stays on land and does not go into the water, even though the air and it are getting colder and colder. In contrast, if the light dims but the temperature remains warm, the alligator will nonetheless enter the water even though the trip isn't needed to keep warm. The purpose, or *function*, of the evening river trips is temperature regulation. The how-it-works, or *mechanism*, is light sensitivity.[1]

So when we ask, "Why do people gesture?" we are actually asking two distinct questions. The first concerns the events that precede gesture and whether those events cause gesturing—the mechanisms that underlie gesture, the *how* of gesturing. The second is about the events that follow gesture and whether gesturing plays a causal role in bringing those events about—the functions that gesture serves, the *why* of gesture. We first explore the mechanisms that underlie gesturing and then turn to its functions, recognizing that the two can be distinct processes.

THE MECHANISMS THAT UNDERLIE GESTURING: *HOW* DO WE GESTURE?

All gestures are acts of the body, physical movements through space. But many gestures also represent actions that can be performed with the body. Here's a nice example. If I ask you how you tie your shoe, you are likely to gesture along with your description, and your gestures will simulate your shoe-tying movements.

Another example comes from a study done by Susan Cook, one of my former students, and Michael Tanenhaus, her postdoctoral mentor, in which adults solved the Tower of Hanoi (TOH) puzzle, either with real objects or on a computer. TOH is a logical puzzle played out on three poles and a stack of round disks. At the beginning of the puzzle, all of the disks are on one pole, arranged from the smallest on top to the largest on the bottom. The goal is to transfer the stack to another pole by moving one disk at a time and never placing a bigger disk on top of a smaller one. The big difference between the real object and computer versions of the puzzle in this study was that, to move one of the physical disks, you had to lift it up off its pole before transferring it to another pole. To move one of the disks during the computer task, you only had to slide the disk from one pole to another without lifting it up. Solving the puzzle using the real disks versus the computer had a big effect on the gestures the adults later produced when talking about their solutions. When they explained how they solved the task, the adults who had moved the real disks produced gestures that contained an arcing movement, whereas the adults who had moved the computer disks produced gestures without arcs, just a horizontal slide. The adults had captured aspects of the movements that they had actually produced in their gestures—and they did *not* describe these movements in their speech.

Interestingly, when other adults later watched the videos of these two groups of adults, they were influenced by the gestures they saw. When asked to solve the task on a computer, the adults who saw the arcing gestures moved the computer disks up and over the poles even though arcing the disks wasn't necessary. The adults who saw the horizontal gestures slid the computer disks sideways from pole to pole. The first set of adults had incorporated aspects of the physical acts they performed into their gestures, and those gestures kept the physical acts alive in the conversation.[2]

As we have just seen, gestures do a good job of capturing action. This observation led Martha Alibali, a former student who has gone on to make seminal contributions to understanding gesture's role in education, and her student, Autumn Hostetter (my academic grandchild), to propose the Gesture as Simulated Action (GSA) framework. When we say the word *throw*, we simulate a throwing movement. We don't necessarily produce the movement, but activity in our brains indicates that throwing is on our minds—the same brain areas that are activated when we throw are activated when we talk about throwing. The idea that we simulate actions when we think and speak is known as *embodied cognition*. This idea forms the basis for GSA, which hypothesizes that action simulations lead to gesture. When a certain threshold of brain activation is reached (people may have different thresholds), throwing becomes visible in a gestural simulation of the act.[3]

All of this suggests that action is part of the mechanism underlying gesture production. If this theory is correct, speakers should gesture a lot when they describe things that they have acted on. And they do: speakers gesture more when describing patterns they have physically constructed than those they have only viewed. Speakers gesture when they express thoughts that involve simulations of actions they have performed.

More evidence that action is involved in gesture production comes from a famous visual illusion. When asked to judge the lengths of two sticks, you will swear that the stick surrounded by two outward-facing fins (the darker stick below) is longer than the stick surrounded by two inward-facing fins (the lighter stick). In fact, the sticks are exactly the same length (as you can see in the sticks without fins).

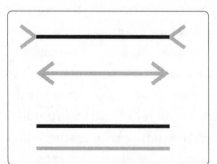

If you are asked to estimate the length of the sticks using your thumb and index finger, you will be susceptible to the illusion. You will spread your thumb and finger wider apart for the darker stick than for the lighter stick when the sticks are surrounded by the fins—your eyes will be misled. This discrepancy is thus captured in your hands when you use them to estimate the lengths of the sticks. But your hands are not always susceptible to the illusion. When you prepare to grasp the sticks, you will spread your thumb and index finger the same distance apart whether you are about to grab the stick with outward-facing fins or the stick with inward-facing fins—your hands will *not* be deceived when they are getting ready to act.[4]

What happens when you use your hands not to estimate or act but to describe—that is, to gesture? The first step is for you to act on a stick displayed within outward-facing fins—to pick it up and move it in space following a prescribed path. Then you describe what you did in speech while gesturing. Later, you act on the same stick displayed within inward-facing fins and describe what you did. The question is whether your gesturing hands look like your acting hands (impervious to the illusion, that is, no difference between your gestures for two sticks of the same size) or your estimating hands (sensitive to the illusion, that is, wider gestures for the stick within outward-facing fins than for the same stick with inward-facing fins).

The answer is that gesturing hands behave like acting hands, not estimating hands. You spread your thumb and index finger the same distance apart whether you are describing the stick within outward-facing fins or the stick within inward-facing fins. Your gesturing hands are no more susceptible to the illusion than your acting hands and much less susceptible to the illusion than your estimating hands. Even though gesture is tightly tied to language, its roots may lie in action.[5]

The final bit of evidence that action is part of the mechanism underlying gesture comes from the responses of our brains. Functional magnetic resonance imaging (fMRI) registers how much blood flow has gone to a particular region of the brain when you do a task: the more flow, the more active that brain region during the task. Children learned how to solve a math equivalence problem $(4 + 6 + 3 = \_\_ + 3)$ by producing either speech alone (saying, "I want to make both sides of the problem equal") or gesture and speech (adding to the speech a sweeping gesture under the left side of the problem and the same sweeping gesture under the right side of the problem) during the lesson. A week after they learned the task, the children were put in the scanner and asked to solve math problems, but this time without producing any movement. The activation patterns differed for the two groups: there was greater activation in brain regions responsible for motor functions in children who had learned through gesture + speech than in children who had learned through speech alone, even though no hand activity was happening anywhere in the scanner. These activated brain regions are very similar to the brain regions that are activated after a child has learned a task through action on physical objects (for example, learning letters by writing them). Learning through gesture leaves a motor signature, just like learning through action on objects. This effect provides at least a partial answer to the question with which we began this chapter: *How* does gesture work? The answer is that action simulation appears to be part of the mechanism underlying gesture production.[6]

But there is a problem. Although all gestures are performed by the body, not all gestures represent acts of the body. When you talk about a rocket shooting up in the air and move your hand upward to capture its trajectory, your gesture represents a movement but not a bodily movement. Or when you trace an *S*-shape in the air to represent the shape of your dog's tail, your gesture is not even representing a movement, let alone a bodily movement. In these cases, the body has not performed an action that could be simulated. The GSA theory may be the right explanation for gestures that represent actions the body performs, but it doesn't easily account for gestures that represent shapes, abstract ideas, or even the movements of objects.

There is additional evidence from a young man called IW that gesture doesn't work exactly like action. IW was nineteen when he suffered an illness of unknown causes. The illness affected the nerves of his spinal cord and caused him to lose his sense of touch and all motor control that depended on feedback indicating body position and orientation, what we call *proprioceptive feedback*. Over time and with great effort, IW learned to control his arm and leg movements by watching and guiding his limbs with his eyes as he moved them. He regained control over his posture and movement but can exercise that control *only* when he can see his limbs. In the dark, he cannot move—with the interesting exception that he can gesture in the dark. In other words, IW is able to move his unseen hands when he talks despite the fact that he is unable to move his unseen hands when asked, for example, to pick up a block. IW's injury affected his actions on objects but not his gestures, suggesting that the mechanisms underlying the two are not identical.[7]

An example from a woman who doesn't have arms but has the sensation of gesturing makes the same point. The book *Phantoms in the Brain* describes a young woman, armless from birth, who should know nothing of gesturing firsthand—but she does. Mirabelle was born with two short stumps below her shoulders but could feel the arms she never had. She had what are known as *phantom limbs*. People typically experience a phantom limb after an arm or leg has been removed. But Mirabelle never had a limb to lose, and her doctor was skeptical. When asked how she knew that she has phantom limbs, she replied, "Well, because as I'm talking to you, they are gesticulating. They point to objects when I point to things, just like your arms and hands. . . . When I walk, doctor, my phantom arms don't swing like normal arms, like your arms. They stay frozen on the side, like this." She stood up, letting her stumps drop straight down on both sides. "But when I talk," she said, "my phantoms gesticulate. In fact, they're moving now as I speak." Gesturing is not just moving your arms.[8]

THE FUNCTIONS THAT GESTURING SERVES:
WHY DO WE GESTURE?

Gesturing might be useful independently of the mechanisms that lead to its production—in other words, gesturing might have a function, or even multiple functions, unrelated to action. Ordinary people can read the gestures you spontaneously produce. This means that your gestures can function to communicate information to your listeners, as suggested in the introduction.[9]

Gesture can even make you a more effective communicator. Here's an example. On Friday, April 9, 2021, the *New York Times* reported on Dr. Martin Tobin's testimony in the trial of Derek Chauvin, accused of killing George Floyd. Mary Moriarty, the former chief public defender of Hennepin County, described Tobin's testimony as follows: "Tobin is a pulmonologist who specializes in the mechanics of breathing. . . . Leaning into the microphone, tie slightly askew, Dr. Tobin used his hands and elbows to demonstrate how people breathe." She went on to say, "He appears to be the world's foremost expert on this, and he explained everything in English, in layman's terms." I believe that what made Tobin's testimony so effective (in addition to his clear thinking) were the gestures he produced as he talked. Tobin may or may not have intended to embellish his testimony with gesture, but it really doesn't matter—once the information is out there, everyone is free to take advantage of it. Your gestures can help *others* understand your thoughts.

You seem to intuitively know this about your own gestures. When placed in a noisy situation, you raise the level of your voice and enunciate your words clearly and distinctly, particularly when speech is the only available mode of communication. But when you have the option of using gesture, you exploit it. You can elaborate gesture in several ways. You can add information to your gestures; for example, when ordering chips and salsa in a noisy room, you precede your EAT gesture with a dipping motion to represent dipping a chip into the salsa before bringing it to your mouth. You can also elaborate gesture by repeating the same motion in a different space or by pausing in between the two motions, which accentuates the movements. Interestingly, when your hands are available, you don't put a lot more effort into intensifying your speech; you allow gesture and exaggerated mouth movements to do the work. In other words, in noisy face-to-face situations, although you adjust both your speech and your gestures to the conditions that make it hard to hear, the visual channel, including gesture, seems to carry the day to make sure that your listener can understand you.[10]

Your gestures help others. Do they also help *you*? It sounds a little wacky, but why else would you gesture on the phone when your listener can't see you? Why do blind individuals gesture when talking to other blind individuals who can't see those gestures? And then there are spoken-language interpreters. Have you ever looked up at the people behind the glass window who interpret at international conferences? Their voices are transmitted to the appropriate listeners, but their visual images are not. No one sees them, but they are constantly gesturing as they translate from one language into another. Our best guess is that those gestures are doing something useful for them.

Let's think a bit about what your gestures could be doing for you that you might not be aware of. You produce gestures along with your speech—maybe your gestures are helping you generate that speech. You might find yourself rotating your hand as you try to think of the word *screwdriver*. Does making this move-ment help you find the word you're looking for? The evidence isn't conclusive: some infer from the evidence that the answer to this question is yes; others, that the answer is no. If gesturing helps you speak, then preventing gesture should get in the way of speaking. But it has been hard to find evidence for this hypo-thesis that convinces everyone. Even if gesturing does play a role in speaking, there is no reason to believe that gesturing has only one function. Gesturing could affect your thinking, and it could do so in many ways.[11]

Gesturing helps you attend. When someone gestures, it catches your eye, and you are more likely to perk up and pay attention. An eye tracker follows the gaze of the person who is wearing it, and we used one to watch children's eyes during a math lesson taught with and without gestures. When the teacher said, "I want to make one side [gesture on left side of the equation] equal to the other side [gesture on right side of the equation]," children tracked her gestures with their eyes and, as a result, looked at the parts of the problem mentioned in her words. Not surprisingly, children who saw gesture in the lesson followed the teacher's words more closely than children who did not see gesture. Someone else's gestures do help you look in the right place.

But we also found something else: if we look *only* at children in both groups who followed the teacher's words, we find that the children who saw gesture were more likely to improve after instruction than children who did not see gesture. This is surprising since the children who didn't see gesture were following the teacher's words on their own and therefore ought to have gotten more out of the words than the children whose attention had been guided by gesture. It looks like gesture got children to glean more from the teacher's words than they would have had they followed the words and *not* seen gesture. Gesture can go beyond controlling attention and help you get more out of the speech you're attending to.[12]

The gestures just discussed are produced by other people. But your own gestures can help keep you focused too. Preschoolers typically point to objects as they count them. Producing these pointing gestures while counting (as opposed to watching a puppet produce the gestures while the children count) helps children coordinate their number words and the objects they are counting. As a result, they count more accurately than if they hadn't gestured.[13]

Producing your own gestures does hold and direct your attention. But gesturing can also help you get more out of what you're looking at than if you don't gesture.

Gesturing helps you remember. If you gesture while describing an event, do you think you'll be able to recall that event better than if you don't gesture? We had adults watch videos of toy objects, animals, and people performing various, sometimes odd, actions: a chicken sliding to a policeman, a woman petting a dog, a dove flying into a wheelbarrow, a jogger bending down to touch his toes, a fence swinging shut on its own. We then tested the adults' memories of these events immediately after the descriptions and three weeks later. Adults who were told to gesture while describing the events remembered more than adults who were told not to gesture, particularly several weeks later. To see if we'd get the same effects if people gestured on their own, we did the study again, but this time we gave the adults no instructions about gesture. We found the same patterns: people remembered items on which they had gestured spontaneously better than items on which they had not gestured. Producing gesture along with speech, either spontaneously or when instructed, makes the information encoded in that speech memorable.[14]

Gesturing lightens the cognitive effort you expend. We've been looking at gestures that are produced along with to-be-remembered items—those gestures make the items easier to remember. But gesture can also have an effect on memory indirectly by lightening the amount of cognitive effort you expend on a task. We showed this by asking adults to *gesture* when explaining how they solved some math problems and *not to gesture* when explaining other comparable problems.

There were four steps to the task. The adults (1) solved a math problem; (2) were given a list of letters to remember (e.g., XR QP BN); (3) explained how they solved the math problem; and (4) tried to recall the letters. Each adult solved twenty-four factoring problems, such as $X^2 - 5x + 6 = (\ )(\ )$. Note that the adults

were trying to remember the letters as they gave their explanations, which means that they were doing the two tasks at the same
time, so the tasks shared cognitive effort. We used the number of
letters the adults remembered as a measure of how much effort
they expended during their explanations: a small number would
mean that they had been working hard on the explanations and
could only recall a few letters; a large number would mean that
they had expended less effort on the explanations and could recall
many letters. This logic, of course, assumes a limited amount of
cognitive effort, what we refer to as *cognitive load*, and a trade-off
between the effort expended on the two tasks performed simultaneously (the explanation task and the letter-recall task). There is
good evidence from previous work for both assumptions.[15]

We were interested in whether gesturing during an explanation
made it easier, or harder, to remember the letters the adult was
trying to keep in mind. In other words, did gesturing decrease or
increase cognitive load? Gesturing is a behavior that is produced
along with speech. Having to integrate gesture with speech might
take effort, which would mean that the explanations would be
harder to produce with gesture than without gesture. On the other
hand, gesture and speech form a single system. So it might take
less effort to produce them together, which would mean that the
explanations would be easier to produce with gesture than without it. What did we find? The adults remembered more letters
when they gestured along with their explanations than when they
did not gesture. Even though producing gestures when you talk
adds a second behavior, the end result is to *lighten* your cognitive
load.[16]

How about children? We adjusted the paradigm slightly for
children and found that gesturing also lightens their cognitive load.
But we could ask another question with the children. We could
contrast children who knew how to solve the addition problems
we gave them and children who didn't—in the case of the adults,
all of them successfully solved the factoring problems. We could

ask whether gesturing worked in the same way when the children's explanations were incorrect as when they were correct—and it did. Gesturing lightened children's cognitive load whether they gave a correct explanation or an incorrect explanation.[17]

But something may be bothering you. We *told* the adults and children not to gesture. Not gesturing by instruction may itself impose a cognitive load. So the adults and children might remember less when they didn't gesture because of the cognitive cost imposed by being told not to gesture. We were able to rule out this possibility because the participants didn't always gesture when they were given the opportunity to gesture. This means that an individual could give three different kinds of explanations: (1) explanations on which the participants chose to gesture; (2) explanations on which the participants chose not to gesture; and (3) explanations on which the participants were told not to gesture. It turned out that both adults and children remembered the same number of items when they *chose* not to gesture as when they were *told* not to gesture—being told to gesture did not add to their cognitive load. In other words, they remembered more items when they gestured than when they didn't gesture, whether by choice or by instruction, which proves that one of gesture's functions is to lighten your cognitive load.

When a verbal task feels hard, you can help yourself by gesturing as you talk.

Gesturing externalizes your thoughts. If you're having trouble solving a math problem in your head, you're likely to grab a piece of paper and write the problem down. Getting the problem onto paper lightens your memory load and gives you a different perspective. Maybe putting your thoughts into your hands can have the same effect.

We have some evidence for this possibility from a study on moral reasoning in children. As an example of a dilemma, two brothers need money and try to get it illegally: one brother cheats an old man; the other steals from a store. The children were asked to decide which is worse, cheating or stealing, and to gesture as they explained their decision. They did as they were told and gestured as they talked. While they talked, they placed their gesturing hands in different spaces, each reflecting a different perspective. Gesture in a single space depicted the perspective of one individual (the illustration on the left); gesture in more than one space depicted multiple perspectives (the illustration on the right where each hand depicts a different perspective).

Placing their hands in different locations in space was the first sign that the children could take multiple perspectives on a moral dilemma. Multiple perspectives also began to appear in the children's speech but, importantly, *only* if the children had been told to gesture. Later, after they were given training in moral reasoning, children who had been told to gesture gave more advanced moral reasoning—reasoning that took more than one perspective into account—to explain the dilemma. Children who had been told not to gesture did not. Note that morality is an abstract concept—not spatial at all. By using gesture, the children "spatialized" their thoughts (they literally put them out into space), which, in this instance, helped them take more than one perspective on a moral dilemma.[18]

By locating ideas in space, gesture not only externalizes ideas but situates them within a spatial framework. Barbara Tversky, a well-known authority in the areas of visuo-spatial reasoning and collaborative cognition, writes about this in *Mind in Motion: How Action Shapes Thought*. In her view, spatial thinking is the basis of thought—not the entire edifice but the foundation. Human activity, including gesture, takes place in space and can establish a ground for our mental representations. The actions involved in gesture can lay the framework for discovering that there can be different perspectives on the same problem.[19]

Laying ideas out in space, even ideas that are not inherently spatial, paves the way for using cognitive operations that rely on space. Take, for example, the *method of loci*, a strategy for recalling lists of items. It works like this: You first imagine yourself placing the items that you want to remember in different locations around a room (e.g., on the couch, on the table, near the lamp, etc.). You then recall each of the items by revisiting in your mind the locations you have used and calling up the image of the item in that location (i.e., the item on the couch, the item on the table, the item near the lamp, etc.). Perhaps gesture could be used in comparable ways. By gesturing about different ideas in space, you are grounding them in those spaces and can perhaps use the spaces to recall them. Someone should test this idea.[20]

Gesturing brings a second modality into thinking. We have been discussing rather subtle functions that gesturing might serve. One less subtle function is that gesture brings a second modality (in addition to speech) into communication. This second modality has the potential to affect thinking and learning. Richard Mayer, author of *Multimedia Learning*, argues that learning is enhanced when two modalities (which are not entirely redundant) are presented simultaneously. Verbal learning is a powerful tool, but a

mixture of verbal and visual materials has the potential to promote deeper, more lasting learning than either material on its own.
For example, building a meaningful connection between the words
"the piston moves forward in the master cylinder" and a diagram
of how a piston moves in a car's braking system can lead to a
more complete understanding than thinking about the words or
the diagram on their own. Mayer's book focuses on learning in the
context of words and pictures. But it's a small step to think about
gestures rather than pictures as the visual material presented along
with words.[21]

There are a few obvious differences between gesture and pictures. Gestures are dynamic and play out over time. Pictures are
static. Some problems lend themselves to dynamic representations—for example, learning how to tie a knot. Pictures of knot
tying are notoriously difficult to interpret, particularly compared
to a verbal description accompanied by a few gestures. Other
problems may do better with a static representation that displays
the relations among elements at a glance—for example, seeing
a picture of what a chest of drawers looks like before trying to
assemble it. Having a model of how the pieces fit together that you
can keep checking throughout the assembly is more helpful than
a fleeting gesture.

But gesture does have one advantage over pictures: it seamlessly integrates with speech in both production and comprehension. This means that you don't have to think about how to put
the two together. You talk, and gesture comes for free. You listen,
and you spontaneously integrate the speaker's gestures into the
message you are receiving. In contrast, you have to do some work
to effectively integrate a picture into talk. In fact, it seems like the
most obvious way to integrate word and picture would be to join
the two via gesture—for example, pointing at the part of the picture as you describe that part. Very little research has been done
on how gesture and pictures can be best used together in a lesson,

but it seems like a promising direction for the future. I'd start by watching how teachers do it since they are the professionals.

Gesturing brings a second representational format into thinking. Gesture is performed in a different modality from speech, but it is also different in another sense: gesture represents information in a continuous way; it paints a picture in the air. By contrast, speech relies on discrete categories combined into larger units—sounds combined to form words, which combine to form sentences. Perhaps it's the fact that gesture introduces a pictorial format, and not just that it brings in a second modality, that gives gesture its power in learning. We can't explore this possibility in speakers because they always use two modalities when they gesture: language in the oral-auditory modality and gesture in the manual-visual modality. But we can tackle the question in signers.

Sign language makes use of categories in the same way that speech does. And signers gesture as they sign. The difference is that their gestures are produced in the same modality as their signs: the manual modality. So signers use two representational formats when they sign and gesture, but only one modality—a discrete format in sign and a continuous format in gesture, both produced by the hands. In contrast, speakers use two representational formats in two different modalities—a discrete format in speech produced by the mouth and a continuous format in gesture produced by the hands. This arrangement allows us to pit using two representational formats against using two modalities. Is it the juxtaposition of two representational formats (discrete for language, continuous for gesture) or of two modalities (hand and mouth) that gives gesture its cognitive power?[22]

Do signers' gestures have the same cognitive effects as a speaker's gestures? We taught a math concept to hearing children who used English and to deaf children who used American Sign Language (ASL) to address this question. The signers should perform like the speakers if it's the juxtaposition of two representational formats that matters—discrete for language, both speech and sign; continuous for gesture. But if it's the juxtaposition of two modalities that matters, the signers should perform differently because they are using only one modality: the hands.

The first question was whether the two groups of children would gesture on these problems. They did, and at approximately the same rates. Here's an example: For the problem 3 + 6 + 8 = 3 + __ , a speaking child and a signing child each (incorrectly) put 20 in the blank, having added up all four numbers in the problem. In her words, the speaker said, "I added up all of the numbers in the problem," while pointing at each of the four numbers. In her signs, the signer produced the sign ADD, followed by the sign ALL; in her gestures, she first swept her index finger under the 3 on the right, then the 8, 6, and 3 on the left, and then produced individuated points under the left 3, the 6, the 8, and the right 3. Both children conveyed the same information—adding up all of the numbers in the problem—in their respective language (speech or sign) and in gesture.

The next question was whether the children ever produced gestures that conveyed *different* information from that conveyed in their language. They did, and again at roughly the same rate. Here's an example: For the problem 7 + 4 + 2 = 7 + __, both children put 13 in the blank, having added up the numbers to the left of the equals sign. In their language, the speaker and signer told us that they had done just that: The speaker said, "I added the 7 and the 4 and the 2 and put 13 in the blank," and the signer (pictured below) produced an ADD sign over the 7, 4, and 2 on the left and signed PUT in the blank. But in their gestures, both children conveyed different information. The speaker produced a TAKE-AWAY gesture on the 7 on the right side of the equation. The signer put a flat palm over the 7 on the right side of the equation as though canceling it out (this movement is a gesture, not a sign in ASL). In both cases, gesture conveyed information that was not found in the speaker's words or the signer's signs. In other words, there was a "mismatch" between the children's language and their gesture. In previous work, we found that the number of times a speaking child produced a "mismatch" between speech and gesture on this type of problem before a math lesson predicted how likely that child was to profit from the lesson.[23]

The crucial question for us here is whether signers behave in the same way: Does the number of mismatches between *sign* and gesture produced by signers before the lesson predict their success on the problems after the lesson? We divided children up according to how many gesture-sign mismatches they produced prior to the lesson, from none to six, out of six possible. Then we looked at whether they successfully solved the problems after the lesson (they could get one wrong and still be considered successful). If mismatch prior to instruction predicts success after instruction, children who produced zero mismatches should do the worst, and children who produced six mismatches should do the best, with the others falling into line in between. This is precisely what we found. The signers performed just like the speakers, suggesting that the juxtaposition of two representational formats (discrete for language, continuous for gesture), rather than the juxtaposition of two modalities (hand and mouth), gives gesture its cognitive power.[24]

Gesturing brings the body into cognition. The representational format that gesture brings to thinking and learning is important, but the modality in which that format is produced might also be important. Gesture is produced by the body and is itself an action. And how we act can influence how we think by grounding our perceptions, feelings, emotions, and even the way we understand language, in the sensorimotor systems we use to interact with the world. For example, if you learn a new dance step without seeing your own movements, later you will be able to identify and distinguish these movements with your eyes despite never having seen them. Your actions have an impact on how you see the world.[25]

Just as action can influence subsequent thought, so can gesture. Recall the studies of the Tower of Hanoi puzzle described earlier. The disks were graduated not only in size but also in weight. The biggest disk was the heaviest and had to be lifted with two hands. The littlest disk was the lightest and could be lifted with one hand. After the adults finished solving the puzzle, we asked them to describe what they had done, and, of course, they gestured. Some adults chose to produce a one-handed gesture to describe moving the littlest disk in their explanations of the task; some adults chose to produce a two-handed gesture.

All of the adults were asked to solve the problem again, but we got tricky: unbeknownst to the problem solvers, we switched the disk weights. Now the biggest disk was the lightest, and the littlest disk was the heaviest and had to be lifted with two hands; the disks did not look different though. The surprising result is that the problem solvers' choice of gesture during their descriptions influenced their ability to solve the puzzle after we had switched the weights, but not the appearance, of the disks. Using a one-handed gesture before solving the puzzle with the switched disks set subjects up to think about the little disk as light. When it ended up being heavy, their performance suffered. The information about the disks' weight was encoded bodily in the adults' hands—and only in their hands—and that information affected how they ended up solving the problem.[26]

What happens to gesture if your hand is not your own? Will you gesture even if you use an artificial limb, and does it matter if you think of the limb as part of your body? Individuals with congenital or acquired loss of one arm are often outfitted with prostheses. It turns out that they gesture with these prostheses when they talk. But they don't all gesture at the same rates. Those individuals who report on a questionnaire that they think of their prosthesis as part of their body gesture more with their pros- thetic hand than individuals who report less embodiment. This is an interesting result for two reasons. First, practitioners can use how much people gesture with their prosthesis as an index of how much they "own" their new arm, the ultimate goal of any human- machine interface. Since gesturing was never explicitly mentioned as part of the task, it's an unbiased and easy-to-implement mea- sure of embodiment. Second, if your arm (natural or prosthetic) is part of you, you will use it to gesture.[27]

It's obvious that your own gesturing engages your body. But can watching *someone else* gesture also engage your body? It turns out that there is overlap between the neural circuitry activated when you *see* someone perform an action on an object and the neu- ral circuitry activated when you yourself plan and *do* that same action. These overlapping neurons are called *mirror neurons*. If your motor system is engaged in an action just as you attempt to understand the same action performed by someone else, you will have fewer motor resources to devote to understanding the action and your performance will suffer.[28]

We used the same logic to figure out whether watching some- one gesture works this way too. We asked adults to move either their arms and hands, or their legs and feet (thus taking up dif- ferent motor resources) as they performed a task that required them to use information conveyed in a speaker's hand gestures. Moving their arms and hands made it harder to understand the speaker's hand gestures, whereas moving their legs and feet did not. So moving your arms and hands—but not your legs and feet—gets in the way of your ability to use information conveyed in a speaker's hand gestures. Understanding someone else's gesture relies, at least in part, on your own motor system.[29]

Gesturing promotes abstraction. Gesturing and acting both have an effect on cognition. But the effects are not identical. Actions on objects have a direct effect on the world. You twist the cap of a bottle, and the cap comes off. In contrast, if you do a twisting gesture near (but not on) the bottle, the bottle cap stays where it is—unless, of course, someone takes your gesture as a request for them to open the bottle and complies. But that is just the point. Action has a direct effect on bottle opening. Gesture has an indirect effect through its communicative and representational properties. This difference might mean that gesture and action have some differing functions.

Miriam Novack, one of my former students, took the lead in exploring this possibility by teaching nine- and ten-year-old children how to solve mathematical equivalence problems in one of three ways. One group was taught movements that simulated a *grouping* problem-solving strategy in action. Two other groups were taught movements that represented the same strategy either in a concrete or abstract gesture. Take the problem 4 + 2 + 8 = __ + 8, which was displayed on a board with magnetic numbers. In the action condition, children were taught to pick up the 4 and the 2 and hold the two number magnets under the blank, simulating adding the 4 and 2 and putting the sum in the blank. In the concrete gesture condition, children were taught to gesture picking up the 4 and the 2 and then to gesture holding them under the blank. In the abstract gesture condition, children were taught to point with their index and middle fingers extended at the 4 and the 2 and then to point with an index finger at the blank. All of the children were taught to make these movements while saying, "I want to make one side equal to the other side," before the math lesson began. During the lesson, the children were told to say the words and do their hand movements before and after attempting to solve each math problem. The teacher produced no movements herself during the lesson.

After the lesson, all of the children were tested on mathematical equivalence—they had solved no equivalence problems correctly before the lesson. All three groups improved in equal measure on problems that had the same format as those on which they were taught—for example, 3 + 4 + 7 = __ + 7. Action and gesture both led to learning.

But the similarities ended there. Children in the action condition were unable to generalize what they had learned to a mathematical equivalence problem in a new format—for example, 3 + 4 + 7 = 3 + __. Note that you can't just add up the two first numbers on the left and put them in the blank to solve these problems. You really need to understand what's happening in an equation—that it states that two quantities are the same—to solve the problem. Children in the action condition failed on these problems. Children in the concrete and abstract gesture conditions succeeded.

We gave them one more test of generalization: problems without any equal addends at all—for example, 3 + 4 + 7 = __ + 5. Again, children in the action condition failed. This time, some children in the concrete gesture condition also failed, but children in the abstract gesture condition did well. It seems that gesture is good at getting the learner to abstract away from the details of the problem and think more deeply about how to solve it.[30]

Now you might say that the actions we had the children do weren't typical: they were produced on objects but didn't solve the problem. So we did the study again. This time Elizabeth Wakefield, a former postdoctoral student of mine, took the lead and used action and gesture to teach three- and four-year-old children new words for actions. We taught children that *tiffing* meant to squeeze the round part of a novel toy. Children in the action

condition did the squeezing on a purple toy (the illustration on the left). Children in the gesture condition did the squeezing near, but not on, the same toy (the illustration on the right). All the children said the word *tiffing* as they did their movements.

After the lesson, the children were tested on how well they had learned the new words. Children in both conditions learned that *tiffing* could be applied to squeezing the purple toy, the one on which they had been taught. But when we asked them to generalize *tiffing* to an orange toy that could also be squeezed, children in the action condition did worse than children in the gesture condition, particularly when we tested them a week and four weeks later. The children who had been taught words via gesture were able to generalize their knowledge and apply it to squeezing in general. The children who had been taught via action were more likely to assume that *tiffing* meant specifically squeezing the purple toy rather than squeezing in general. They weren't wrong, but they were being conservative and slow to generalize what they had learned beyond the conditions of learning.[31]

Action and gesture can both help you learn. But gesture helps you generalize beyond the particulars of the learning situation. Action and gesture both also bring the body into cognition, which can be helpful in promoting learning. However, to explain why gesture promotes generalization better than action does, we need to go beyond the body.

Gesturing fills in the gaps left by speech. We've established that language is rule governed and packages information into categories. The particular language you speak has ready-made categories that make it easy to convey certain types of information. But these categories leave out information that you might have wanted to express. For example, if you say, "The cup is near the milk," you are indicating that the cup and milk are side by side. But you're not saying how much distance there is between the two. They could be quite close to each other, or there could be a sizable gap between them. You could use gesture to clear this up. It works the same way with the word *over*. You could say, "The box of cereal is over the sugar," but this sentence doesn't tell me whether the box is directly over the sugar, over but to the right of the sugar, or over and to the left of the sugar. You could, of course, add words to your sentence to clarify, but gesture also does the trick, and likely more efficiently.

Gesture allows you to fill in the picture with ideas that are hard to fit into the prepackaged units your language provides, tailoring an imperfect language to be more useful to the speaker or listener at the moment. That tailoring can come about because your language may need a lot of words to express a thought that is more easily expressed in gesture, as in the examples about locating objects in space. The tailoring can also come about because you don't have the ability to express an idea in speech at that moment. Recall the chemistry learner in the introduction who wasn't yet able to bring the word *rotation* to bear on the stereoisomer problem but was able to produce a gesture for rotation. The tailoring can also come about because you're uncomfortable expressing an idea in speech, like the friend who insisted upon his belief that men and women are equally competent leaders but then put his gesture for men in a higher gestural space than his gesture for women. Gesture can reveal ideas that you have but do not express in speech.

Gesture can bring out information that is implicit in a picture and difficult to express in words. Mary Hegarty, an expert on spatial thinking, has explored with her colleagues the role gesture plays in mental animation. They showed adults diagrams of mechanical systems and asked them to figure out how parts of the systems moved. The adults gestured on more than 90 percent of problems, and most of their gestures portrayed mechanical motions not described in their words and not explicitly shown in the diagram. Gesture is a natural way for speakers to express the inferences they make about a mechanical system from a picture of that system.[32]

This discussion brings us back to comparing gestures and pictures. Gesture's advantage over pictures is that it incorporates motion into its form. Mathematics involves moving and transforming numbers, but those movements and transformations are not explicitly represented in mathematical equations. Rafael Núñez, known for his studies of mathematics and gesture, asked mathematics graduate students to work in pairs and prove theorems at the board. Some of the theorems involved dynamic mathematical concepts—concepts like increasing function, continuity, and intersection. Others involved relatively static concepts—concepts like containment and closeness. All of the pairs produced proofs that were nearly complete, and all but one of the students gestured. The gestures were later coded as dynamic (gestures with movement) or static (gestures without movement).[33]

As we might expect, gestures produced along with talk about dynamic notions (increase, continuity, and intersection) involved movement; gestures produced along with talk about static notions (containment and closeness) did not. For example, one student working with inequalities in set notation said, "So that contradicts uhhh increasing," as his hand flew upward with his index finger extended in a pointing handshape as if tracing a path. The student produced this movement gesture after he had written down a sequence of equations. His gesture shows us that, despite his depictions, which have no movement, his understanding of increasing functions is fundamentally dynamic. In other words, he conceptualizes increasing functions and sequences as dynamic, moving entities, and we can tell that from his gestures. Concepts in calculus that have been defined entirely in static terms are nevertheless conceptualized dynamically by advanced mathematicians, and that dynamism is visible in their gestures. Note that teachers who produce a dynamic gesture while describing a set of static representations are revealing the dynamic nature of the mathematical concept with their hands. If students can glean meaning from their teacher's gestures (and we know that they can), they will be getting important instruction in these mathematical concepts that is found only in the hands.[34]

GESTURING IS THE PERFECT STORM

So why do you gesture when you talk? We don't really know, but we've got lots of good leads. Action is part of the mechanism that drives gesture but not the whole story. And gesture has many, many functions. Your gesturing communicates information to your listeners, whether or not you want it to. But your gesturing also helps (or hurts) you, again whether or not you want it to. The jury is still out on whether gesture affects your speaking, but it does affect your thinking. Gesturing helps you attend to and focus your thoughts. Gesturing helps you remember the information you gestured. Gesturing lightens your cognitive load. Gesturing externalizes your thoughts and situates them in a spatial framework, which paves the way for using cognitive operations that rely on space. Gesturing brings a second modality into thinking, and two modalities are often better than one. Gesturing brings a second representational format into thinking, one that makes conveying imagistic information relatively easy. Gesturing brings the body into cognition, which helps you learn many tasks. Gesturing promotes abstraction and does it more effectively than doing the same movements on physical objects. Gesturing can fill in the gaps left by spoken language (and probably by sign language too) and is particularly good at bringing perceptual-motor information into representations and conversation. There is no one function that defines gesture.

Each function that gesture serves can be performed by other devices. For example, a highlighter can focus your attention. Pictures bring a second representational format into thinking. Acting brings the body into cognition. But gesture is unique in that it does these things, and others, all at the same time. In fact, gesture is likely a powerful teaching and learning tool *because* it serves all these functions at the same time. Gesture is a perfect storm in that it is a unique combination of circumstances that drastically alters an event—in this case, a learning event. Although the term is typically used to describe a destructive phenomenon, I use it here to describe a *powerful* and natural confluence of factors. Less may be more in certain circumstances, but the fact that gesturing can have so many different effects on your cognition *at the same time* suggests that, in this instance, more is more—gesturing brings it all together in a perfect storm.

2

OUR HANDS REFLECT OUR MINDS

WE HAVE SEEN WHY IT IS BENEFICIAL FOR YOU TO MOVE YOUR hands when you speak, which strongly suggests that your gestures are more than just hand waving. In this chapter I aim to show you that gesture can offer a privileged window into peoples' minds. But first I need to tell you where gesture fits into other nonverbal behaviors and what makes it unique.

FITTING GESTURE INTO NONVERBAL BEHAVIOR

Your body communicates messages about you. Arm movements, facial expressions, and vocal tone are all examples of body language. You cross your hands over your chest and send a message that you're not open to interaction or that you may be feeling a bit defensive. You put your hands on your hips and signal that you're ready for action or that you may be feeling a bit aggressive. A great deal has been written in the popular press about how to read—and produce—body cues and about how we share some of these body cues with other animals. For example, animals, including humans, display their dominance through expansive nonverbal poses. These power poses have the expected effect: animals cower before members of their species who have assumed a dominant pose. The pose communicates strength and is typically used, at least by nonhuman animals, to avoid physical conflict rather than to promote it.[1]

In humans, the power pose not only tells others how you see yourself but can also affect your own feelings about yourself. Individuals were told to assume either a high-powered pose (an expansive position with open limbs) or a low-powered pose (a contractive position with closed limbs) and to hold the position for two minutes. After posing, the individuals participated in a gambling task and rated how "powerful" and "in charge" they felt during the task. The high-power posers took more risks when gambling than the low-power posers, and they reported feeling more powerful and in charge. Hormonal changes have, in some studies, been found to co-occur with feelings of power, but these physiological changes have been difficult to replicate. So it isn't clear whether hormonal changes underlie the feelings of power that you get from putting your body into an expansive pose, but there is solid evidence that assuming a power pose alters your feelings and self-perceptions.[2]

The body communicates, which is why people like to call it *body language*. But body language isn't language in the traditional sense. It doesn't have the structures found in spoken or signed languages, and it doesn't even have to occur with language. You can strike a power pose without saying anything at all; doing so silently might even be more effective. By contrast, in this part of the book I focus on body movements—hand movements, in particular—that co-occur with language. The influence of these hand movements comes, at least in part, from the fact that they are intimately tied to language, our most powerful communication system.

In 1969, psychologists Paul Ekman and Walter Friesen, pioneers in studying emotions and their relation to facial expressions, classified nonverbal behaviors into five types: (1) facial expressions, which display your emotions—for example, a smile, knitted brows, or a wrinkled nose; (2) regulators, which pace the flow of conversation—for example, nodding to encourage a speaker to keep talking; (3) self-adaptors, which have a function but are produced even when that function is gone—for example, pushing your "glasses" up your nose when you're not wearing glasses; (4) emblems, which are conventional gestures with a standardized form that can be produced with speech but need not be—for example, waving good-bye or holding up a finger in front of your mouth to quiet everyone; and (5) illustrators, which must be produced along with speech and are interlaced with its moment-to-moment fluctuations—for example, saying, "You open it by twisting to the left," while rotating your hand counterclockwise. As noted in the introduction, illustrators are called *co-speech gestures* and, as the name suggests, are intimately tied to speech.[3]

GESTURE IS AN INTEGRAL PART OF SPEECH

Many years ago, Jana Iverson came to my lab as a first-year graduate student with a very interesting question in mind. She wondered whether individuals who are blind from birth will gesture. Congenitally blind individuals have never seen anyone gesture. Does this matter? Jana observed congenitally blind children and adolescents doing a task on which sighted people typically gesture and found that congenitally blind individuals do gesture—even when they know they are talking to another blind individual who, of course, can't see their hands. And they use the same kinds of gestures on this task that sighted children and adolescents use. You don't need to have seen gesturing in order to do it when you speak.[4]

Jana's finding tells us about the mechanism underlying gesturing—how it works—but not whether seeing gesture is necessary to use gesture like a native speaker of a particular language.

For sighted people, the gestures we produce when we talk are influenced by the structure of that talk. For example, English speakers describe path (across) and manner (skipping) within a single clause, "I skipped across the street," and also produce one gesture containing manner and path, wiggling fingers at the same time as the hand moves across; the manner is incorporated into the path. But there are other languages in the world—Turkish is one—that package path and manner separately; path is in one clause and manner is in another (the English equivalent of "I went across the street skipping"). Not only do Turkish speakers describe path and manner in separate clauses, but their gestures are also separate—they either produce two gestures (wiggling fingers first, then moving the nonwiggling hand across space) or, more typically, one gesture containing only path (moving the nonwiggling hand across space). The drawings below illustrate both patterns, an English speaker on the left, a Turkish speaker on the right.

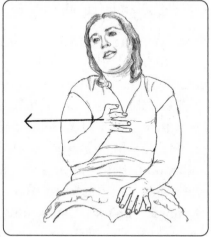

Do *blind* English and Turkish speakers show these same language-specific features in their gestures? It all depends on *how* gesture is formed—its mechanism. If it's essential to *watch someone* who speaks English or Turkish gesture in order to learn how to gesture like an English or Turkish speaker, congenitally blind individuals should *not* show cultural differences—all blind individuals ought to gesture in the same way. But if you only need to *learn how to speak* English or Turkish in order to gesture like a speaker of English or Turkish, then blind English speakers should gesture like sighted English speakers, and blind Turkish speakers should gesture like sighted Turkish speakers—which is precisely what we find, as illustrated below (the blind English speaker is on the left; the blind Turkish speaker is on the right).[5]

 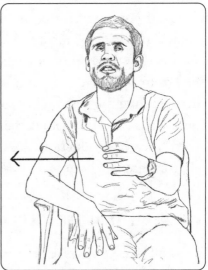

All you need to do is learn a spoken language in order to gesture like a native speaker of that language—although it takes time to learn how to gesture like a native, just as it takes time to learn how to speak like a native. Of course, this doesn't mean that blind gesturers will be indistinguishable from hearing gesturers. Culture-specific emblems like *okay* and *thumbs-up* need to be learned, either by seeing them or, if you're blind, by reading about them or being explicitly taught them. The gestures that follow the structure of language, however, come for free when you learn the language.

Finding any kind of gesture in congenitally blind speakers addresses another important point about gesture. Who is it *for*? A person who has never seen gesture, who gestures when speaking to someone who has also never seen gesture, is not likely to be gesturing for the listener. The blind speakers are likely gesturing for themselves—their gestures help organize their own thoughts. This doesn't mean that their gestures aren't used by their (sighted) listeners. But it does mean that they are not likely *intended for* the listener.

But let's get back to the different ways gesture is integrated with speech. Gesture is perfectly timed with the words it accompanies. If you say, "To fix the pipe, you'll need to bend it back," you will produce the most forceful part of your BENDING-BACK gesture, the stroke, just as you say the phrase *bend it back*. If you slow your speech down, you will also slow your gesture down, often holding the gesture in place to wait until speech catches up. I've always found it striking that gesture is timed with speech even when speech production goes awry—stutterers stop gesturing when caught in a bout of stuttering. Hand and mouth go together.[6]

WHAT WE ALL KNOW, AND DON'T KNOW, ABOUT GESTURE

We think we know all about gesture—or, more likely, we ignore gesture completely. But I've shown you in the introduction that we have misconceptions about gesture, the biggest being that it reveals only feelings and not thoughts. In 1975, a decade after Ekman and Friesen came up with their classification of nonverbal behavior, British social psychologist Michael Argyle listed the roles that nonverbal behavior plays in human communication. For Argyle, nonverbal behavior can express the emotions you're feeling, convey your attitude toward your communication partner, and display aspects of your personality, as well as help you manage taking turns, getting and giving feedback, and controlling your partner's attention. The striking omission from this list is any acknowledgment of the role of nonverbal behavior in communicating the substance of your message.[7]

As far as I can tell, Argyle had his finger on the folk view of nonverbal behavior and gesture. Recall from the introduction that Lady Diana's teacher didn't want her to gesture when she spoke lest she reveal her emotions to those who could use them against her. She wasn't worried about Diana revealing her thoughts or opinions in her gestures—although perhaps she should have been, given Diana's free spirit. Along the same lines, we think that gesture can brand us as liars, but we don't believe that gesture can reveal the content of our lies. The folk view is correct as far as it goes—our hand gestures *can* identify us as liars and reveal our emotions. But they can also give our lies away and even our truths. In other words, nonverbal behavior—gesture—can reveal the substantive ideas we have, as well as our feelings about those ideas. Recall the example from Amy Franklin's dissertation described in the introduction: Adults did as they were told and mis-described the cartoon cat as jumping to the pole, while revealing the cat's true running movements in gesture. Some adults even went so far as to shake their heads *no* while telling these untruths, as though telling the world not to believe them. New work is also finding that facial expressions, another type of nonverbal behavior typically believed to reflect feelings and emotions, can serve as a source of information about others' attitudes toward events. People's reactions to the world are often registered on their faces, and others, including infants and children, can read those emotional reactions. Both facial expressions and gestures can give observers insight into a speaker's emotional state, but only gesture offers insight into the speaker's ideas.[8]

We might still be tempted to restrict conversation to the words that come out of our mouths and not include gesture. The traditional view of communication does just that—it divides communication into its verbal and nonverbal components, with little attention paid to the way the two interact to convey meaning.

Adam Kendon, one of the world's authorities on gesture, was the first to challenge this view. He argued that at least one form of nonverbal behavior—gesture—cannot be separated from the conversation itself. David McNeill, an American psychologist whose name is also synonymous with "gesture," took up Kendon's mantle in his groundbreaking studies. He showed that the gestures you produce as you talk are tightly intertwined with your words. And they are intertwined not only in their timing but also in their meaning. To close your eyes to gesture is to close your eyes to part of the conversation.[9]

So far we've thought about why you gesture and learned that your gestures differ from other nonverbal communication by contributing substantive ideas to a conversation. What can gesture add to a conversation? It can draw attention to people, places, and things in the room: pointing at your communication partner, the ceiling, or a book. It can also draw attention to absent people and things: pointing at the chair where your friend previously sat to refer to him or pointing at a book in the room to refer to the book you keep upstairs. It can highlight the shapes of objects and the trajectories of actions: tracing the S-shape of a snake or moving your hand to illustrate its slithery movements. It can draw "metaphors" in the air: intertwining your fingers to form a single shape while talking about your close relationship with your spouse.

All of the things gesture can "say" could have been said in speech, but the message gesture conveys is never *identical* to the message in speech. If you point at a coffee pot while talking about it, you are saying *what* it is with your words and *where* it is with your gestures. The manual modality is really good at drawing pictures in the air, tracing trajectories, and indicating where to look. It adds a pictorial and dynamic texture to speech and also makes speech more colorful.

But there are times when gesture does more. It adds information that *cannot* be found in the accompanying speech but is essential to comprehending that speech. An adult talking about a cartoon he just saw says, "So the hand is now trying to start the car." This odd formulation is difficult to make sense of without the accompanying gesture: a hand rotating in a circle. The gesture lets the listener know that the car is very old and must be started with a crank. In other instances, speech *can* stand on its own but is clarified when interpreted in the context of gesture. A husband is sitting in the living room and talking with his wife about what their children did that day. He says, "They made a cake, didn't they?" This sentence seems straightforward enough and unambiguous. But while saying the word *cake*, the husband gestures toward the garden. The gesture makes clear that the activity took place not in the kitchen but in the garden and that the cake was made not of flour but of mud. Gesture can convey information that cannot be found in, and is not even implied by, the accompanying speech. If you shut your eyes, you will miss it and risk misinterpreting the speaker's intended, or perhaps unintended, message. Again we see that there's more to a conversation than speech alone.[10]

We've seen how gesture can have a range of different relationships to speech. On the one hand, gesture can reinforce and flesh out the message conveyed in the speech it accompanies, bringing a pictorial and dynamic dimension to that speech. On the other hand, gesture can add information to speech that cannot be found *anywhere* in that speech. In the remainder of this chapter, I focus on this second type of gesture-speech combination simply because it highlights how much you are missing if you don't pay attention to gesture.

WHEN GESTURE CONVEYS DIFFERENT INFORMATION FROM SPEECH

My first graduate student, R. Breckinridge Church—known as Breckie—discovered what we later called *gesture-speech mismatches*. For context, every year in my developmental psychology course, I showed a videotape given to me by Rochel Gelman, a well-known developmental psychologist and one of my two

advisors at the University of Pennsylvania. The video illustrates a
child participating in a conservation task developed by acclaimed
Swiss psychologist Jean Piaget. The experimenter shows a child
two rows containing an equal number of checkers and asks if the
rows have the same or a different number of checkers. The child
looks at the rows and says they have the same number. Then the
experimenter spreads out the checkers in one of the rows and asks
the child if the two rows still have the same number of checkers.
You or I would say, "Yes, of course," as do children who realize that the number of checkers is not affected by moving them
around. But *nonconservers*, as they are known, are certain that
the number has changed. This was Piaget's insightful discovery. To
fully understand what was going on in their minds, he asked children to explain their answers. The nonconservers would say that
the spread-out row of checkers had more than the non-spread-
out row because "you moved them" or because "they take up
more space." But Piaget missed something in those explanations:
every single child gestured in explaining his or her nonconserving
beliefs. After looking at this videotape every year when I showed
it to my class, I finally *saw* the gestures and suggested to Breckie
that she develop a system for describing them.[11]

Each type of explanation that Piaget had identified in the children's speech had a counterpart in gesture, and Breckie developed
a coding system for those gestures. At some point, we decided that
we had to make sure that our speech codes weren't influencing our
gesture codes. So Breckie coded speech with the picture turned off,
and gesture with the sound turned off. And she made an interesting
discovery: sometimes the explanation that a child gave in gesture
did not match the explanation that the child gave in speech. Here's
an example: The child says, "They're different because you moved
them," an explanation that focuses on what the experimenter did.
But, at the same time, the child zigzags his index finger from the
first checker in row 1 to the first checker in row 2, then from the
second checker in row 1 to the second checker in row 2, and so

on. In his gestures, he is pointing out the one-to-one correspondence between the checkers in the two rows, an important step in understanding conservation of number. This nonconserving child, illustrated below, who *says* that the numbers of checkers in the two rows are different after one row is spread out, does seem to know something about conservation—or at least his hands know!

Contrast this child with another nonconserving child, who also says, "They're different because you moved them." This second child, illustrated below, conveys movement information in his gestures: he does a spreading-out gesture. This child has produced the same information in his gestures and his speech, a gesture-speech match, and gives no evidence that he knows anything at all about conservation.

As it turned out, some nonconserving children produced a lot of these "mismatching" responses in which gesture conveyed different information from speech, and some produced none at all. We hypothesized that children

who produced many mismatches might know more about the task than children who produced few and might be able to get more out of instruction in conservation. We gave all of the children a lesson in number conservation and counted up how many chil-dren improved their understanding of the concept after the lesson. Just as we thought, children who had produced gesture-speech mismatches prior to the lesson were likely to improve after-ward—more likely than children who produced no mismatches. Gesture-speech mismatch was a good index of who was, and who was not, ready to learn this concept.[12]

Why is this an important discovery? Gesture reflects what's on a learner's mind and tells us how likely the learner is to change that mind. Knowing who is ready to benefit from instruction *before* the lesson begins allows teachers to be more targeted in their teaching: they can give mismatching children different instruction than they give matching children. As we'll see later in this chapter, teachers do this naturally, without any advice from us! So gestures are informative and are not only seen, but also used, by teachers. In addition to having communicative significance, children's ges-tures, taken in relation to their speech, have cognitive significance. All of the children in the conservation study gestured, so it wasn't whether a child did or didn't gesture that predicted readiness to learn conservation. Rather, it's whether a child's gestures conveyed information not found in the accompanying speech that predicted who was ready to make this particular cognitive transition.

But how do we know that gesture-speech mismatch's ability to predict progress isn't specific to conservation tasks or to children aged five to eight years? To explore how general this phenomenon is, we turned to math. Fourth graders in the United States have difficulty solving problems that look like this: $4 + 6 + 3 = \_ + 3$. The 3 on the right side of the equation confuses them—they don't know what to do with it. Some children add up all of the numbers on the left side of the problem and put 13 in the blank. Other children add up all of the numbers in the entire problem and put 16 in the blank.

Michelle Perry, my second graduate student, gave nine- and ten-year-old children a set of these problems and then asked them to explain how they got their answers, all of which were incorrect. By this time, we knew we had to look at gesture and speech independently, so Michelle coded speech with the picture turned off and gesture with the sound turned off. She noticed that most children gestured as they gave their explanations. Some children expressed the same problem-solving strategy in speech and gesture—they were matchers. For example, they said, "I added the 4, and the 6, and the 3, and got 13," and pointed at the same numbers (the 4, 6, and 3 on the left side of the equation), the *add-to-the-equals-sign* strategy. But about a third of the children expressed different problem-solving strategies in speech and gesture—they were mismatchers. For example, they expressed the *add-to-the-equals-sign* strategy in speech but used a V-shaped hand to point at the 4 and 6 and then pointed with an index finger at the blank— the *grouping* strategy, which highlights the two numbers on the left side of the equation that can be grouped together and added and their sum put in the blank. Again, we thought that the mismatchers might know more about the problem than they revealed in their speech, and more than the matchers. We selected children who solved none of the problems correctly and gave them a math lesson. If mismatching children are ready to learn how to solve mathematical equivalence problems, they should do better after the lesson than matching children—and they did! Gesture-speech mismatch is not unique to five- to eight-year-old children solving conservation problems.[13]

In fact, gesture-speech mismatches are found in many tasks and at many ages—toddlers growing the size of their vocabularies exponentially; preschoolers explaining a game or counting a set of objects; elementary school children talking about seasonal change; adolescents predicting when rods of different materials and thicknesses will bend; adults explaining how gears work or problems involving constant change; and all ages discussing moral dilemmas or explaining how they solved a logical puzzle (the Tower of Hanoi).[14]

Anjana Lakshmi, a graduate student in my lab, is taking gesture-speech mismatch into a new domain: social evaluation. She asks adults to talk about the competence of different groups and watches the gestures they produce as they talk. Most people use the vertical axis when gesturing about competence. In other words, they locate their hands higher on the up-down continuum when gesturing about groups generally considered to be competent (e.g., surgeons, successful businessmen, skilled athletes) and locate their hands lower down on the continuum when gesturing about groups considered less competent (e.g., the elderly, homeless people, children). Anjana then asks them to compare two groups, men and women, for example, with respect to competence. In many circles, it is not acceptable to say that men are more competent than women, but, of course, many people hold this belief nonetheless. Anjana finds, as described in the introduction, that some speakers say that men and women are equally competent, but when talking about men, they produce gestures higher on the vertical axis than the gestures they produce when talking about women. Although these speakers may think they believe that men and women are equally competent, their gestures suggest that, subconsciously perhaps, they think otherwise. At the least, the fact that an adult says that men and women are equally competent but gestures that there is inequality reflects ambivalence on the speaker's part, which suggests that the speaker may be in a state of flux. Whether the speaker becomes more, or less, convinced of male-female equality may depend on the type and persuasiveness of the input he or she receives while in this state.[15]

Gesture gives away unspoken beliefs in people of all ages and on a range of tasks and, when taken in relation to the speech it accompanies, can predict openness to change. Toddlers just learning to talk can only produce one word at a time—they're in the one-word stage. But they are able to combine words with gestures. Sometimes, there is overlap between the meaning of the gesture and the meaning of the word: a point at a bird combined with the word *bird*.

But, in other combinations, there is essentially no overlap between gesture and word: a point at the bird combined with the word *nap*, to describe a picture of a bird with its eyes closed. This second type of combination does the work of a two-word sentence: *bird nap*. Sure enough, when we look several months later, we find that children who had produced combinations in which gesture conveyed different information from speech (point at bird + *nap*) are producing their first two-word sentence (*bird nap*). Children whose gestures routinely overlapped with speech (point at bird + *bird*) are not. Here, too, producing gestures that convey different information from speech sends a signal that you are ready to learn.[16]

We see similar results in older learners. In one study, we tested college students who had taken general chemistry but not organic chemistry on how well they understood stereoisomers, sets of molecules that are mirror images of, and cannot be superimposed onto, one another. They did not understand stereoisomers—no one succeeded on the task, which was to draw the stereoisomer of a molecule if it had one. However, when asked to explain their answers, some students produced gestures relevant to the problem that conveyed different information from their speech. The person pictured in the introduction is one such student: he didn't mention rotation in speech, but he did produce a rotation gesture. We gave all of the students a brief lesson in how to figure out whether two molecules are stereoisomers and then tested them again. The more students produced information in gesture that was relevant to the problem *and* was different from the information conveyed in their speech before the lesson, the more likely they were to improve after instruction. Although most of the gesture studies I have done were conducted with children, I firmly believe that everything we have discovered in children applies to adults as well. Gesture is a window into the minds of young and old.[17]

Our minds speak through our hands, often unbeknownst to us, and tell the world that we are ready to take in new information. But is the world listening?

LISTENERS CAN READ OUR HANDS,
WHICH TELLS THEM ABOUT OUR MINDS

Do ordinary listeners, who do not have the advantage of video replay, notice when gesture and speech convey different information? Perhaps more to the point, can ordinary listeners glean information from gesture when it conveys information that is not found in speech? When Breckie Church first tackled the conservation videotapes, she coded speech and gesture at the same time and wasn't able to see that, at times, gesture conveyed different information from speech. It took an artificial procedure that pulled the two channels apart (coding speech in one pass through the tapes and gesture in a separate pass) for her to recognize that gesture and speech can mismatch. Why was this so hard? As listeners we seamlessly integrate the information we see in gesture with the information we hear in speech—and we have no idea which bits came from where. But that doesn't mean that we can't glean information from gesture. This section assesses whether people who are not trained in gesture coding can glean information from gesture.[18]

The easiest way to find out whether listeners can glean information from a speaker's gestures is to ask them what they heard. David McNeill, a gesture giant and my colleague at the University of Chicago, and his team asked adults to watch a videotape of someone narrating a Tweety Bird cartoon titled "Canary Row." The adults never saw the cartoon; they only heard the narration. Unbeknownst to them, the narrator performed a carefully choreographed program of mismatching gestures. The adults' task was to retell the story, and that retelling was videotaped. Another group of adults heard the soundtrack of the narration but didn't see the narrator.

McNeill and his colleagues found that adults absorbed information from the narrator's gestures and had no idea that they had done so. Let's look at an example. The narrator says, "He comes out the bottom of the pipe," while bouncing his hand up and down. No mention is made in speech of how Sylvester, the bird-chasing cat, came down the pipe, but gesture suggests he did it in a bouncy way. In her retelling, an adult says, he "goes down stairs," while producing a nonbouncy gesture that moves down in a straight line. The adult had picked up the bouncy manner found *only* in the narrator's gesture and translated it into her speech ("goes down stairs"). She must have stored the bouncy manner in some form general enough to serve as the basis for her *linguistic* invention (stairs). She did not say that she got the idea that Sylvester went down *stairs* from the narrator's gestures—my guess is that she had no clue as to where this idea came from. Gesture's power to influence may come, in part, from its subtlety.[19]

We also know that ordinary listeners can glean information from gesture even when we have not artificially constructed the gesture-speech mismatches. We selected examples from the gestures and speech children naturally produced in our conservation and math studies. Half were gesture-speech matches, and half were gesture-speech mismatches. Each example was shown twice to an adult, and the adult was simply asked to give us a sense of the child's reasoning on this particular problem. We thought that adults who interact with children on a daily basis and are constantly called upon to assess their skills might be particularly good gesture readers; we therefore arranged for half of the adults in each study to be teachers and half to be undergraduate students.[20]

How should adults react to a child's gesture-speech mismatch? If they are responding only to the fact that the children are moving their hands (and not to the message conveyed by those hands), they should react to mismatches in the same way that they react to matches. However, if they are responding to the *content* of the children's gestures, they ought to react differently to mismatches versus matches. A mismatch contains two messages, one in speech and one in gesture. If adults are gleaning information from gesture, they ought to say more when they assess a child who produces a mismatch than when they assess a child who produces a match. And they did. In both studies, the adults mentioned information that could not be found anywhere in the speech of the child they were assessing when evaluating mismatchers but not matchers. Importantly, that additional information could, for the most part, be traced back to the gestures the mismatchers produced.

Here's an example. We showed adults the conservation mismatch described earlier in this chapter: the child said that the rows contained different numbers of checkers after the top row had been spread out "because you moved 'em," but in his gestures he indicated that the checkers in one row could be matched in a one-to-one fashion with the checkers in the other row. The adult first repeated what the child said: "you moved 'em." But she also noticed the child's gestures and went on to say, "He pointed . . . he was matching them even though he wasn't verbalizing it." The adult had attributed reasoning to the child that appeared only in the child's gestures (one-to-one correspondence), along with reasoning that appeared in the child's speech (the checkers had been moved). In this example, the adult explicitly refers to the child's gestures, but that doesn't happen in all cases—sometimes the adults translate the information conveyed in the child's gestures into their own speech, just like the participants in McNeill and colleagues' study.

Surprisingly, teachers were no better than undergraduates at gleaning information from children's gestures. But the results really shouldn't have come as a surprise: integrating knowledge from gesture and speech is a basic feature of *everyone's* communication system.[21]

Untrained adults were able to glean substantive meaning from gesture when we pulled out our very best examples of gesture-speech mismatches and displayed them on video. We chose, for example, clear instances of a child using gesture to pair the checkers in one row with the checkers in the second row. Perhaps the adults couldn't help but notice the children's gestures and glean substantive meaning from them. But the situation we set up is a far cry from the real world. We took two steps to create a more natural gesture-reading situation: we had some adults *observe*, and other adults *teach*, real-live children who produced whatever gestures they pleased.

We asked adults to watch a series of children responding to Piagetian conservation tasks. Each adult watched from four to seven children chosen at random from a classroom. Of course, we couldn't stop the child after each task and ask the adult to assess the child's understanding of the task as we had done in our videotape studies. We needed a technique that allowed the adults to make assessments of the children in the moment. To solve this problem, we presented each adult with a checklist, one for each task that the child would perform. Each list contained the typical explanations that children produce on this task, both correct and incorrect. The adult's job was to check off all of the explanations that the child expressed on each task as the child was performing that task. The checklist technique allowed adults to assess the child's performance on a task as it was being administered.

After all of the data in these studies had been collected, we coded and analyzed the explanations that the children had produced. Luckily for us, the children produced both mismatches and matches, so we could tell whether the adults were gleaning information presented only in gesture. As we predicted, the adults did check off explanations that appeared only in a child's gesture (in mismatches), and they did so more often when the child expressed that explanation in gesture than when the child did not express the explanation at all. Adult listeners can get meaning from gesture even when it is unedited and fleeting. Child listeners can do it too.[22]

But the adults in our studies weren't real listeners—they were, at best, overhearers, observers of children doing the task with others. We really needed to study adults when they are part of the conversation. Melissa Singer, a graduate student in the lab at the time, asked professional teachers, first, to watch us giving a child a mathematical equivalence test. Their job was to focus on the child's responses and explanations so that they would know a little bit about each child before teaching them. After watching a child take the math test, the teacher taught the child how to solve problems of this type using any approach she wanted—in other words, she was part of the conversation and a real listener. Eight teachers took part in the study, and each teacher observed and taught approximately five children, one at a time. Interestingly, teachers picked up on whether a child produced gesture-speech mismatches during the math test and during the lesson. They didn't explicitly say that they had read the children's gestures, but we could tell that they had because they treated mismatchers differently from matchers. They gave more different types of problem-solving strategies to children who produced mismatches than to children who didn't produce them, and they produced more of their own mismatches when interacting with children who produced mismatches. The teachers weren't copying the children's mismatches—their mismatches contained two different, but *correct*, strategies to solve these problems; the children's mismatches contained at least one *incorrect* strategy. The teachers generated their own mismatches.[23]

Why would a teacher produce a mismatch? The teachers were not uncertain about their understanding of mathematical equivalence. But I think they may have been uncertain about how to teach a child who says one thing and gestures another. This uncertainty may have led them to produce their own mismatches as they taught children who mismatched.

Instruction containing two correct strategies might seem like a good way to teach a child who is on the brink of change. But is it? To find out, in a subsequent study, Melissa and I gave children the kind of instruction that the teachers spontaneously gave their mismatching students. To our surprise, we found that gesture-speech mismatches were very effective in promoting learning, better than all other kinds of instruction! We'll come back to this in Part III of the book.[24]

The examples in this chapter illustrate how gesture offers a privileged window into peoples' minds. Gesture allows you to quite literally see the ideas that learners, both child and adult, are working on before those ideas appear in their speech. Early insight into a learner's ideas gives you the opportunity to foster those ideas, tailoring your instruction to the learner in front of you. Of course, this tailoring will work only if you are able to glean substantive information from a learner's gestures—and you can. You can read the gestures that all speakers produce, not just child speakers. The final step needed for gesture to play a role in learning is for you to react to the gestures you see and to change your behavior accordingly. And you do, not only when you observe gestures handpicked by experimenters, but also when you interact with others and see the gestures they spontaneously produce.

So here's the bottom line. Speakers often reveal their newly minted thoughts about their understanding of cognitive tasks, as well as their assessments of social groups, through their hands. Their hands also reveal how ready they are to change these understandings and assessments. Listeners can then use those hands to read the speaker's mind and give them input that will promote change. This means that people of all ages have the potential to shape the input they receive from others relevant to their cognitive and social growth just by gesturing as they talk.

3

OUR HANDS CAN CHANGE OUR MINDS

W E'VE SEEN HOW GESTURE CAN REVEAL THOUGHTS YOU DON'T even know you have. But gesture can also change your thoughts. Remember our friend in the introduction whose implicit beliefs about the leadership potential of men and women were visible in his gestures? This belief didn't match his verbally expressed opinion that men and women are equally good leaders—he produced a mismatch between gesture and speech. As we saw in the last chapter, people who produce gesture-speech mismatches on a task are ready to learn that task. The friend who espouses male-female equality in speech and inequality in gesture is on the brink of change. But the direction his change will take—whether he becomes more or less convinced of male-female equality—will depend on the input he gets while he's in this state.

Let's get our friend to interact with someone who not only says that men and women are equally good leaders but also gestures about the equality—perhaps by placing his palms at the same height when talking about men and women. Seeing this person display equality in gesture, combined with a lesson on gender and leadership styles, might propel our friend toward resolving the mismatch and believing unequivocally in equality. If we can get him to produce equality in his own gestures, he might be even more likely to move his beliefs in the direction of equality. I explore these possibilities in this chapter. We will see that gestures—those you see and those you produce—*can* change your mind.

SEEING OTHER PEOPLE GESTURE CAN CHANGE YOUR MIND

Pay attention to gesture in your next conversation: everyone, including you, can read other peoples' gestures—although you might not know you're doing it. But your being able to read gesture does not provide scientific evidence that other peoples' gestures can change your mind. What we need is to give some learners instruction with gesture and other learners instruction without gesture, and observe who learns what. If seeing others gesture changes minds, learners who see gesture in the lesson should do better after the lesson than learners who don't. Martha Alibali and her student Nicole McNeil (my academic grandchild) did just that: she gave grade school children math instruction with and without gesture. Children stacked blocks according to instructions given by a speaker on a video. The speaker said, "Find the block that has an arrow pointing up and a smiley face with a rectangle above it." The speaker used a neutral face and produced one of three types of gestures: reinforcing gesture (gesturing UP and ABOVE while saying *up* and *above*), conflicting gesture (gesturing DOWN and BELOW while saying *up* and *above*), or no gesture. Children who saw reinforcing gesture were more successful after the lesson than children who saw conflicting gesture or no gesture. Martha did a second, comparable manipulation in which she taught preschool children about symmetry (we have symmetry when an object can be divided into two identical halves). She again found that children who saw reinforcing gesture were more successful after the lesson than children who saw no gesture.[1]

Finally, Breckie Church, who you'll recall discovered gesture-speech mismatch, taught conservation—with and without gesture—to two groups of grade school children: native Spanish speakers learning English and monolingual native English speakers. The native English speakers did better on the task after instruction than the Spanish speakers, which is not surprising since the test was conducted in English. What is surprising, however, is the effect of gesture. Children in both groups who saw gesture were more successful after the lesson than children who saw no gesture. Having gesture in instruction helped native and nonnative speakers in equal measure: both groups were twice as likely to improve after instruction when that instruction included gesture than when it didn't. Gesture can help children learn whether they are proficient speakers or just learning the language.[2]

In all three of these studies, the gestures in the lesson matched the speech in the lesson. Melissa Singer and I were emboldened to include mismatching gesture in the lesson particularly because we had found that teachers spontaneously produce mismatches in their math lessons. Our question was whether a lesson containing mismatching gesture (a correct strategy in gesture that was different from another correct strategy in speech) would promote learning. Full disclosure: we didn't think it would work. But we were wrong.

As described earlier, we gave all of the children mathematical equivalence instruction in speech (the *equalizer* strategy). For example, for the problem, $5 + 2 + 7 = \_\_ + 7$, all children heard the experimenter say, "You need to make one side equal to the other side." Some also saw matching gesture: a sweep of the palm under the left side of the equation, followed by a sweep under the right side. Some saw mismatching gesture: pointing at the 5, 2, and 7 on the left, followed by a pull-away gesture under the 7 on the right, representing an *add-subtract* strategy ("add all of the numbers on the left, and subtract the duplicate number on the right"). Some saw no gesture at all. After the lesson, the children were tested again on mathematical equivalence.

The big surprise was that children who got mismatching gestures in their math lesson performed the best—better than children who got either matching gestures or no gestures. Presenting one strategy in gesture and a different strategy in speech turns out to be very good for learning. You might say, "Of course, a mismatch contains more information than a match—an *equalizer* strategy in speech and an *add-subtract* in gesture, compared to a single *equalizer* strategy in both speech and gesture. Two strategies *should* be better for learning than one strategy." But we took care of that problem by giving another group two different strategies (an *equalizer* strategy and an *add-subtract* strategy) entirely in speech. This group did worse than all of the children who got only one strategy in speech, with or without gesture. Two strategies are fine but only if one is presented in speech and the other in gesture. When gesture adds relevant information to speech, it is a very effective teaching tool.[3]

Co-speech gesture is, by definition, produced along with speech. Is it important for gesture to be produced *at the same time as* speech in order for it to promote learning? A teacher could produce one strategy in speech and then follow it up with a second strategy in gesture. Maybe presenting the two pieces of information sequentially would be even better for learning than presenting them simultaneously.

To find out, one of my former graduate students, Eliza Congdon, took the lead on a study that gave children the equalizer strategy in speech. One group heard this strategy in speech at the same time as they saw the add-subtract strategy in gesture (S1 + G2). Another group heard the equalizer strategy in speech before they saw the add-subtract strategy in gesture (S1 then G2). A third group heard the equalizer strategy in speech before they heard the add-subtract strategy in speech (S1 then S2).

Whenever we teach, our first goal is for students to do better after the lesson than before it. But our second goal is for the learning to last—we want students to remember what they learn. So we tested children not only immediately after the lesson but also one week and four weeks afterward. We were looking for *retention* of what children had learned.

A third goal is for students to be able to extend what they learn. At each time point, we tested children on problems that were identical (except for the specific numbers) to the ones on which they had been taught. For instance, children were taught on the problem $4 + 5 + 7 = \_\_ + 7$, then were tested on $3 + 4 + 6 = \_\_ + 6$; only the numbers were different. We also tested children on problems that required generalization beyond the format on which they were taught. After being taught on $4 + 5 + 7 = \_\_ + 7$, children were tested on $3 + 4 + 6 = \_\_ + 8$. Note that not only were the numbers different, but there was no duplicated number on the right side of the equation; to solve the problem, children couldn't follow a rote strategy but had to truly understand what the equals sign means. We were looking for *generalization* of what children had learned.

Not surprisingly, given the study Melissa Singer and I had done together, gesture presented simultaneously with speech worked really well. Children who were given simultaneous speech and gesture in the lesson *retained* what they had learned better than children who were given the same information entirely in speech. In fact, the children who got simultaneous speech and gesture got better and better over time, even though no additional instruction was provided. These children were also able to *generalize* what they had learned better than the children who got the same information entirely in speech, and they got better and better over time on the problems that required generalization. It looks like gesture sets the stage for continued improvement, even without additional instruction. Gesture is the gift that keeps on giving.

Did timing matter? The short answer is yes. Gesture was only effective in the lesson when presented simultaneously with, not after, speech. In fact, children who received sequential gesture and speech (and children who received sequential speech and speech) got worse and worse over time, particularly on problems requiring generalization. In other words, it's not gesture per se that makes a good lesson; it's gesture presented simultaneously with speech. When gesture is presented after speech, learners have difficulty integrating information across the two modalities. Simultaneous presentation makes that step seamless.[4]

Does including gesture in instruction *always* promote learning? Consider the following interchange that occurred when we asked a teacher to instruct a child in mathematical equivalence. When the teacher asked the child to solve the problem 7 + 6 + 5 = __ + 5, the child added up all of the numbers on the left side of the problem and put 18 in the blank. In her *speech*, the teacher pointed out to the child that he was using the *add-to-the-equals-sign* strategy. She said, "So you got this answer by adding these three numbers." However, in her *gestures*, she pointed at the 7, 6, and 5 on the left side of the equation *and* to the 5 on the right side of the equation. She then went on to try to explain how to solve the problem correctly, but before she could finish, the child offered a new solution: 23. Notice that 23 is the number you get when you add up the numbers at which the teacher had pointed. The teacher was genuinely surprised at her student's new answer and completely unaware of the fact that she herself might have given him the idea to add up all of the numbers in the problem. The gestures children see have an impact on what they take from their lessons, for better or for worse. Gesture can promote learning, but it can also obstruct learning. The bottom line is that gesture is always powerful.

PRODUCING YOUR OWN GESTURES CAN CHANGE YOUR MIND BY SHAPING THE INPUT YOU GET

What about when you produce your own gestures? Your gestures tell others what's on your mind. If others can glean information from those gestures and use the information to tailor their input to you, you will have better input than had you not gestured. We have seen that ordinary listeners can read the spontaneous gestures speakers produce, although they are likely to gather this information subconsciously. But for this mechanism to work, listeners not only have to pay attention to the speaker's gestures but also have to change their input in response to those gestures, preferably to a type of input that helps the speaker.

We saw in Melissa Singer's study that teachers gave different input to children who produced mismatching gestures than to children who produced matching gestures. Interestingly, the input they spontaneously gave mismatching children was better for learning than the input they gave matching children. In general, teachers are advised to provide children with multiple ways of solving problems because this kind of instruction maximizes learning. What was new in our study was that the teachers spontaneously gave multiple strategies specifically to mismatching children, who were ready to take advantage of it. The children's mismatching gestures seemed to tune the teachers in to the fact that they were ready to learn, and the teachers responded with instruction that promoted that learning.[5]

We see the same coordinated dance between child and teacher— or, in this case, parent—in early language learning. As we saw earlier with the point at bird + *nap* example, toddlers combine single words with gestures to produce a string that conveys the meaning of a two-word sentence (e.g., point at mommy + *cup*), and they do this *before* they start producing two-word sentences (e.g., *mommy cup*). These gesture + word combinations signal the child's readiness to take the next step and produce two-word sentences. Do parents respond to this signal? Yes, they translate the child's gesture + word into a spoken sentence, saying, "Yes, that's mommy's cup." But parents vary in how often they produce these translations, and this variability matters. Children whose parents often translated their gesture + word "sentences" into spoken sentences were the first to produce two-word sentences. The parents' targeted responses helped their children take their first step into sentences. Notice, however, that the children's gesture + word combinations elicited these targeted responses from the parents. The children were eliciting the input they needed just by moving their hands.[6]

PRODUCING YOUR OWN GESTURES
CAN CHANGE YOUR MIND BY AFFECTING HOW YOU THINK

The gestures you produce not only change your mind indirectly by influencing the input you get from others, but can also have a direct effect on your mind by changing what you're thinking. I first tell you about situations where your own gestures get in the way of thinking and then move on to situations where your gestures help you think.

Your own gestures can set you up for failure. When Sian Beilock was my colleague at the University of Chicago, we set up a situation in which the gestures adults produced on a task had the potential to affect their subsequent performance on the task. We used the Tower of Hanoi (TOH) task because it's almost impossible for people to explain how they performed this task without gesturing. As mentioned earlier, TOH is a logical puzzle containing three poles and a stack of round disks. The goal is to move all of the disks, which are stacked from largest to smallest on one pole, to one of the other poles following two rules: you can only move one disk at a time, and you can never put a bigger disk on top of a smaller disk. All of the adults successfully solved the problem, although some needed more time, and more disk moves, than others. We then asked them to explain how they solved the problem. The disks we used were weighted—the biggest disk weighed the most, the littlest disk the least—but no one talked about the weight of the disks. They talked only about where they moved the big, little, and medium-sized disks. They did, however, introduce the weight of the disks into their explanations through

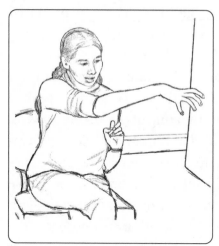

their gestures. When they talked about the littlest disk, some of the adults used one hand in their gestures (illustration on the left); others used two hands (illustration on the right).[7]

The littlest disk could be moved with either one hand or two, so it was perfectly reasonable for the adults to split on this dimension. But as it turned out, the choice of one hand versus two had implications for the next time they solved the puzzle, right after their explanations.

As I told you earlier, the second time the adults solved the TOH task, some of them got a surprise. One group of adults solved the puzzle a second time using the same stack of disks, where the heaviest disk was the biggest disk. But another group solved the puzzle on a stack of disks that looked the same but differed in one crucial respect: the heaviest disk was now the littlest disk, and the lightest was the biggest disk. What this meant was that, for this group on the second time, the littlest disk could no longer be lifted with one hand and required two.

The group that solved the puzzle with the same set of disks got faster and used fewer moves the second time around. But the group that had the disks switched on them was slower and used more moves when solving the puzzle the second time. The interesting finding is that we could predict who would get slower on the second TOH task by looking at the gestures the adults produced in their explanations. Adults who had used a one-handed gesture when talking about the littlest disk did worse the second time around than adults who had used a two-handed gesture. Using a one-handed gesture right before doing the task with the switched disks set the adults up for failure—thinking about the littlest disk as a light disk that could be lifted with one hand was not helpful since lifting the disk now required two hands. The more one-handed gestures a person used in their explanations, the worse they did on the second TOH puzzle—but only in the group with the switched disks. The gestures that the adults produced in the other group who used the same disks both times did *not* predict their subsequent performance since the littlest disk could be lifted with either one or two hands.

Maybe the adults who used a one-handed gesture when describing the littlest disk were already thinking about the disk as light, and that's why they used this gesture. If so, then the gestures that the adults produced did *not* shape their thinking; rather their thinking shaped their gestures. To see if this was the case, we did the task again using the same procedure, but this time the adults were not asked to explain how they solved the task so that they produced no gestures. This shouldn't matter if their gestures were *reflecting* their thinking—the results should be unchanged. But if their gestures were *changing* their thinking, the results should look very different simply because they hadn't gestured. It turned out that the results changed dramatically. Now both groups looked the same on the second TOH task: both got faster and used fewer moves. What this means is that, when the adults gestured, the one-handed gestures they produced influenced how they viewed the littlest disk (they now saw it as a light disk), which in turn affected how they solved the second TOH task (they took more time and used more moves). When they produced no gestures, they had no problem with the second TOH task.[8]

People gesture when they describe how they tie their shoes, rotate gears, or balance blocks. The information conveyed in these gestures often reflects the actions they have executed on these objects and is found only in gesture—in other words it is not conveyed in the accompanying speech. Our TOH study shows that these action gestures have consequences not only for listeners but also for the gesturers themselves—and the consequences aren't always positive.[9]

Your own gestures can slow down learning. As another example of your own gestures getting in your way, take a study done by two PhDs from the University of Chicago: Martha Alibali, who applies work on gesture to math education; and Sotaro Kita, who helped spread gesture studies to Europe and Great Britain. The two reasoned that if gesture is good at highlighting and structuring perceptual-motor information—movements that can be seen and felt—then it should promote ideas that perceptual-motor information supports. They asked adults to imagine strings of connected gears and had them predict which way the last gear would rotate if the first gear was rotated in a particular direction. There are two ways to solve gear problems: (1) You can use the parity strategy: count up the number of gears in the string—if it's an odd number, the last gear in the string will rotate in the same direction as the first gear; if it's an even number, the last gear will rotate in the opposite direction. (2) You can simulate the gear movements by tracing the path of each gear in the string in sequence and observe whether the last gear is moving in the same direction as the first gear.

One group of adults was allowed to use gesture as they talked aloud while solving the problems. Another group was not allowed to use their hands. Adults who were allowed to gesture used the simulation strategy more than adults who were not allowed to gesture (they used the parity strategy). The adults' gestures highlighted perceptual-motor information, which, in turn, made the discovery of the parity solution less likely. Note that, in this case, gesturing is doing more harm than good since it gets in the way of finding an efficient strategy for solving the gears problem. Although both strategies help you arrive at the correct solution, the parity strategy gets you there more quickly and is more easily generalizable to a new set of gears. The bottom line is that gesture goes beyond reflecting thought—gesture changes thought, in this case, by introducing a particular action into our minds. Gesture can force us to think with our hands, and those thoughts have cognitive consequences, good and bad.[10]

In the TOH task, we set up the situation so that gesture had the potential to affect the adults' subsequent performances. But we didn't control the adults' gestures—they gestured whenever and however they wanted. Making people gesture in a particular way is another approach to this question. If we make them gesture, and if gesturing affects how they think, their thinking should change accordingly. Let's take a look at a series of studies following this approach, first controlling the gestures that young children make when they learn words, and then controlling the gestures that school-aged children make when they learn about mathematical equivalence. In both cases, gesturing improves learning.

Encouraging toddlers to produce their own gestures increases their vocabulary. Before children speak, most communicate using gesture, and these gestures predict later word learning in infancy and through preschool. For instance, the more different kinds of objects children point at when they are eighteen months old, the larger their vocabulary on entering school. The big question is whether these early pointing gestures play a causal role in fostering vocabulary development. Does gesturing help children become better word learners? If gesture does play a causal role, and if child gesture can be increased experimentally, we should be able to increase the number of words children produce by increasing their gestures.[11]

Eve LeBarton, a graduate student in my lab, first asked whether she could increase children's gesturing through an experimental manipulation. She went to children's homes when they were sixteen months old and observed them interacting with a parent in a naturalistic setting. That observation gave her a good estimate of both the number of gestures and the number of words the children produced at home. That was step one.

She then showed each child a book of pictures. Looking at one of the pictures—say, a picture of a dress—she said, "Look, that's a dress." At the same time, she pointed at the picture of the dress, and asked the child to put his or her index finger on the dress ("Can you do this?"). All of the children cooperated and pointed at the pictures when asked to. Two other groups of children also heard Eve's speech but had different gesture experiences: the second group saw Eve point at the dress and the other target pictures but didn't point themselves, and the last group experienced no gesture at all (they neither saw nor produced gesture). That was step two.

Eve came back to the child's home and repeated these two steps every week for seven weeks. She observed children interacting naturally with their parents for the first half hour and then interacted with them herself for the second half hour. The eighth visit was designed to be a poststudy assessment of parent-child interaction at home (Eve did not interact with the children at all during this visit).

At the end of the eight weeks, the children who were asked to gesture, not surprisingly, increased their gestures during the experimental sessions with Eve. They did what they were told. More interestingly, they also increased the number of gestures they produced *with their parents* in their naturalistic interactions. Eve was successful in getting children to increase their gesturing. The other two groups didn't increase their gesturing in either the experimental sessions or the naturalistic sessions with their parents.

But our question is whether increased gesture in the children who were told to gesture led to an increase in spoken vocabulary. It did. On the eighth visit, when children interacted with their parents, children who had been told to gesture during the study produced more words than children in the other two groups. Importantly for our causal argument, the more gestures the children in this group produced during the preceding seven visits, the more words they produced at the end of the study. Note that, in this case, seeing the experimenter point was *not* enough to increase a child's spoken vocabulary. The children had to do the pointing themselves.[12]

We also told young word-learning children which iconic gestures to produce. We found that telling children to perform a squeezing motion in the air, for example, helps them learn words for a squeezing action. To be certain they didn't know the words we taught them, we made the words up. As mentioned earlier, Elizabeth Wakefield, a former postdoc in my lab, taught children a new word for an action (for example, *tiff*). She asked some children to produce a particular iconic gesture for the action and asked others to watch an experimenter produce the iconic gesture. Doing the gesture led to learning. It also helped children generalize the word to new contexts and retain what they had learned. Interestingly, in this study, seeing the experimenter gesture led to as much learning, generalization, and retention as doing the gesture.[13]

Encouraging children to produce their own gestures improves their math learning. We have also controlled the gestures that older children produce on mathematical equivalence tasks. We trained them in how to move their hands before the math lesson and asked them to produce those hand movements before and after each problem they attempted during the lesson. For example, children were taught movements to make on the problem $4 + 2 + 7 = \_\_ + 7$, which was written out in magnetic numbers. The experimenter showed the child how to point with a *V*-shaped hand at the first two numbers (4 and 2) and then point with an index finger at the blank, while saying, "I want to make one side equal to the other side." Children who gestured learned as much as children taught to move the magnetic numbers around (put the 4 and the 2 together and hold them under the blank). But the children who gestured were better at generalizing their new knowledge to problems in another format ($4 + 2 + 7 = \_\_ + 5$) than children who moved the numbers around. Producing particular gestures on a task helps you *learn* the task, *retain* what you learned, and *generalize* that knowledge to new contexts—just the things we want learners to be able to do after a lesson.[14]

But can gesture really be used as a general teaching device if we have to teach children a new set of gestures for each task? What would happen if we just told children to gesture as they explained their answers to a problem? Would that help them get more out of a lesson? Sara Broaders, a graduate student in my lab, wanted to find out. She first asked children to solve mathematical equivalence problems and explain their answers—that gave her a good sense of the kinds of gestures each child produced on these problems. She then asked them to solve another set of problems of the same type, but this time she either asked them to gesture when they explained their answers to the problems or not to gesture.

Not surprisingly, the children who were told to gesture did, and the children who were told not to gesture didn't. In other words, they followed instructions. But what did the gesturers do with their gestures? In the spirit of full disclosure, we had thought that asking children to focus on gestures might mean that they would no longer produce mismatches—that the content of their gestures would match the content of their words. But we were wrong. When we told children to gesture, they produced many new problem-solving strategies in gesture that they had not produced before, and those strategies were *not* ones they produced in speech. In other words, they produced lots of gesture-speech mismatches. Most surprisingly, a lot of the new strategies that they produced in gesture (and not in speech) were correct. So these children, who continued to solve the problems incorrectly and give incorrect explanations in speech, were at the same time giving *correct* explanations in gesture—all because they were told to gesture.

Now for the important part: After all of this, we gave all the children instruction in mathematical equivalence. The children who had been told to gesture before the lesson were more likely to improve after the lesson than the children who had been told not to gesture. Gesturing prior to the lesson helped children benefit from the teacher's instructions. The promising point is that the gestures the children produced were entirely of their own choosing. This approach could scale up and make gesture a powerful teaching tool for a range of classroom topics.[15]

Encouraging children to produce their own gestures improves their abstract reasoning. Can gesture be used to teach topics even more abstract than math? If so, that would dramatically increase gesture's reach. Before turning to this question, we need to think about whether gesture is used to convey abstract ideas. Let's take *time*, an inherently abstract idea, as an example. Do we try to capture it with gesture?

When they visualize time, people in many cultures think of the future as being in front of them and the past as being behind them. The gestures produced with descriptions of time in these cultures move forward from the body for the future and backward for the past. But another way of thinking about time is illustrated by the Aymara language, an Amerindian language spoken in the Andean highlands of western Bolivia, southeastern Peru, and northern Chile. In Aymara, the basic word for *front* (*nayra*, "eye/front/sight") is also a basic expression meaning *past*, and the basic word for *back* (*qhipa*, "back/behind") is a basic expression meaning *future*. In other words, the past is treated as being in front of you (since you've experienced it and it is known) and the future is treated as being behind you (unknown and yet unseen). The gestures that Aymara speakers produce go hand in hand with this framing—gestures in front for the past, gestures behind for the future. The Aymara speakers' gestures capture their conceptualization of time.[16]

Now we can think about whether gesture can change a speaker's conception of time. No one, to my knowledge, has encouraged speakers to gesture in particular ways when talking about time, but Barbara Tversky and her student gave listeners the same scenario, accompanied by either a forward-moving gesture or a backward-moving gesture. The experimenter approached each adult and when side by side said, "Next Wednesday's meeting has been moved forward two days. What day is the meeting now that it has been rescheduled?" Half of the adults saw the experimenter produce a forward-moving gesture; half saw a backward-moving gesture. The adults who saw the forward-moving gestures thought the meeting had been rescheduled for Friday. Those who saw the backward-moving gestures thought the meeting had been rescheduled for Monday. The gestures that the adults saw influenced how they interpreted the experimenter's statement about the timing of the meeting. Gesture can influence our conception of abstract ideas as well as concrete ideas.[17]

Let's take another example: moral reasoning. Moral education is an important topic these days because it prepares children to be fully informed and thoughtful citizens. As described earlier, when asked to reason about moral dilemmas, children gesture. The gestures they produce on this task are often metaphoric and display abstract relations. Adults gesture too, and their gestures are also abstract. An adult says, "When you have two opportunities like this with interests that compete with one another, this is the point where people develop skills of negotiation." As shown in the illustration on the next page, the speaker displays these rather abstract ideas in his hands: He first holds up two C-shaped hands, representing the two different interests. He then faces the C's toward each other, representing the competition between the two interests. He finally alternates moving each C in a circle, representing negotiation. This verbal response and the accompanying gestures display two points of view, indicating that the adult has considered multiple perspectives.

If we could increase a child's ability to consider more than one perspective, we might be able to improve that child's moral reasoning. We thought that gesture might be helpful in getting children to consider multiple perspectives simply because, as in the example just given, the hands can easily be used to represent more than one point of view. As in our math tasks, we told some children to move their hands when they explained a moral dilemma but didn't tell them *how* to move them. Just telling children to move their hands led them to produce, *for the first time*, multiple-perspective gestures of the sort seen in the adult example. And these gestures led to multiple-perspective *spoken* responses.

We then gave the children a lesson in moral reasoning. All children received instruction on the two-brothers dilemma, one brother who cheats and one who steals. Children had to decide which is worse, cheating or stealing. As in earlier studies of moral training, which made use of the Socratic method, we had two experimenters participate in the lesson: one agreed with whatever choice the child had made, and the other disagreed; neither gestured. The experimenters argued back and forth, giving reasons that illustrated multiple perspectives on the dilemma. Our manipulation worked, but only with the children who had been told to gesture before the lesson; they improved in their moral reasoning after the lesson. Children who had been told not to gesture did not.[18]

This easily implemented method, which hinges on gesture, is a good way to get children to take the first step toward improving how they reason about moral dilemmas. This step is necessary for the development of moral reasoning but on its own is not sufficient. The next question is whether this first step can have a ripple effect, leading to mature moral reasoning across topics, over time, and in more heterogeneous populations.

This is an important result because it allows us to scale up the impact of gesture. Merely telling your students to gesture when explaining hard topics can get them to express new ideas. If they are then given a lesson on the topic, they are more likely to make progress on the topic than if they had not gestured. And this works for topics as different as math and moral reasoning. We'll come back to this result later when we talk about how gesture can be harnessed in the classroom.

This result is important for another, related reason. When we first told people to focus on their hands, I thought that the focus might ruin gesture's ability to capture unspoken knowledge. If you concentrate on your hands while you talk, you might try to align your hands with your words, which would mean that you would not produce gesture-speech mismatches. But I was wrong. Telling people to gesture brought out implicit, unspoken ideas in both the math task and the moral reasoning task. And expressing those ideas in gesture made people ready to learn the task. This result frees us to put the focus on gesture as a legitimate part of our conversation—and still have it serve as an effective learning tool.

DOES SEEING OTHERS GESTURE HAVE THE SAME IMPACT ON LEARNING AS MAKING YOUR OWN GESTURES?

Let's take a moment to think about whether seeing people gesture works in the same way as performing your own gestures. Seeing gesture and gesturing yourself both promote learning, retention, and generalization in math- and word-learning tasks. And seeing a teacher inadvertently point at an extra number can lead a child to the wrong answer on a math task, just as using one versus two hands in your own gestures on the Tower of Hanoi puzzle can, when the weights of the disks are switched, lead you to perform less well the next time you solve the task. In other words, gesture helps you think and learn and can also hurt your thinking and learning, not only when you see gesture but also when you produce it. Gesture is powerful in someone else's hands *and* in your own hands.

But the timing of gesture and speech can have different effects on learning for seeing gesture versus doing gesture. Children learn, retain, and generalize more when their *teacher* produces gesture simultaneously with speech than when she produces gesture and speech sequentially. But the findings are different when *children* produce their own gestures. We taught some children to simultaneously produce a grouping strategy in gesture and an equalizer in speech and others to produce the same two strategies sequentially. We found that the two groups of children were equally good at learning and retaining the content of their lessons when they produced gesture sequentially with speech as when they produced it simultaneously with speech. In other words, aligning gesture and speech is important for learning and retention when gesture is in the hands of the teacher, but not when it is in the hands of the learner.[19]

We don't know why seeing and doing gesture differ in this respect, but we can speculate. When you see gesture produced at the same time as speech, speech provides a context that helps you interpret somebody else's gesture. But when *you* produce gesture along with your speech, you don't need the context since you already know what you're saying. As a result, your own gesture and your own speech don't have to occur simultaneously. Whatever the reason, these findings have serious implications for teaching: producing gestures yourself as a teacher may work differently from asking your students to produce gesture. This means that we can't just generalize from seeing gesture to doing gesture—we need to study both situations before we can advise teachers.

But there's no doubt that both watching someone else gesture and performing your own have an effect on learning—a positive effect if the gestures align with the to-be-learned concept, a negative effect if they don't. The gestures you spontaneously produce when you talk not only tell the world what you're thinking; they—along with the gestures others produce—can also change the way you think. Gesturing is not a decorative frill but is instead a critical part of interpersonal communication—even if most people don't recognize its role or importance.

We have been looking at gestures that are produced along with speech. But what about gestures that occur without speech? We often use gesture to get an idea across when speech is difficult or inappropriate—an index finger held over the mouth to get everyone to quiet down or a hand pretending to write in the air to call for the check in a busy restaurant. These gestures are used without speech, although they can also be used with speech. As mentioned earlier, they are *emblems*, conventionalized hand signals that vary from culture to culture. But what about a different type of gesture that is used without speech: gestures used by a child who does not know a conventional language and is using gesture as a primary communication system. Do the child's hands move in the same way that hands do when they co-occur with speech? In other words, can the gestures that typically accompany speech be used on their own to form a language?

Part II delves into this question and finds that the answer is *no*. The hands take on a different form, one that looks like the discrete building blocks of language, when they are forced to take on the full burden of communication. You might be thinking that we know this already—sign languages, used by deaf communities as their primary communication system, are characterized by combinations of discrete units at many levels. But sign languages are conventional systems of hand movements transmitted from one generation to the next. My focus in Part II is on hand movements that are *spontaneously* created to serve the full needs of communication. This phenomenon has important implications for our journey into gesture as it shows us that spontaneous gesture doesn't *have* to look like the gestures we have been exploring in Part I. Probing gesturing hands that take on the full burden of communication puts into bold relief gesturing hands that accompany language.

Part II
SPEAKING WITH OUR HANDS

4

AS LONG AS THERE ARE HUMANS, THERE WILL BE LANGUAGE

S O HOW DO YOU COMMUNICATE WHEN YOU AREN'T GIVEN A LAN-guage to learn? This question really asks about how the mind expresses itself when it doesn't have access to an established language. To find out, let's return to the scenario I asked you to imagine in the introduction—a world in which all forms of language (spoken, signed, written) and your knowledge of these forms are wiped out, but everything else human about you remains. Do you think you could reinvent language? And if you did, what would it look like? Would it resemble human language as we know it?

The answers to these questions depend on answers to an age-old question: Are languages the products primarily of *culture* or of the *mind*? Human languages differ on the surface—it's obvious that knowing English does not mean that you automatically know Turkish, Swahili, or any other language. The linguistic properties that *differ* across languages could be the result of handing language down from one generation to the next—that is, the result of *cultural transmission*. However, you know something about how all languages work from having learned

English. All human languages have structural similarities: each draws from a constrained set of sounds, and specific rules dictate how those sounds form words and how those words form sentences. The particular rules differ from language to language, but all languages draw from the same set of elements and have rules for combining the elements. The linguistic properties that are the *same* across languages could reflect how our *minds* structure communication.

If language is strictly the end product of cultural transmission, a tradition handed down from generation to generation, there is no guarantee that it would be reinvented if it were wiped out. And even if we did reinvent language, we might invent a system that doesn't have the units and combinatorial rules found in modern languages. But if language is the way it is because the capacity for language is hardwired in our brains, not only would we be able to reinvent language if it were wiped out, but we would invent a language that shares characteristics with the language we lost.

This may seem like a purely hypothetical debate. Short of the outright eradication of cultures, languages don't just disappear. And when they do, there is no one around to compare them to what comes next. One way to figure out whether language was a onetime invention or can be reinvented anew is to find a child who has not been exposed to a usable model for language and see what that child does. As you can imagine, this is a rare event. But due to a confluence of social and physical factors described in detail later, some deaf children end up being unable to acquire the spoken language that surrounds them and are not exposed to sign language. They live in the modern-day world but don't have access to a usable language model. It turns out that children in this circumstance communicate and use their hands to do so. For you to understand how this spontaneously created gestural communication could resemble human language, I need to give you a little background on how the hands are used in established sign languages of the deaf.

WHAT IS SIGN LANGUAGE?

People who can hear process language through the mouth and ears. But deaf people use sight, gesture, and even touch—deaf people who are also blind have invented a tactile language that involves "speaker" and "listener" touching each other's hands and arms with both of their hands. These manual languages are very different from spoken languages on the surface, but they serve the same functions as spoken language and, deep down, are organized in similar ways.[1]

Before talking about the functions and forms of sign language, let's get a few common misconceptions out of the way. First of all, there is not just one universal sign language. Sign languages differ from culture to culture, just like spoken languages. Someone who is fluent in Chinese Sign Language will not necessarily be able to communicate with someone who is fluent in American Sign Language (ASL). Second, sign languages are not derived from spoken languages. In fact, ASL has more lexical items and syntactic structures in common with French Sign Language (FSL) than with British Sign Language (BSL). ASL is a descendent of FSL and thus has a stronger historical connection to it than to BSL. This connection explains the commonalities between ASL and FSL—just as the historical connection between American English and British English explains the commonalities between those two spoken languages.[2]

Just like spoken languages, sign languages are used to comment on things, to question things, to demand things, to negate things, and so on. They are also used for less obvious functions—talking to yourself, mumbling, whispering, cursing, storytelling, reciting poetry, and performing theater. Sign language can serve any function served by spoken language, including promoting the acquisition of object categories in young infants.[3]

Sign languages also have many of the same types of linguistic structures as spoken languages. For example, in English, if you say, "The cat bit the dog," the cat is doing the biting, and the dog is receiving the bite. The *order* of the words tells you who is doing what to whom. So too in sign language. The order in which the signs are produced can tell you who is biting and who is being bitten. Sign languages have other devices besides word order that can get this information across (as do spoken languages). For example, a signer can produce the sign for cat on his right and the sign for dog on his left, then move the sign for bite from right to left to indicate that the cat is the biter. All languages, including sign languages, have systematic ways of indicating who is acting and who is acted upon.[4]

One last point of commonality between sign and speech is essential to the argument I'm making here: deaf children who are exposed to a sign language from birth by their deaf parents acquire that language as naturally as hearing children exposed to a spoken language by their hearing parents. They follow comparable steps, on roughly the same timetable, as hearing children acquiring spoken language. Deaf children babble with their fingers (they make repetitive, meaningless finger movements just like a hearing child saying *Ba-ba-ba-ba*), then produce single signs, then two-sign sentences, and finally long sign sentences that convey complicated ideas and tell stories. And they express the same ideas in their signs and sign sentences as children learning spoken language.[5]

DEAF CHILDREN BORN TO HEARING PARENTS

We've established that deaf children born to deaf parents who use sign language learn that language just like any child learns language. But what most people don't know is that the vast majority of deaf children are *not* born to deaf parents. In the United States, 90 percent of deaf children are born to hearing parents. These parents are not likely to know sign language—they may not even know a deaf person. They want their children to learn their spoken language so that the children can communicate with them and their friends and relations. But learning a spoken language is not easy for a child with a profound hearing loss—even when the child is taught with the oralist method. Oralism gives deaf children hearing amplification and teaches them to use visual cues (like lip-reading) to learn spoken language. But it's really hard to learn spoken language by reading lips, and most profoundly deaf children fail to learn speech well enough to use it freely in natural-istic situations.[6]

When I began my studies fifty years ago, oralism was a popular way to educate deaf children. There were schools (mostly board-ing schools) where sign language was taught, but sending a deaf child to a signing school is difficult for hearing parents. First of all, sending a small child away to school is hard, and, once there, the child will learn a sign language that the parents (and grandparents and neighbors) don't know. Learning an entirely new language, in a new modality, is not easy for young parents. So many hearing parents sent their deaf children to local oral schools for the deaf even though learning spoken language is difficult.

The deaf children I began studying in 1972 were all born to hearing parents who didn't know sign language. The children were not able to learn spoken language, even with hearing aids (cochlear implants were not widely used at the time), and they had not been exposed to sign language anywhere in their worlds. In this sense, the children in my studies were living the far-fetched scenario I asked you to imagine earlier—surrounded by the mod-ern world without a usable language.

What did these children do? They used their hands to communicate—they gestured. But did their gestures resemble human language? Had they really reinvented language on their own? Together with Lila Gleitman and Heidi Feldman at the Uni-versity of Pennsylvania, I was determined to find out.

I still remember the first family we visited, a family I remain in contact with. The child was profoundly deaf and attended a local oral school. Heidi and I walked into the house and were astounded. Here was a deaf child, whom we called David, gesturing up a storm at two years, ten months of age. He gestured to his hearing parents, to his hearing siblings, and to us. We had brought with us a toy bear that beat a drum when turned on, and David described it by producing a beating motion in the air to ask us if he could play with it. Here was a child who had invented a communication system.

Seeing David use his hands to comment, request, and question told us that deaf children who can't learn speech and aren't exposed to sign, growing up in caring families, can communicate. But it doesn't tell us whether their communication is *language*.

DO THE GESTURES DEAF CHILDREN CREATE FORM A LANGUAGE?

People have different definitions of what constitutes a language. And we have the additional problem that our participants are children and so could invent, at best, child language. We decided to operationalize language as what young children who are learning either speech or sign from their parents do when they communicate. To determine whether the deaf children's gestures qualified as language, we used the methods that researchers use to analyze hearing children's speech and deaf children's sign. We used these methods to look for patterns in the deaf children's gestures and then compared whatever patterns we found to patterns reported in hearing children's speech and deaf children's signs. The first hint that the deaf children might be doing something that could be considered language was the fact they were *not* using pantomime to communicate.[7]

A story from my time in Philadelphia illustrates the difference between pantomime and homesign. I was at a performance of a mime who was behaving as he should, reenacting events using a series of exaggerated motions that the audience could easily identify—and he did it quite well. At some point in the performance, he needed to introduce the next act, which was a singer. This was new information that he needed to generate and communicate,

not reenact. He didn't want to break his silence to do the introduction, but pantomime was no longer adequate. So he pointed at
the singer and opened his mouth wide to represent singing before
pointing at himself and moving his fingers up and down as though
he were playing the piano (he was going to accompany the singer
on the piano). When the mime needed to convey a message to the
audience, he abandoned pantomime and turned to the types of
gestures homesigners produce.

You'll remember from the introduction that when a mime
describes eating an apple, he uses his whole body to reenact the
scene—he moves as though picking up an apple, shining it on
his shirt, moving his hand to his mouth and taking a large bite
out of the invisible object, and then slowly chewing. But that's
not what the deaf children did. To talk about eating an apple, a
homesigner points at the apple and then jabs his hand (fingers and
thumb touching) toward his mouth, an EAT gesture. If he wants
to indicate who should be doing the eating, he might then point at
someone in the room, for example, at Heidi, me, or himself. The
child breaks the event up into pieces, each piece represented by a
separate gesture—like the mime introducing his singer. He then
has to combine these gestures into a string to convey the complete
message. Our task was to figure out what each of the pieces represented (actors, objects, relations, and so forth) and how the pieces
were combined.

Heidi and I watched scores and scores of videotapes of David
and five other deaf children of hearing parents in the Philadelphia
area. We didn't know what would be important to capture, so we
wrote down as much as we could—every movement, every change
in handshape, even eye and eyebrow changes—on large drawing
pads. We looked for patterns, and over time we found ourselves
concentrating on what the children did with their hands—their
shapes, movements, and locations. Following common practice,
we called these hand gestures *homesigns* (because, as noted earlier,
they were created in the home) and the children *homesigners*.

From birth up until around eighteen months, the homesigners used gestures just like hearing children do. They pointed at objects that they wanted you to look at, they held out an open palm when they wanted you to give them something, and they occasionally produced a gesture that looked like an action—an *iconic gesture*. The EAT gesture mentioned earlier is an example of an iconic gesture, as is twisting the hand as though trying to open a jar to get mom to open the bubbles. The two groups' paths begin to diverge at about eighteen months. Hearing children start to combine their gestures with words; they very rarely combine two gestures. But the homesigners do combine gestures: points with points, points with iconic gestures, and iconic gestures with other iconic gestures.

These combinations expressed the same ideas that hearing children express with their word + gesture combinations and word + word combinations. When a homesigner pointed at the toy duck in my hand and then at his mother, he was asking me to give the duck to his mother, just as an English-learning hearing child might use the two words *that momma* to mean "give the duck to momma." When he pointed at a jar and then produced a TWIST gesture in the air, the homesigner was asking me to twist the jar lid open so that he could blow bubbles, just as a hearing child might say *twist that* to mean "twist open the jar."

Homesigners create gesture sentences that are structured. The homesigners' gesture combinations were like hearing children's word combinations in another way: they followed a consistent ordering. In the sentence requesting me to give mother the duck, the gesture for duck, the object of the action—what we typically call the *patient* in linguistics—came first, and the gesture for mother, the patient's landing place, the *location*, came second. In the sentence asking me to twist open the jar of bubbles, the gesture for jar, the *patient*, came first, and the TWIST gesture, the *action*, followed. The homesigners followed this patient-action ordering even when the sentence contained two iconic gestures: an EAT gesture referring to a grape, the *patient*, came first, followed by the GIVE gesture for the *action*.[8]

I find it striking that the homesigners used a consistent ordering for their gesture sentences. As I noted earlier, the ordering rules of established languages help listeners determine who is doing what to whom. If I said, "Jack push" and then "push Jill," you would infer from the ordering of the words, *Jack, push, Jill*, that Jack pushed Jill and not the other way around because doers (agents) precede verbs in English, and done-to's (patients) follow verbs. As just described, in homesign, patients precede verbs: *jar* TWIST; *grape* GIVE. Note that producing gestures that follow a consistent ordering is not really needed for someone to figure out what's going on here: a jar can be twisted but cannot twist something else; grapes can be given but cannot themselves give. So the homesigners followed a consistent ordering in their gestures even when it wasn't necessary to get their message across. In other words, ordering principles must be neither handed down from generation to generation nor useful to the listener to crop up in human language. They seem to reflect an innate desire to organize our thoughts when we communicate them to others.

Homesigners distinguish between nouns and verbs. Homesigners also use the same iconic gesture to refer to an object and an action—much like we do in English when we use the word *hammer* to refer to the tool and to the action performed with the tool. Homesigners use TWIST to refer to the jar and to the twisting action required to open it. But, importantly, homesigners abbreviate a gesture when it's used as a noun to refer to an object—they produce one rotation in TWIST when it refers to the jar (page 106, illustration on the left) rather than several twists when it refers to the twisting act (illustration on the right). And they produce the TWIST gesture at chest level (illustration on the left) when it refers to the jar itself but near, though not on, the jar when it refers to the twisting act (illustration on the right).[9]

In other words, homesigners introduce a distinction between nouns and verbs into their gestures, a characteristic of human languages. This is another property of language that does not depend exclusively on language being handed down from generation to generation within a culture.

Homesigners create sentences with hierarchical structure. One last property of homesign is worth mentioning. All languages (including sign languages) have hierarchical structure in which smaller units are embedded within larger units. This is a key property of human languages (but it is not a characteristic of the gestures that accompany speech). In English, you can say, "Dogs bite," which is a simple two-word structure (illustration on the left). Or you can say, "That dog bites," specifying which dog is doing the biting. *That* modifies the word *dog*, and the two-word phrase *that dog* serves as the subject of the sentence. The sentence thus contains hierarchical structure: [[*that dog*] *bites*] (illustration on the right).[10]

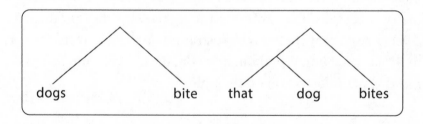

Homesigners refer to objects either by pointing at them or by producing an iconic gesture. For instance, they might simply point at a grape if it's within view, or gesture GRAPE, with fingers and thumb jabbed at the mouth, to indicate that the grape is a member of the category *edible things* (in this instance, the child was talking about a plastic grape so was not likely to be gesturing about eating). When homesigners ask for the grape, they either point at the grape and gesture GIVE (*that give*) (illustration on the left) or gesture GRAPE and then GIVE (*grape give*) (illustration on the right).

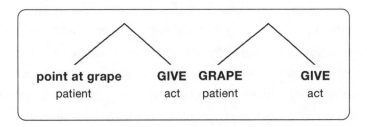

A little later in their development, homesigners begin to combine iconic gestures and points within the same sentence to refer to the same object: point at grape + GRAPE. Why would homesigners use two gestures when either gesture alone would do? The point at the grape indicates which object is in the child's focus, but the GRAPE gesture indicates the object's category (edible things). I could say *that* with a point at a cookie and you'd know which object I'm talking about. But you wouldn't know whether my intent is to talk about the object as a member of the food category, the dessert category, or the cookie category. Producing *cookie* along with *that* narrows down the possibilities.

So too for the homesigner who points at the grape *and* gestures GRAPE. When combined with a GIVE gesture, the two gestures, point at grape + GRAPE, function as a unit within the larger sentence unit: [[point at grape + GRAPE] + [GIVE]] = [[*that grape*] [*give*]] (see illustration on next page).

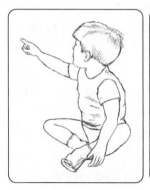

If the point at grape + GRAPE combination is functioning as a unit and substituting for a single gesture in the sentence, it ought to serve the same semantic role as the single gesture (either GRAPE alone or point at grape alone), and it does: it represents the object on which the action is done, the patient. The combination also ought to occur in the same position in a sentence as the single gesture, and again it does ([that-GRAPE]-GIVE): it occupies first position in the sentence, where the patient typically goes, as does GRAPE alone (GRAPE-GIVE) or point at grape alone (point-GIVE) (compare the illustration below to the illustrations of point at grape–GIVE and GRAPE-GIVE on the previous page).

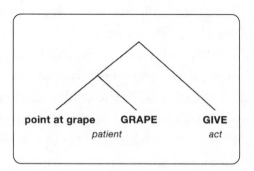

Psychologists call these units *chunks*. When things are chunked in your mind, they take up less cognitive effort than when they are not. Think of how many numbers you can remember when they are presented as one telephone number, compared to how many you can remember when they are presented as one long list of numbers. Point + GRAPE takes up less cognitive effort when the two gestures form a chunk than when they are *not* chunked, as in the sentence below, which has the same number of gestures, but each gesture plays a separate semantic role [point at sister–GRAPE–GIVE] = [*sister give grape*].

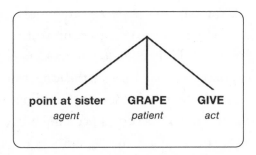

The homesigners created longer sentences than we expected them to, all because their two-gesture chunks took up less cognitive effort than two gestures that were not chunked. The bottom line is that their gesture sentences had hierarchical structure. Chunking and hierarchical structure are not only important characteristics of all human languages but also mark homesign as different from the gestures that accompany speech, which are not chunked and have a flat structure. Finally, hierarchical structure is yet another property of language that does not depend on language being an exclusively cultural phenomenon. The fact that hierarchical structure is found in homesign tells us that this type of structure does *not* require teaching or cultural transmission to arise in language—individual children can invent it themselves.

HOMESIGN SERVES THE FUNCTIONS OF HUMAN LANGUAGE

We now know that homesigners' gestures follow the patterns of human language: they have words and sentences, and those sentences are structured. Homesigners also use their gestures to serve the functions of language—to request, comment, question, tell stories, talk to themselves, talk about talking, and so on. It's not surprising that the homesigners use their gestures to make requests. After all, chimpanzees use their natural gestures to ask for food and to ask to play, be tickled, or be scratched. But chimpanzees don't use their natural gestures to comment on the world. Even when taught a sign language, chimpanzees use the signs they are taught to ask for things. Very, very rarely (less than 1 percent of the time) do they use those signs to comment to someone else on the state of their world. In contrast, homesigners routinely use their gestures to comment—to describe the long, thin tail of a dog, to note the height of the tower they are building with mom, to indicate that the bird in the picture is pedaling a bike.[11]

Chimpanzees also don't use the signs they are taught to ask questions, but homesigners do. Homesigners borrow the gesture that hearing people use to express doubt and lack of knowledge—an open hand rotated from palm down to palm up—to ask all sorts of questions: *what*, *where*, *who*, and even *how* and *why* questions. They put their question gestures at the end of their sentences, for example, producing a GO gesture, followed by a BEAT gesture, and then the PALM-UP gesture (see illustration) to ask, "Where is the toy that goes forward and beats a drum?"

Homesigners also borrow from hearing peoples' gestures to say no—they adopt the headshake to comment on the absence of an object, to reject an object or action, or to make a denial. For example, one homesigner told us that a toy bear, which he thought was broken, wasn't really broken: he shook his head *no* while holding two fists together, side by side, and then broke them apart in the air, a BROKEN gesture—all with a big smile to express his joy that the toy was not broken. Interestingly, negative headshakes often come at the beginning of the homesigners' sentences, whereas questions come at the end. The fact that negative and question markers are placed at the ends of sentences, and at different ends, suggests that this type of linguistic patterning can be brought to communication by the child and need not be learned from a language model. The homesigners' hearing parents spoke English, and that's not the way negatives and questions work in English. Nor do they work that way in co-speech gesture: side-to-side headshakes are not restricted to the beginnings of utterances, and palm-up question gestures are not found primarily at the ends.[12]

There are also more elaborate ways to use language. You can talk to yourself, and at times the homesigners used their gestures to do just that. David was sitting on the floor playing with blocks. He had a sheet that pictured a particularly nice block tower that he wanted to build, but he needed a block with an arc to build the tower. He started looking around for the block and produced an ARCED gesture. I then tried to hand him the appropriate block, and he ignored me. This was an instruction to himself, not to anyone else. He eventually found the block and finished the tower without my help.

You can also use your speech to talk about talking ("I said, 'I want the duck'"). It's not easy to gesture about your own gestures, but the homesigners do it occasionally. David was looking for the Donald Duck toy, and he created a DUCK face with his lips—this gesture was intended for me, but I wasn't paying enough attention. He then pointed at his DUCK lips as if to say, "I said, 'Donald Duck.'"

Finally, you can tell stories with language, and the homesigners tell lots of stories with their gestures. David used his homesigns to tell us about the bus route that his grandpa followed when he picked the kids up for school. He told us how Santa Claus came down the chimney and got the seat of his pants dirty. And he told us how he fell off his bike and hurt his chin. One day, David was looking at a picture of a shovel stuck in sand. Inspired by this picture, without pausing or breaking the flow of his motion, he produced the following complex gesture sentence describing what you do with a *snow* shovel: he gestured DIG, pointed at a picture of a shovel, gestured PULL-ON-BOOTS, pointed outside, pointed downstairs, pointed at the shovel picture, gestured DIG, and gestured PULL-ON-BOOTS (see illustrations on page 113). David linked a string of gestures together to tell us what he knew about the snow shovel: how it's used (to dig), when it's used (when boots are worn), where it's used (outside), and where it's kept (downstairs)—a pretty elaborate story generated from a picture of a sand shovel.[13]

DO HOMESIGNERS AROUND THE WORLD
DISPLAY THE SAME STRUCTURES?

Heidi and I studied six homesigners in Philadelphia, and with Carolyn Mylander, my lab manager of many years, I studied another four homesigners in Chicago. We began our project expecting that each homesigner would gesture and hypothesized that their gestures would be systematically organized. But we didn't expect all of the homesigners to come up with the same systematic structures—after all, they lived in different cities, and even the children who lived in the same city didn't all know one another. But they did come up with the same structures. Could the structures reflect

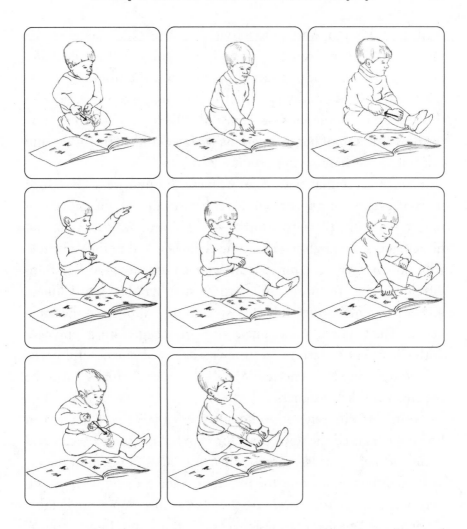

some as-yet-unknown aspect of how American culture organizes the lives of children?

To tackle this question, when I got to Chicago, my lab started studying homesigners in another culture: a Chinese culture, where parents were reported to interact differently with their children than American parents. Chinese parents ask more probing questions when they talk with their children and give more elaborate descriptions of objects than American parents do. We thought this difference might impact how Chinese hearing parents interact with their deaf children. And it did in one salient respect: Chinese hearing parents gestured much more with their children, both deaf and hearing, than American hearing parents. But the homesigns that the Chinese deaf children created looked just like the American deaf children's homesigns—and just like the homesigns created by the deaf children of hearing parents we later studied in Turkey and Nicaragua, with a few important exceptions.[14]

First, the similarities: The Chinese homesigners described motion events—events in which a person moves, or moves an object, from one place to another—in the same way as American homesigners, highlighting the same elements, and in the same distribution. In fact, the Chinese and American homesigners' gestural descriptions were more similar to each other than are Chinese and American *hearing* children's spoken descriptions of the same events. The Chinese homesigners also produced gesture sentences with consistent orderings, gestures made up of meaningful parts, and gestures used as generics (labels for classes of things), just like the American homesigners.[15]

Now the differences: Although the Chinese and American homesigners used the same signs for many of the same objects and events in their worlds—moving their fists up and down in the air as though hitting a drum for BEAT, creating a circle with thumb and index finger for PENNY—there were also some predictable differences. American homesigners jabbed a hand, fingers touching the thumb, at their mouths for EAT. The Chinese homesigners also used this sign but, in addition, they moved two straight fingers in a V toward their mouths as though moving chopsticks for EAT. In other words, their gestural labels were culturally appropriate, which is not a surprise since the way we label objects and actions varies around the globe. *Dog* is but one word for the animal known in other languages as *chien*, *perro*, *pas*, and *hund*.

The stories Chinese and American homesigners told with their gestures were also different and culturally appropriate. Before looking at examples of Chinese and American homesign stories,

let's take a look at stories that hearing parents spontaneously produce when talking about interactions with their hearing children.
Chinese hearing parents use stories to make moral statements.
An aunt, for example, told the following story about her niece:
"She was really bad. She cried—such a big deal. And this after
I hadn't scolded her for writing on my wall! If she weren't my
sister's child . . . At midnight, just before going to bed, she scrib-
bled on the wall with chalk. And we had [just had] our home
painted." By contrast, American hearing parents tell stories to
entertain their audience. A mother told the following story about
her daughter, Molly: "I was napping and [as I was waking up] I
saw Molly writing on the dining room wall, [so I woke up and]
said, 'Mol, you didn't write on Mommy's wall with a pencil, did
you?' Oh! She was so relieved! She said, 'No! Me no use pencil,
me use key!' . . . And I was like 'OH GOD! Not a key!' . . . But it
was so funny! You look at her and she's like 'I didn't use a pencil.'"
The two stories dealt with a similar topic—children writing on a
wall—but the purpose of the story was different in each culture.[16]

The Chinese homesigners told stories with their gestures that
had the evaluative edge found in the stories told by Chinese hearing adults and children. Qing, at age four, told a story in homesign, which we translated as follows: "Uncle threw a ball. That is
not good. Uncle was not good—he was bad." Qing got her evaluative message across by drawing an X in the air and by shaking
her pinky; both are evaluative gestures used by hearing adults in
Taiwan. American homesigners also saw hearing adults use evaluative gestures—*thumbs-up* and *thumbs-down* are examples—but
the children very rarely reproduced these evaluative gestures and
never incorporated them into their stories. Instead, they used their
stories to entertain and inform, as do American hearing story-
tellers. David, at age five, told a story in homesign, which we
translated as follows: "We have a rabbit like this one out there.
Someone opened the cage and the rabbit hopped out and ate a
carrot in the backyard."[17]

The homesigners produced culturally appropriate narrations even though they couldn't hear their parents' stories, which suggests that this particular cultural message is accessible through nonverbal channels—stories can be heard, watched, and felt, separately or all at once. Some aspects of culture seem to be so important that they are not entrusted to a single medium. Homesigners can tell us what these culturally important messages are.

This brings us to a nagging question. We see the building blocks of language in the hands of a homesigning child. But maybe it's *not* the children who are inventing homesign. After all, we know from the stories they tell with their gestures that homesigners are influenced by their respective cultures. Maybe the hearing parents came up with the gestures, which the children then copied. If so, the children wouldn't be responsible for inventing homesign; their hearing parents would be the creators.

WHO REALLY CREATES HOMESIGN?

Everybody gestures when talking, including the homesigners' hearing parents. So before we can make any real claim about the innateness of language, we have to find out if the hearing parents' gestures look like homesign. We looked at the gestures that the hearing parents produced when they interacted with their deaf children. We ignored the speech that came along with those gestures simply because we wanted to view the gestures as their deaf children would. The deaf children couldn't hear and decode the speech, so we shouldn't use it either. We then analyzed the parents' gestures using the same tools that we used to analyze the homesigners' gestures.[18]

The parents at times used *emblems*, gestures that have an agreed-upon meaning and form within a culture. In the United States, a thumbs-up means *good*, a thumb and index finger forming a circle with three fingers extended means *okay*, and an index finger held over the mouth means *be quiet*. Homesigners copied their parents' emblems and used them but often extended their meanings. Hearing mothers in the United States hold up an index finger to children who are anxious to get moving, while saying, "Wait, wait a minute." Homesigners will use this held-up index finger to mean *wait*, but they also use it to indicate an event that is going to happen soon. In other words, they use it as a marker for the future, a use never found in the hearing parents. The parents' emblems provided a starting point for the homesigners, who then extended the meaning of gestures in a sensible way. It's not surprising that the homesigners would pick up their hearing parents' gestural emblems—emblems are, after all, word-like gestures even for hearing folks. But remarkably the homesigners used their hearing parents' emblems as raw material to iterate upon, assigning them new, extended meanings. The children take their parents' gestural emblems and incorporate them into their own linguistic systems to fit the needs of their minds. By doing so, they reveal the contents of their minds to us.[19]

Parents also used iconic gestures created on the spot that imagistically represented an object, action, or attribute (e.g., BEAT, DUCK, ROUND). But there was little overlap between the parents' iconic gestures and their child's iconic gestures—much less overlap than between the parents' and children's emblem gestures. The children and parents had different gestural vocabularies. This means that the homesigners were creating at least some of their gesture words themselves.[20]

More striking is the difference in how the parents and children combined their gestures. The parents often produced one gesture at a time, most likely because they were talking as they gestured and English speakers tend to produce one gesture per clause. This means that the parents produced very few gesture + gesture combinations. So if the deaf children were looking at their hearing parents' gestures to learn how to structure their own gestures, they would have had a very hollow model. In fact, the homesigning children in the United States and China displayed statistically reliable ordering patterns in their gestures, but their hearing parents didn't. Along the same lines, both the American and Chinese homesigners produced complex gesture sentences, which contained more than one proposition ("You build the tower, and I will hit it"). But their hearing parents didn't—or at least they produced far fewer complex sentences than their children and began producing them only after their children had already produced them. Finally, the American and Nicaraguan homesigners displayed hierarchical structure in their sentences, as when they combined a point at a grape with the gesture GRAPE before gesturing GIVE. But the hearing parents never combined these two types of gestures. The bottom line is that the children produced homesigns with combinatorial and hierarchical structure—two essential properties of human language. The hearing parents did not provide a model for this degree of complexity in the co-speech gestures that they used with their homesigning children.[21]

The hearing parents did not provide a model for the particular gestures or gesture sentences that their homesigning children produced. But they did provide a model for gesturing in general, since they all gestured when they talked to their children. In addition, the parents found it easy to understand the gestures that their homesigning children produced because those gestures transparently depicted what the children wanted to say—and because children at the beginning of language acquisition talk mostly about what's in front of them. Think about what an odd communicative situation this creates. Children produce homesign when they converse with their hearing family members, but they do *not* receive homesign in return. It's like talking to your French friend who understands English but doesn't speak it. She speaks to you in French, and you perhaps understand her French but are not proficient enough to carry on a conversation in French yourself, so you respond in English. The difference is that the homesigning children invented their language, and the hearing parents don't really consider the homesigners' gestures to be a language.

But maybe we're jumping to conclusions about the origin of homesign. There are other ways that the hearing parents could have influenced and shaped their children's homesigns. Perhaps they responded positively to gestures in one form and negatively to gestures in another form. Maybe the parents were more likely to respond to gesture sentences in which the child produced a gesture for the *patient* before a gesture for the *action* (grape-GIVE), as opposed to a gesture for the *action* before a gesture for the *patient* (GIVE-grape), which could perhaps explain homesigners' tendency to produce gesture sentences following a patient-action order.

Although this sounds like a good hypothesis, hearing parents aren't this systematic when they respond even to their hearing children's words. They respond to the content of their children's spoken sentences rather than the form. When a child says, "Walt Disney is on TV on Tuesdays," the mother will correct the child, stating that Walt Disney is in fact on TV on Wednesdays, even though the child's sentence is grammatically perfect. By contrast, when a child says, "Me love you, mommy," it's the rare mother who will correct her child's grammar before reciprocating the affection. But maybe hearing parents respond differently to their deaf children's homesigns.[22]

To find out, we looked at gesture sentences that each homesigner produced and classified them into sentences that fit or did not fit the child's preferred ordering pattern. None of the children produced sentences that were 100 percent consistent—they were children, after all. We then looked at how the parents responded to these two different types of sentences. We calculated how often the parents responded with *approval* (smiles, head nods, generally positive affect) to sentences that did and did not follow the child's ordering patterns. We also calculated how often the parents responded with *sequiturs* to the two types of sentences—for example, if they gave the child what he or she wanted or provided a gesture that built on what the child said. If the parents' responses were shaping the ordering in the children's gesture sentences, we should find more approvals and more sequiturs after sentences that did follow the children's preferred ordering patterns than after sentences that did not. But instead we found that the parents responded with approval to about 65 percent of the children's well-ordered sentences and 65 percent of the children's mis-ordered sentences. And they responded with sequiturs to about 50 percent of the children's well-ordered sentences and 50 percent of the children's mis-ordered sentences. There was nothing to go on in the parents' responses. Interestingly, Roger Brown, a premier researcher of language acquisition, and his student Camille Hanlon found the same rates—65 percent approval and 50 percent sequiturs—when studying how hearing parents respond to the sentences of their young English-learning hearing children. The homesigners' hearing parents behaved just like other hearing parents in the United States.[23]

But maybe we missed something; maybe there were subtle ways in which the parents were responding to well-ordered versus mis-ordered sentences, ways that we didn't code in our analyses. We can never argue that we have looked at all possible cues, but to be as sure as possible, we ran an experiment. We asked a child actor to produce either well-ordered or mis-ordered gesture sentences—for example, the actor produced one sentence that contained a point at the grape followed by a GIVE gesture (patient-action ordering) and another that contained a GIVE gesture followed by a point at the grape (action-patient ordering). We then showed these gesture sentences to English-speaking adults and asked them to tell us the meanings of the sentences and to rate their confidence in their responses. We thought that maybe the well-ordered gesture sentences would be more easily understood than the mis-ordered gesture sentences. But here again we turned up short: hearing speakers gave correct translations equally often to the well-ordered and the mis-ordered sentences, and were equally confident of their responses to both types. In other words, well-ordered sentences were not easier to comprehend than mis-ordered sentences. Nonetheless, the children preferred to produce gesture sentences following the well-ordered pattern. The urge to produce consistently ordered gesture sentences and the tendency to adhere to a particular order came from the home-signing children. This suggests that the children themselves, not their hearing parents, were responsible for the structure found in their homesign systems.

Our experiment also suggests that hearing people are not looking for consistent ordering in the gestures they see and that they can understand gestures arranged in any order. The pressure to use consistent linear order in communication is *not* coming from co-speech gesture.

If, as we've seen, children themselves, and not their hearing parents, are responsible for the structure found in their home-sign systems, we have evidence that the structures in homesign are a robust part of language. Children are predisposed to learn them when they find them in the languages they are exposed to, and are predisposed to invent them when they are not exposed to language. If language disappeared, we humans would very likely reinvent it, and it would look (at deep levels) like the languages we speak now. The bottom line is that homesign tells us about the powerful connections between our hands and our thoughts. If we are exposed to a conventional language, we use our hands to express the thoughts that are not so easily expressed in discrete, linguistic categories. If we are not exposed to a conventional language, we use our hands to invent one.

LANGUAGE IS MORE RESILIENT THAN NUMBER

Language comes naturally to homesigners, which tells us that having language is part of being human. If you aren't exposed to it, you will create it nevertheless. Is this true of other representational systems, like music or numbers?

Hearing speakers use their fingers to enumerate things—one finger for one object, two fingers for two objects, and so on. Can a number system also grow out of gesture? Previous literature suggests that homesigners might need a model for a number system in order to develop one. The Mundurukú and Pirahã are Amazonian peoples in rural Brazil whose languages do not contain words for exact numbers larger than five (the Mundurukú) or any exact number words at all (the Pirahã). Hearing adults in these cultures can match a set of objects to another set if the number is small, fewer than three or four. But they can't match larger sets. When asked to pick out a set of apples to match a set of six pears, they might come up with six, but they also might come up with five or seven—their response will be approximate, not exact.[24]

Not only do these two cultures lack words for large numbers, but they also don't often put people in contexts where exact numbers are needed. Maybe it's the lack of cultural pressure to use large exact numbers that prevents the Mundurukú and Pirahã from doing so, not the lack of a language model. What we need are homesigners who don't have a model for a number system but who are living in a culture where *exact* number is valued. Nicaragua is such a culture. It has, for example, a monetary system comparable to the one we have in the United States, whereas the Mundurukú and Pirahã do not. It also has homesigners who are adults. Homesigners in the United States are typically exposed to a conventional sign language like American Sign Language as they grow older. As a result, adult homesigners are rare in the United States, but in Nicaragua deaf individuals can stay homesigners throughout adulthood. If living and working in a culture that values the precise number of items is sufficient to develop an understanding of large, exact numbers (numbers larger than three or four), adult and maybe even child homesigners in Nicaragua ought to have a notion of large, exact numbers.[25]

Liesje Spaepen, a graduate student in my lab, along with Liz Spelke and Susan Carey, two well-known psychologists who know a lot about number, and Marie Coppola, a former post-doc and expert in Nicaraguan homesign, took the lead on a study of four adult homesigners in Nicaragua. The homesigners held jobs, made money, and interacted socially with hearing friends and family. They knew no other deaf individuals, and none had attended school regularly. We presented ten short animated stories on video in which number was critical to the plot and asked the homesigners to retell the stories to a relative or friend who had not watched the video but was familiar with the storyteller's homesign—we did a PALM-UP gesture (two palms rotating from palm down to palm up) to ask them what had happened in the video. All four homesigners extended their fingers to indicate the number of objects in the videos. As the number of objects grew, so did the average number of fingers that the homesigners extended. But the number of extended fingers was exactly correct *only* when there were fewer than three objects. When there were four or more objects, the homesigners came close but were not always accurate. For example, when there were five sheep on the screen, the home-signers might hold up five fingers, but they were just as likely to hold up four or six fingers. Homesigners were using their gestures to track the approximate values of large sets rather than the exact values, at least when they told stories. Child homesigners in Nica-ragua show the same pattern.[26]

We also designed a nonnarrative task to elicit exact numbers in order to figure out whether the lack of exactness was connected to the narrative form. If you give adult homesigners two sets that contain one, two, or three objects, they will solve the task flaw-lessly and match ones to ones, twos to twos, and threes to threes. But if you give them two sets that contain four or more objects, homesigners will again approximate—they will match a set con-taining six objects with a set containing six objects, but they will also match the set with sets containing five or seven objects (as the Pirahã did). You might say that this is to be expected—when the numbers get large, it gets hard to be exactly correct. But you would be exactly correct if you had unlimited time to match the two sets. Homesigners are not: they display this approximate pattern to numbers greater than four even if they have an unlimited amount of time to match the two sets. Large exact numbers are a fundamental aspect of our number system, just as fundamental as imposing linguistic structure on our thoughts when we communicate them. Yet homesigners can invent linguistic structures but can't come up with large exact numbers.

Language and number are both worldwide phenomena. Before learning about our studies, you might have guessed that language and number would reflect the structure of our minds in equal measure. But you would have been wrong. Language can be created by a child. Large exact numbers cannot. The capacity for language seems to be hardwired in humans in a way that the capacity to represent large numbers exactly is not. If language were inadvertently wiped out, it could regenerate with many of the same traits and organizing principles as modern languages. By contrast, if number were inadvertently wiped out, it might or might not be reinvented. And even if it were reinvented, it would likely require many inventors and would not likely be reconstructed by a child working alone—even if the child were provided with gestures that mapped onto numbers of objects. Gesture can grow into a structured linguistic system, but not into a structured system of large exact numbers. Language is resilient; number is not.

BACK TO LANGUAGE

Children, of course, learn the language that surrounds them as they develop. The homesign findings tell us that children begin language learning expecting a communication system with the properties of homesign. Their job, if they are exposed to a language, is to figure out how the properties we've seen in homesign are expressed in that language. In this sense, children are prepared to learn language.

Are they also prepared to learn co-speech gesture? We know that people who are congenitally blind and have never seen anyone gesture nevertheless gesture when they talk. In this sense, people are prepared to gesture along with their language. But note that a child's first step in *creating* a communication system is homesign, a system of discrete units that are combined into larger units, not the co-speech (or co-sign) gestures that are used along with discrete forms. When, then, does co-speech or co-sign gesture appear in an emerging human communication system? In other words, when do homesigners begin to produce gestures along with their discrete language forms? We haven't noticed anything that resembles co-speech gesture in our American homesigners' sentences, but it's an understudied area. So we don't really know the point in language emergence when co-speech gesture appears; we just know that it does *not* appear in the first step of language emergence.

Homesign is a system of gestures that reveals how children who are not exposed to language structure their thoughts during communication. These structures resemble those found in human languages, signed and spoken. The structures that make homesign language also make it distinct from co-speech and co-sign gestures. Co-language gestures reveal our thoughts too, but typically thoughts that fit the imagistic format that the hands are particularly good at capturing. We have discovered just how versatile our hands are: in Part I, we saw that our hands can reveal our thoughts through imagistic gestures when we have a conventional language and, in Part II, that they can reveal our thoughts through linguistic categories when a conventional language is not available.

Deaf children all over the globe invent homesigns, and those homesigns embody fundamental aspects of language. But it's hard to imagine that homesigners, on their own, are able to invent all aspects of a fully developed language. How far can an individual inventing a means of communicating go toward creating a modern-day language? Some properties of language really might need to be handed down from generation to generation in order to emerge in language. These are the properties that homesigners fail to develop on their own. When and how do these properties emerge in a young language? This is the question that organizes the next chapter. Answering it will help us begin to understand why modern-day language is structured the way it is.

5

WATCHING LANGUAGE GROW NATURALLY AND IN THE LAB

HOMESIGN REVEALS HOW CHILDREN ORGANIZE THEIR THOUGHTS when not exposed to language. Interestingly, this organization looks like the organization in languages that have been handed down from generation to generation—discrete elements that combine with other elements at many different levels. Homesign tells us that it is our minds, and not the handed-down languages, that provide structure for these thoughts.

But homesign does not display all of the properties found in human languages. In fact, all over the globe, homesign systems gain linguistic properties and turn into full-fledged sign languages as homesigners come together and communicate with one another on a daily basis. To see how, we can look at an instance of language emergence—which happens to be taking place right now in Nicaragua. Sign languages all over the world have grown out of homesign systems as deaf individuals form communities. But the Nicaraguan situation is exciting because researchers have been present from the start and have charted the changes to the language in real time.[1]

EMERGING LANGUAGE IN THE REAL WORLD:
NICARAGUAN SIGN LANGUAGE

Fifty years ago, there was no deaf community in Nicaragua. Deaf children were born into hearing families and had no contact with each other. As a result, these deaf children used their homesigns with the hearing people who surrounded them. In 1977, a center for special education began a program for deaf children, which attracted fifty students. In 1980, a vocational school for deaf adolescents opened, and by 1983, the two schools had over four hundred enrollees. At the start, the schools taught Spanish, but the students had trouble learning it (remember how difficult it is to learn a spoken language from watching the speaker's lips). They did, however, bring their own homesigns, which they began to share with one another. For the first time, these homesigners were not only *producing* homesign but also *seeing* others use it. These exchanges among homesigners led to the birth of a new language, Nicaraguan Sign Language (NSL), and the homesigners who came together and began to create NSL are known as its first cohort.[2]

To understand which elements of language were added to homesign as it took its first steps toward NSL, my colleagues and I compared homesigners, who do not share their systems with the people they interact with, to the first cohort of NSL signers, who do share their systems with each other. We identified properties of language that homesigners *don't* develop but that the first cohort of signers *do*. These properties are interesting: they seem to arise only when communication takes place between people who share a system. Homesigners produce structured gestures but have no opportunity to see those gestures because their hearing parents use their own form of co-speech gestures. When they came together decades ago, Nicaraguan homesigners, for the first time, saw homesign being produced by others, which may have prompted them to introduce into their gestures the properties that now differentiate NSL from homesign. These new properties require *shared communication* to emerge in language.

Eventually, the school started teaching NSL to its students and began hiring deaf adults to teach them. Now deaf children who attended saw a model for a sign language and learned it rapidly. But in the process of learning, they changed the language, just as hearing children often change the spoken language they hear as they learn it. Take my granddaughter, who frequently says *I amn't*. She has invented a new pattern that follows other patterns in the language (*he isn't, you aren't, we aren't, they aren't*). She is sticking with the pattern at the moment, but it doesn't seem to be catching on with her friends. Eventually, she will drop it too. The difference in Nicaragua is that many of the changes introduced by deaf children learning NSL have stuck and have changed the language—after all, there are no older language prescriptivists around to keep the changes from sticking. The properties of language that homesigners and the first cohort of NSL signers *don't* develop, but that subsequent cohorts of NSL signers *do*, require transmission from one person to another to arise in an emerging language. They are created in the context of *learning*.

So we have three types of linguistic properties that differ as a function of the conditions that support their development. I provide an example of each type in the next paragraphs.

Properties that are resilient. The first is a linguistic property that homesigners develop and the first and subsequent cohorts of NSL signers continue to use. Human languages have ways of distinguishing between symmetrical and reciprocal events. Two people shaking hands, high-fiving, or meeting are all *symmetrical events*: both participants play an equal and necessary role in creating a single act. In *reciprocal events*, two people are involved in two separate acts rather than one: two people punching, kicking, or tickling each other at the same time constitute reciprocal events. One person can punch another without having that person punch back, but one person can never high-five alone. We describe a symmetrical event in English by saying, "Charlie and Joe met yesterday" or "Charlie and Joe met each other yesterday." Importantly, we cannot say, "Charlie and Joe punched yesterday"—we have to include *each other*, or the sentence isn't grammatical in English.

Adult homesigners in Nicaragua also mark this abstract distinction in their communication systems, although in a different way. When asked to describe an event in which two people are meeting each other, they create a MEET gesture in which two index fingers come together mid-air, which looks like what happens when two people meet (see illustration).

But when homesigners describe an event in which two people are punching each other at the same time, they produce a PUNCH gesture going in one direction *followed by* another PUNCH gesture in the other direction (see illustration on the next page).

It is physically possible (and not hard) to produce these two PUNCH gestures at the same time—and producing them simultaneously would be a more accurate depiction of the simultaneously occurring punching events that the homesigners are describing.

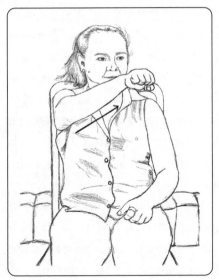 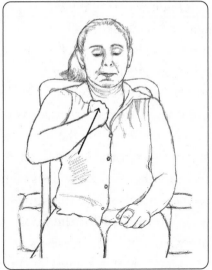

But that's not what homesigners do. They describe punching in a way that doesn't look very much like the actual event. Doing so allows them to signal the difference between symmetrical and reciprocal events. All cohorts of NSL signers make this same differentiation. The distinction between symmetrical and reciprocal events is abstract, but it is a fundamental property of language—so fundamental that it can be reinvented by individuals who don't share a communication system with the people around them.[3]

Properties that need shared communication. The second type of linguistic property is one that homesigners *don't* develop but members of the first cohort of NSL signers *do*. It has turned out to be a lot harder than I expected to find properties that cohort 1 signers develop and homesigners don't. This means that many properties of language can be invented by homesigners who produce the forms *without ever seeing those forms*. These properties do not require shared communication to emerge. We have, however, found one aspect of language where cohort 1 signers excel and homesigners don't: having a stable set of labels for objects. This linguistic property *does* require shared communication to emerge.

Diane Brentari, my colleague at the University of Chicago, and I, along with Laura Horton, a former student, compared Nicaraguan homesigners to NSL signers from cohorts 1 and 2. We asked all of the groups to describe short videos displayed on a computer screen—for example, a book falling on its side or a hand placing a book on its side. We then looked at how often the same handshape was used every time the object was described. We found that each signer in cohorts 1 and 2 used the same handshape to describe the book in all of the videos (signers were consistent within themselves) and also used the same handshape that the other signers in that cohort used for the book (signers were consistent with each other). In contrast, homesigners used different handshapes for the book in different videos. This may not surprise you: after all, the homesigners didn't know one another so shouldn't be expected to all invent the same handshape for a book. What may surprise you—as it did me—is that individual homesigners did not use the same handshape every time they labeled the book. For example, a homesigner might extend four straight fingers when labeling a book that someone had laid flat but only two fingers when labeling a book that fell on its own. Signers in cohorts 1 and 2 use the same handshape in both contexts. Stability in the form of a word, even within an individual's own vocabulary, doesn't seem to emerge without pressure from a peer linguistic community, which happens in cohorts 1 and 2 but not in homesign.[4]

Properties that need learning. The third type of linguistic property is one that neither homesigners nor the first cohort of NSL develops but that subsequent cohorts of NSL do. Lilia Rissman, one of my postdoctoral fellows, took the lead on a project that examined agent backgrounding in adult Nicaraguan homesigners, cohort 1 signers, and cohort 2 and 3 signers. When describing a video in which a fully visible person was placing a book on its side, all signers, even homesigners, produced gestures with a C handshape, as though holding a book incorporated into the verb (a *handle* handshape). By contrast, when describing a video in which the book fell over on its own, all signers produced gestures with a flat palm representing the book incorporated into the verb (an *object* handshape). The difference between groups was how they responded to a third video in which only the hand of the agent was visible: the hand placed the book on its side, and the head and torso of the placer were *not* visible.

In English, if we want to background who is performing the action, we can use the passive voice and say, "The book was placed on the table." NSL signers in cohorts 2 and 3 invented a way of backgrounding the agent. They did it by using both types of verbs to describe the book event: the PLACE verb with a *handle* handshape, followed by the PLACE verb with an *object* handshape. This combination hedges its bets: the first verb highlights the actor who put down the book, and the second verb highlights the book itself as the object, putting a focus on both at once. Importantly, this was the preferred strategy *only* for cohorts 2 and 3 and *only* for videos in which the hand, and not the whole body, could be seen moving the book. It is a way of taking some of the focus off of the agent, a passivizing structure that only made it into the language when cohort 2 signers learned NSL from cohort 1 signers. Cohort 2 signers had the advantage of seeing cohort 1 signers and homesigners use the *handle* and *object* forms in separate contexts. They could then make use of these forms and combine them in order to signal a new situation in which the agent was not salient. In other words, this passive voice equivalent was introduced into NSL when one cohort learned the developing language from another in an iterative process. Cohort 2 signers stood on the shoulders of cohort 1 signers who had come before them.[5]

So far we have examined the steps a naturally emerging language takes as it moves toward becoming a full-fledged language. Homesigners can go only so far toward inventing language on their own. The properties that homesigners are unable to develop require additional conditions; shared communication among users leads to the lexical stability not found in homesign, and transmission of that lexically stable language from one generation of users to the next leads to the agent backgrounding not found in homesign or the first generation of signers. Note that these properties are not found in co-speech gesture under any conditions: there is no stability of form in gesture apart from emblems, which are, in effect, soundless words, and there is no standard way of backgrounding the agent in gesture. Sharing a communication system with another and learning it from others are pressures that turn homesign into a full-fledged language. But these pressures do *not* have the same effect on co-speech gesture. It's only when applied to the structures homesigners use to communicate their thoughts that these pressures mold human language into what it is today.

EMERGING LANGUAGE IN THE LAB: SILENT GESTURE

We can learn a great deal about the forces that shape language from studying languages like NSL that emerge under natural circumstances. But the real world is messy, which means we have very little control over the circumstances of emergence. We can't always tell what's causing the changes and what's resulting from them. Setting up an analog to a language-emergence situation in the lab can help us determine what levers impact the course of a language's evolution.

Simon Kirby, a British cognitive scientist who holds the chair of language evolution at the University of Edinburgh, was one of the first to attempt to experimentally explore language emergence. He and his colleagues set up an experiment in which English speakers were asked to learn a "language" in which a randomly selected string of letters (e.g., "kamone," "gaku," "hokako") was paired with a picture. There were twelve "words" and twelve pictures. The pictures differed on two dimensions: (1) shape: there were three different shapes—a lima bean shape with one protrusion, a prickly shape with three protrusions, and a starlike shape with six protrusions; and (2) filling: there were four different textures and colors—solid white, solid black, checked, and spotted. The learn-ers saw each of the twelve words as text, paired with a different shape, on a computer screen. They saw each word-picture pairing six times, and their job was to learn the label for each picture. This was the *learning* phase.

Next came the *communication* phase. Two learners then inter-acted with one another over the computer, taking turns producing and receiving. In each trial, the producer saw a picture and had to type its label into the computer so that the receiver could identify it out of an array of six pictures. After each trial, the pair learned whether they had "communicated" correctly, and if so, they got a point. The two then switched roles, and the receiver became the producer.

The final step was the *transmission* phase. The labels that one of the learners produced during the communication phase were used to teach the next generation. This next generation saw the labels paired with their pictures. Some of the labels were exactly the same as the ones presented originally, while others varied from the orig-inal. It's a bit like a game of telephone, where errors that are intro-duced get passed along to the next player. This process continued until there were six generations of learners.

In order to confirm that transmission across *different learners* was shaping the emergence process, Kirby and colleagues included a second group. The learning and communication phases were the same for this group, but the transmission phase was differ-ent. Instead of passing down the labels to a new pair of learners, the experimenters gave the labels to the same learners—in other words, the learners completed all six trials themselves in the *same learners* group.

When we play telephone, we evaluate success in terms of whether the original message remained intact across the players. The *same learners* group turned out to be the big winners using this metric. They were not perfect, but after the first generation, they gave labels that were much closer to the original labels than

those given by the *different learners* group. In fact, the labels that
the *different learners* group gave moved further and further away
from the original labels—they were terrible telephone players.

What was happening to the "language" over the six generations
in the *different learners* group? Interestingly, their labels became
more and more systematic and structured. For example, one pair
in the *different learners* group ended up with different labels for
each of the three shapes ("ege" for the lima bean, "mega" for
the star, and "gamene" for the prickly shape) and different labels
for the four fillings ("wawu" for black, "wawa" for checkered,
"wuwu" for spotted, and no label for white). They then combined
these labels systematically: "mega-wawa" was used for the star
shape that was checkered; "ege-wawa" was used for the lima bean
shape that was checkered; and "ege-wuwu" was used for the lima
bean shape that was spotted. Not all of the pairs in the *different
learners* group were this systematic, but all of them were moving
in this "compositional" direction.[6]

What does this study tell us about language emergence? In an
artificial lab situation, when "language" is passed down from generation to generation in a communicative setting, over time the
language changes and becomes more structured and systematic.
This paradigm is an analog to what happened in Nicaragua when
cohort 2 learned the language from cohort 1 and changed it, then
cohort 3 learned the language from cohort 2 and changed it, and
so on.

Although these artificial language-learning studies simulate
some aspects of language emergence, they don't simulate the initial creation stage—in other words, there's no analog to homesign.
They are studies of how language changes as it is *learned* but not
of how the fundamentals of language are *created* in the first place.

A new line of studies is, however, bringing language *creation*
into the lab. Most of these studies ask individuals to create gestures, as opposed to sounds, to describe scenes or objects, simply

because it's easier for us to create gestural labels than spoken labels. Creating *silent gestures*, as they have come to be called, turns out to be easy for adults. This process is reminiscent of charades, but silent gesturers don't build off their spoken language as people do in charades—as you'll soon see, that's one of the most interesting findings.[7]

The first study of silent gesture compared the gestures that we spontaneously use when we talk (co-speech gestures) to the gestures that we produce when asked to describe a scene without talking (silent gestures). We asked English-speaking adults to describe a set of videotaped events in speech, then to describe the same events again using only their hands, and we compared the gestures under the two conditions. The two types of gestures looked very different. The gestures used with speech contained lax handshapes and floppy movements—they looked like typical co-speech gestures. In contrast, the gestures used in place of speech were crisp, with clearly defined handshapes and movements—they looked like homesign![8]

Let's take an example. We showed an adult a picture of a doughnut arcing out of an ashtray.

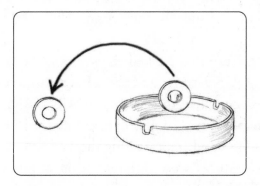

The adult described the scene by saying, "The doughnut jumped out of the ashtray," while producing the following movements with his hands (see next page).

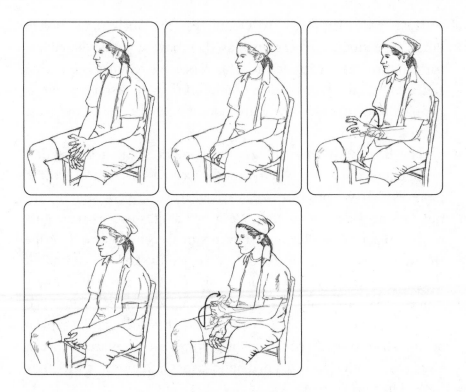

When asked to describe the same event without speech, he produced a string of clearly articulated gestures: two gestures for the ashtray (SMOKE, STUB-OUT), a gesture for the doughnut (ROUND), and a gesture for the action (ARC-OUT) (see illustration on page 139).

The only gesture that looked the same in the two renditions was the ARC-OUT gesture, and the adult's co-speech ARC-OUT was much less complete than his silent ARC-OUT, in which his right hand shaped like a circle (representing the doughnut) arced out of his flat left hand (representing the ashtray).

The silent gestures were different from co-speech gesture in another way. The co-speech gestures, if connected at all, did not follow a consistent ordering. The silent gestures did. This adult, and all of the other adults in the study, produced gestures for the stationary location first (the ashtray), the moving object second (the doughnut), and the action last (the arc). Note that this order

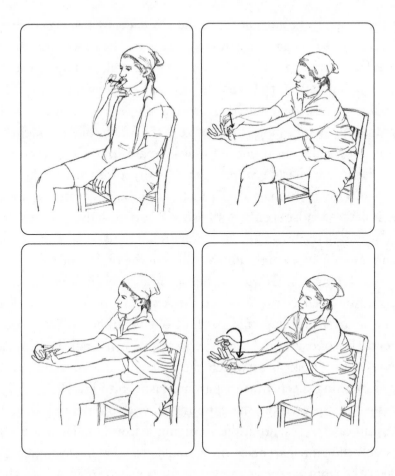

is not the default order found in English: we would say, "The doughnut jumped out of the ashtray," not "Out of the ashtray the doughnut jumped." These differences underscore the versatility of our hands—they are typically used along with our speech to enrich what we say, but they can be instantly transformed into a system that takes on the full communicative burden.[9]

Having set up a gesture-creation situation in the lab, we expanded the repertoire of scenes the adults described and also broadened the scope of the study to include speakers of other languages—Turkish, Chinese, and Spanish, as well as English. For example, speakers were asked to use their hands to describe a video of a captain swinging a pail. The English speaker produced a gesture for the captain, the subject (S) of the sentence, by tracing the brim of a cap on her head; a gesture for the pail, the object (O) of the sentence, by tracing the round shape of the pail; and a gesture for the swinging action, the verb (V), by making a swinging motion. Speakers of all four languages produced gestures in this order—captain-pail-swing, subject-object-verb (SOV), despite the fact that this is not the default order in English, Spanish, or Chinese.

This finding has been replicated many times in speakers of many different languages—Turkish, Chinese, Korean, Japanese, and Italian—whose speakers all use SOV order in the gestures they produce to describe scenes in which an animate person acts on an inanimate object, even though SOV is not the typical order in most of these languages. Gesture, when produced on its own without speech, may reflect the way we think about the elements of an event, apart from language. To find out whether the SOV order extends beyond gesture, we asked speakers of English, Spanish, Chinese, and Turkish to watch the videos and reconstruct what they saw using sheets of transparent plastic with line drawings on them—one representing the captain (S), one representing the pail (O), and one representing the swinging action (V). Their job was to stack the transparencies on a hook after having watched the video. The transparencies recreated the scene no matter how they were stacked—the sheets were transparent so the order in which you placed them on the hook didn't matter. Nevertheless, all of the participants picked up the transparent pictures of the captain (S) first, then the pail (O) second, then the swinging action (V) last, recreating the SOV order in a very different context. Silent gesture may reveal how we structure the world when we are not talking.[10]

In keeping with this hypothesis, silent gesture looks the same no matter who is producing it—in other words, no matter what language you speak, you will structure your silent gestures like everyone else. This is particularly surprising given that your co-speech gestures *are* influenced by the structure of the language you know. Remember from Chapter 2 that English speakers typically describe the path taken (across) and the manner used on that path (skipping) within a single clause: "I skipped across the street." They also produce one gesture containing manner and path, wiggling their fingers at the same time as they move them across. In contrast, Turkish speakers describe path and manner in separate clauses, and they either produce two gestures (wiggling their fingers first and then moving their hand across) or just one representing the path (moving their hand across). But when they produce silent gestures, English and Turkish speakers both combine path and manner into the same gesture, which is the way homesigners gesture about motion along a path. The Turkish speaker used two hands to represent two feet walking (illustration on the right); the English speaker used two fingers (illustration on the left). But both embedded their walking movements within their path movement when asked to gesture without speech. Contrast these silent gestures with the co-speech gestures Turkish and English speakers (both sighted and blind) produce, which are illustrated in Chapter 2, pages 54 and 55.[11]

All of the gesturers in the studies we've looked at so far were adults. Can children create a gesture language? Getting children to produce silent gestures requires a clever paradigm. Two four- to six-year-old children were placed in different rooms and told to communicate with one another via a video channel. One child was the producer and had to communicate the content of a picture to the other child, the receiver. Initially, both the sound and picture on the camera worked and the children learned how to play the game. Then the experimenter cut the audio connection and told the children that the system had broken and that they had to try to communicate with their bodies and not their mouths. The children, particularly the six-year-olds, readily created gestures to convey the contents of the pictures. And the gestures that the children created contained fundamental features of human language and emergent sign languages, which is very impressive. But, of course, young silent gesturers all know a language (as do adult silent gesturers) and so are not really *creating* language; they are creating structures outside their spoken language. The best evidence for language creation still comes from homesign.[12]

But if we can show parallels between homesign and silent gesture, then we can be more confident that the lab studies really do have something to say about language creation and emergence. Take, for example, a silent gesture lab study investigating ordering in descriptions of different types of events. In an *intensional event*, the object of the action does not exist at the beginning of the event: "I baked a cake," "I drew a picture"—the event involves creating the object. In contrast, in an *extensional event*, the object is present at the start: "I cut the cake," "I ripped the picture"—the event involves acting on an existing object. It turns out that silent gesturers use different gesture orders to describe these two types of events: SVO for intensional events, SOV for extensional events. Is this difference, discovered in the lab, also found in a human language-emergence situation? Do NSL signers use these same two orders to describe intensional and extensional events?[13]

Molly Flaherty, one of my graduate students who is fluent in Nicaraguan Sign Language, and her collaborator, Marieke Schouwstra, found that they do. This means that the ordering phenomenon discovered under controlled conditions in the lab is a good simulation of naturally occurring language emergence. We haven't tested homesigners yet, but we predict, based on the silent gesture study, that homesigners will make this distinction: the silent gesturers needed neither to see a model of a gesture system nor to share their gestures with another to make the distinction, so homesigners should be able to develop it too. The lab study led to the hypothesis that marking the difference between intensional and extensional events is part of the apparatus humans bring to language. We can test this hypothesis by looking at the naturally occurring language that is emerging in Nicaragua.[14]

Another way to determine whether there are parallels between human language emergence and silent gesture is to start with a phenomenon in the real world and take it to the lab. Natasha Abner, one of my postdoctoral fellows, took the lead on a study that we did with homesigners and cohort 1 and 2 signers in Nicaragua. We asked whether any or all of these groups mark the distinction between nouns and verbs. All languages make this distinction but do so using different techniques. Does NSL make the distinction, and if so, when does it emerge and how is it marked? In English, nouns and verbs are produced in different positions in a sentence and take different endings: nouns occur after determiners (*the, a*) and take plural endings (*-s, -es*); verbs occur after auxiliaries (*is, do, have*) and take tense endings (*-ing, -ed*). Does NSL mark this distinction in some way? To find out, we developed a set of videos that we thought might elicit noun forms versus verb forms. We showed a person hammering a nail; the HAMMER gesture for this video would likely describe the action and function as a verb. We also showed a person performing an action that the hammer was not designed for, like dropping it into a cup; the HAMMER gesture for this video would likely describe the object and function as a noun.

All of the signers in Nicaragua, including the homesigners, distinguished between noun and verb uses: verb gestures were produced at the end of the sentence; noun gestures were produced earlier in the sentence. As we saw in the young American homesigners, humans introduce the noun-verb distinction into their language even if they are not learning that language from or sharing it with anyone.

But homesigners did not use all of the markers that signers used. NSL signers used bigger gestures (involving more joints: wrist, elbow, shoulder) for verbs and smaller gestures (involving fewer joints: only the wrist) for nouns. The longer a signer had been part of the deaf community, the more likely he or she was to use size to mark the noun-verb distinction. This raises an interesting question: Is learning language from someone else necessary to use size as a marker of nouns and verbs (cohort 2 signers and beyond)? Or is it sufficient to share the language with someone else (cohort 1 signers)?[15]

Lab studies give us some purchase here. We are now giving the same videos to hearing English speakers and asking them to describe the videos using their hands and not their mouths. Some of them create their gestures on their own over a series of trials; they simulate homesigners. Some create their gestures with another English speaker, also using hand and not mouth; they simulate the first NSL cohort. In keeping with the NSL findings, all of the hearing adults in this study use order to distinguish between nouns and verbs, placing verbs at the end of their gesture sentences and nouns earlier in the sentences. But none of the adults use size to mark the distinction, which suggests that creating and sharing language with someone else does not create enough pressure for this distinction to arise. Our next step is to use the videos created by this "first generation" as input for a new group of adults, repeating the process for six generations. Our question is whether silent gesturers will at some point start marking the distinction between nouns and verbs with size. If they do, we will have good evidence that transmission is necessary for this particular property to appear in an emerging language, and at least in a lab setting, we will know how many generations it takes.[16]

Silent gesture reveals deep-seated cognitive structures that humans call upon when we need to communicate—no matter what language we speak or whether we have a language at all. This could be useful when you visit a foreign country and don't speak the native language. People in foreign countries often gesture as they try to make themselves understood. That may be just the wrong strategy. If you gesture when you talk, your gestures will take on the characteristics of your speech. But if you don't speak and use silent gesture, you are likely to use the same structures in your gestures that your addressees would use—making it more likely that you will be understood. Take my college roommate who was visiting Rwanda and wanted to find a food market. She said nothing but produced an EAT gesture and then a WHERE gesture (she flipped both of her palms over), just as a homesigner might. She risked getting sent to a restaurant instead of a market, but if you're hungry in a strange place, that's good enough. Silent gesture brings out the communicative strategies that we all share, independent of language. Importantly, silent gesture is categorically different from co-speech gesture, the gestures you use when you speak.

We have spent two chapters exploring the gestures that children produce when they are *not* exposed to a language. Why? First, this phenomenon illustrates just how important structured communication is to humans. A child who has no experience with language as we know it can nevertheless invent a system of homesigns. This system has many (but not all) of the properties of human language. Homesign reveals the properties of human minds that structure language, not the other way around. In other words, this is where our *minds* shape language, not where language is shaping our minds.

The second reason is related to the first. Before studying homesigners, we might have guessed that children not exposed to a language would have no communication ability at all, and if they did, it would be no more sophisticated than animal communication, lacking rules for combining units at several levels. But that guess would be wrong: children have quite a lot to say, and they say it in a structured way, even when they can't learn speech, and sign language is not their parents' primary language. Language is resilient in humans.

With these findings as a backdrop, we now turn to the payoff for having spent five chapters learning about gesture. *Silent gesture*, created by a child without linguistic input or by hearing individuals who are not talking, provides a unique window into the ideas humans like to express in language, unfettered by the actual languages of the world. These gestures have the potential to be used, or taught, when speaking is difficult—for example, during developmental delay, after injury, in noisy speaking conditions, when languages are incompatible, and so forth. *Co-speech gesture* also reveals your thoughts to the world, but these thoughts don't necessarily fit easily into language. They have the potential to get the world to pay attention to you and also to respond to you in a different way than if you had not gestured. And the gestures that accompany speech participate in and can bring about change in your own thinking. Gesture has a role to play in a wide range of circumstances, from everyday conversation to the courts of law. Part III explores three of these circumstances, with an eye toward revealing how to make the world a better place through your hands.

Part III
WHY YOU SHOULD CARE ABOUT HANDS

6

USING HANDS TO PARENT

THIS FINAL PART OF THE BOOK TAKES WHAT WE'VE LEARNED AND tells us how understanding gesture, in all of its guises, allows us to better understand others and ourselves in real contexts, including child development, clinical settings, and education. Much of this chapter and the next two focuses on children (parenting, treating, and teaching children) because, as I mentioned in the introduction, I am a developmental psychologist, and my expertise is in child development. But the takeaways from this part of the book are relevant to you even if you are not a parent, clinician, or teacher. Learning how gesture helps you better understand others and yourself is useful even if you infrequently interact with children—after all, adults gesture too. And remember, as mentioned in the introduction, the few studies done on adults paralleling those done on children find the same results. I'm betting that everything I've shown you about gesturing in interactions with children can be extrapolated to gesturing in interactions with adults.

The gestures you produce with your hands complete your thoughts, which means that an encompassing picture of human communication contains both language and gesture. In order to fully understand ourselves and others—how we develop, how we teach, how we know what others know, even how we know what we ourselves know—we have to reconceptualize communication as a dynamic between language and gesture.

Gesture can help you be a more sensitive parent in many ways—beginning when your child is first learning to talk and continuing through and beyond the adolescent years. Because gesture taps into hidden thoughts, you have a ready-made way to identify thoughts your children might not even know they have—a useful parenting tool at any age. The first step is watching how your children move their hands when they talk and knowing what to look for.

PAY ATTENTION TO YOUR CHILD'S GESTURES

Children enter language hands first. This means that gesture can be helpful to parenting even before your child is able to speak. If your child points at you when she sees your hat, she is effectively telling you that she knows it's your hat. You can then begin a conversation that will be of mutual interest around that point: "Yes, that's mommy's hat. Where's your hat?" Later, as adolescents, when children tend to be more private and less communicative, their hands can continue to give them away. Your adolescent who produces a hand flip and shrug while insisting you are wrong is revealing some uncertainty and maybe even an openness to compromise.

As I have noted many times, gesture often provides the first evidence that a child is ready to take the next developmental step. This means that you can use your children's gestures—or lack thereof—as both an early indicator of their progress and as an early warning that they are not on track. In order to know what to look for, you need to know what the typical developmental trajectory looks like for a child's gesturing. So let's begin at the beginning.

Early in the language-learning process, children have limited vocabularies, and so gestures give children a way to extend their communicative range. Children begin to gesture between eight and twelve months. They use their first gestures to draw attention to objects: they point at objects, people, and places, and they hold up objects so that you will look at them (but not take them). These are known as *declarative* deictic gestures. Children also point to get things done: they point at objects that they want or that they'd like you to act on. These are known as *imperative* deictic gestures. Later on, children produce *iconic* gestures (gestures that capture aspects of the objects, actions, or attributes they represent), just as adults do. For example, a child flaps his arms to indicate a bird or the act of flying.[1]

These early gestures not only precede but also predict speech. The more a child gestures early on, the more words his or her vocabulary is likely to have later in development. Interestingly, it's the child's declarative points—the ones that feel conversational—that predict later linguistic skills, not the imperative points that tell others to do something. We can even predict which particular nouns will enter a child's spoken vocabulary by looking at the objects that that child indicated with pointing gestures several months earlier. Take a child who doesn't know the word *bird* but indicates an interest in birds by pointing at them. Within approximately three months, that child is likely to learn and produce the word *bird*—more likely than learning a word for an object the child hadn't pointed at earlier. Gesture paves the way for children's early nouns. Interestingly, gesture doesn't seem to pave the way for early verbs. Children produce their first iconic action gestures (a TWIST-OPEN gesture) six months *after* using their first verbs (*open*). So don't worry if your child isn't producing iconic gestures early in development—they'll get there eventually.[2]

I find it really interesting and potentially useful that children's gestures predict the onset of phrases and sentences. Hearing children, at least in the United States, rarely combine gestures with other gestures. But they do combine gestures with words, and they do it before they combine words with words. Their earliest gesture + speech combinations are points combined with a label for the object at the end of the point—for example, point at dog + *dog*. In these constructions, gesture *complements* speech. Complementary gesture + speech combinations predict the onset of phrases in which one word, the noun (*dog*), specifies the category to which the object belongs, and the other word, the determiner (*the*), specifies a particular member of the category. Once children begin to produce constructions like *the dog* in their speech, they decrease their point at dog + *dog* combinations. This developmental progression suggests that the point at dog + *dog* combination serves a purpose eventually taken over by *the dog*.[3]

After producing complementary gesture + speech combinations, the child's next step is to produce gesture + speech combinations in which gesture conveys information that is different from, and *supplementary* to, the information conveyed in the accompanying speech. For example, the child points at a ball while saying *here* to request that the ball be moved to a particular spot. The information conveyed in gesture, when taken in relation to the information conveyed in speech, creates a meaning that could be expressed in the short sentence *ball here*. And sure enough, about three months after they have produced their first supplementary gesture + speech combination, children produce their first two-word sentences.[4]

As the findings in the previous paragraphs suggest, gesture is not merely an early index of overall communicative skill. It's a prelude to *specific* linguistic steps a child will soon take. This becomes clear when we look at the same gestural devices within a child. Early gestures for objects predict later spoken vocabulary— for instance, pointing at a toy bear at eighteen months foreshadows the word *bear* entering the child's vocabulary at forty-two months—but not the onset of two-word speech. Conversely, early

gesture + speech sentences, such as point at bear + *growl*, produced at eighteen months predict the onset of two-word speech
(*bear growls*) at forty-two months but don't predict later spoken
vocabulary.[5]

Gesture does more than open the door to sentence construction.
The particular gesture + speech combinations that a child produces
predict the achievement of particular linguistic milestones. Take a
child who produces a DRINK gesture by cupping his hand at his
mouth and tilting his head back, followed by the spoken word
you. Several months later, the child is producing spoken sentences
that contain these elements: a word for the agent (*you* in the earlier combination) and a word for the action (*drink* in the earlier
combination)—for example, *you paint*. Or take a child who points
at a car and says *drive*. Several months later, this child is producing spoken sentences that contain a word for the action (*drive* in
the earlier combination) and a word for the object of the action
(*car* in the earlier combination)—for example, *ride horsie*. Finally,
consider the child who produces an EAT gesture, jabbing a fist at
his mouth, before saying *I like it*. Several months later, this child is
producing complex spoken sentences that contain two verbs (*like*
and *eat* in the earlier combination)—for example, *help me find*.
Supplementary gesture + speech combinations continue to provide
stepping stones to increasingly complex linguistic constructions.[6]

Gesture also predicts changes in a child's stories later in development. At five years of age, some children are able to take the
viewpoint of a character into account when they tell their own
stories—but only in gesture, not speech. For example, to describe
a woodpecker's pecking, a child moves her upper body and head
back and forth, assuming the perspective of the bird as he is pecking (a *character* perspective), as opposed to moving her hand
shaped like a beak back and forth, which would illustrate the perspective of an *observer* looking at the bird. The interesting result
is that children who produced character-viewpoint gestures at age
five were more likely than children who did not produce these

gestures to tell well-structured stories at ages six and seven. Good stories manipulate perspective, which may be why children who can display character viewpoint in gesture early in development later produce well-structured stories. Gesture continues to act as a harbinger of change as it assumes new roles in relation to discourse and narrative structure.[7]

We know that, early in development, young children can produce meaningful gesture + speech combinations that do the work of sentences. This means that even toddlers are able to integrate information across the manual and oral modalities when they *produce* the two together. Can toddlers also integrate the two modalities when they *see* them produced? We gave one-word speakers, all of whom were able to produce gesture + speech combinations, commands in English that either did or didn't contain gesture. For example, we said *push* without gesture or *push* with a point at the ball; or we said *cookie* without gesture or *cookie* with a GIVE gesture, an open palm extended outward. We also gave the children spoken sentences that expressed the meaning conveyed by the gesture + speech combination: *push the ball* or *give the cookie*. All of the children were able to integrate the information presented in speech with the information presented in gesture—they were more likely to push the ball when they received *push* + point at ball than *push* alone and more likely to give the cookie when they received *cookie* + GIVE gesture than *cookie* alone. In fact, they pushed the ball and gave the cookie just as often in response to the gesture + speech combinations as to the parallel spoken sentences *push the ball* and *give the cookie*. Young children can integrate information given manually and orally in both production and comprehension. So don't be afraid to use gestures that convey different information from your speech when you interact with your child: your child will understand and, as we'll soon see, benefit from them.[8]

Once children have mastered spoken sentences, they no longer need gesture to fill in the blanks and function like words. But they continue to gesture, as do we all. As adults, we use gesture not just to convey word-like meanings but also to convey broader ideas that influence the interpretation of our speech. From this point on, gesture helps children and adults learn domains other than language, such as conservation, math, the balance scale, chemistry, and so on. As we've seen, gesture is seamlessly integrated with the speech adults both produce and hear. Are children able to integrate speech with gestures that are not functioning as words per se but are nevertheless adding ideas to the mix?

Gesture-speech integration is an important hallmark of human communication. Vocalizations combined with gestures are routine in human children but far less common in apes. Being able to integrate information across modalities (gesture and speech) may have been a crucial step in supporting the emergence of language in our ancestors. So when do we have good evidence of gesture-speech integration in children?[9]

To address this question, we first tackled gesture-speech integration in adults. We showed adults a video of a speaker producing the same sentences with and without gesture. For example, consider this short story: "Stacie was excited when her parents brought home her new pet. Sparky, who was cute as could be, tried to bite her when she fed him." Everyone, including you, would guess that Stacie's pet was a dog on hearing this little story *without* gesture—but not on hearing the same sentences accompanied by an arms-flapping gesture produced as the speaker says the word *pet*. Everything changes with the gesture—you now assume that the pet is a bird. But you come to this interpretation *only if* you can understand the information conveyed in gesture and integrate it with the information conveyed in speech.

All of the adults in our study inferred that the pet was a bird with the flapping gesture—they were able to integrate gesture and speech. To understand what's going on in the brain when we integrate gesture and speech, and to get another measure of integration, we gave the adults these little stories while they were in a functional magnetic resonance imaging (fMRI) scanner, which measures brain activity by detecting changes associated with blood flow. We asked which brain regions were activated when the sentences were presented with and without gesture. We also gave the adults sentences in which gesture conveyed the same information as speech—we replaced the word *pet* with the word *parrot*—so that gesture wasn't essential to understand that the pet was a bird. Three regions of the brain—the left inferior frontal gyrus triangular, the opercular portions, and the left posterior middle temporal gyrus—responded more strongly when the flapping gesture added information to *pet*, compared with when the flapping gesture conveyed the same information as *parrot*. In other words, these three areas were active when gesture was integrated with speech and not when gesture merely occurred with speech.[10]

We used the same sentences and the same brain-imaging techniques with children ages eight to ten years. Some of the children realized that the pet was a bird when they saw the flapping gesture combined with *pet*; they were able to integrate gesture with speech. Some of the children did not. Importantly, the brain areas activated in these two groups of children differed. There was more activity in three brain areas (inferior frontal gyri; right middle temporal gyrus; left superior temporal gyrus) when the flapping gesture was produced with *pet* than with *parrot*. This activation pattern was found *only* in children who realized that the pet was a bird after hearing *pet* and seeing the flapping gesture.

At both behavioral and brain levels, the children who could do gesture-speech integration differed from the children who could not. The brain-activation patterns for gesture-speech integration in the children overlapped with the patterns in adults performing the same task, but the patterns were broader. This suggests that children have more developmental work to do to home in on adult levels of gesture-speech integration. Whether the moment of gesture-speech integration (between ages eight and ten years) found in this study cuts across other domains or is specific to story comprehension is a matter for future research. But the study does offer a possible neurobiological mechanism that could underlie children's increasing ability to integrate gesture and speech over childhood and might even account for individual differences across children in that integration.[11]

I once told a colleague (a linguist, no less) about this gesture phenomenon. I told him that early gesture + speech combinations predicted the onset of two-word sentences in young language-learning children. On going home, he listened to and looked at his toddler grandson and found that he was in fact producing supplementary gesture + speech combinations (*open* + point at box). My colleague predicted that his grandson would soon be producing two-word sentences, and that's exactly what happened. His son, the child's father, was very impressed. So at the least, you can use this information about gesture to impress people. You can also use it to tailor your responses to your child and promote the child's language learning, as the next section describes.

RESPOND TO YOUR CHILD'S GESTURES

Your child doesn't know the word *dog* and points at a dog to draw your attention to it. A very natural response on your part is to say, "Yes, that's a dog." This seems like a really good time to say *dog* to the child because this is a moment when the child is clearly interested in the animal and might be open to learning its label. It feels like a "teachable moment"—a time when teaching a particular topic or idea is relatively easy, often because the learner is focused on what needs to be learned. The concept of a teachable moment was popularized by Robert Havighurst, then a faculty member in education at the University of Chicago, in his 1952 book *Human Development and Education*. Havighurst used the phrase to refer to a child's developmental readiness to learn a particular concept. But it is often used (as I use it here) to refer to a child's heightened interest in a topic, which makes the child particularly receptive to input that targets that topic.[12]

Because saying *dog* when your child points at one is finely tuned to the child's state of mind at the moment, your response to the gesture could be very effective in teaching the child how this object is labeled in English. This scenario assumes that young children intend to convey messages with their gestures, and the literature provides good evidence for this assumption. When twelve- to sixteen-month-old infants use gesture, they have a particular message in mind. We know this because they negotiate with their mothers over the meanings of their gestures. For example, a child points toward a tumble of objects and says, "Uh." Mother says, "Oh, you want a grape," and hands the child a grape. The child pushes the grape away and continues to point toward the objects, making it clear that he knew exactly what he wanted (and it wasn't the grape). Along the same lines, thirty-month-olds engage in a range of behaviors to ensure that an experimenter understands their requests, expressed primarily through gesture.[13]

Responding *dog* to a child's point can facilitate word learning only if parents understand the messages conveyed in their child's gestures and respond accordingly. There is evidence for this assumption as well. Adults typically react to the gestures speakers produce along with their speech, often recasting the information conveyed in gesture into speech. Mothers of young infants are no exception. Mothers respond to the gestures that their young children produce and translate what they think those gestures mean into words, as in the *dog* example. The big question is whether parents' translations of their children's gestures have a positive impact on their children's subsequent language development.[14]

We began to address this question by looking at naturalistic interactions in the home between mothers and their children aged ten to twenty-four months. The children were all learning English and were producing only one word at a time, and, of course, they gestured. We had taken videotapes of many mother-child interactions over time and could observe developmental trajectories in each child.

Let's focus first on word learning during this period. We looked at the sessions when a child indicated objects in gesture *only* and never in speech. Mother responded to some, but not all, of these gestures by "translating" them into speech—saying *bottle* after the child pointed at the bottle. When she didn't translate, her response was sensible but not as useful as her translation of the pointing gesture: the child pointed at a blue chicken, and mother said, "That's the blue one," which isn't too helpful if the word the child needs to learn is *chicken*. The question is whether mother's translations of her child's gestures influenced which words the child learned first. They did: a few sessions later, the child said *bottle* but not *chicken*. In general, when mother translated her child's gestures into words, those words were likely to soon become part of the child's spoken vocabulary. For the most part, a mother didn't determine which objects her child pointed at. But once the child pointed at an object, mother could have an influence on whether the child would soon learn a word for that object.[15]

Mothers respond not only with object labels to children's declarative gestures (e.g., saying, "That's a bear," in response to a child's point at the bear) but also with action labels to children's imperative gestures (e.g., saying, "Do you want me to open that?" in response to a child's point at a bubble jar). Mother's responses to declarative gestures at twelve months predict the child's *noun* vocabulary at seventeen months, and her responses to imperative gestures at twelve months predict the child's *verb* vocabulary at seventeen months. Responding to your children's gestures in a targeted way can have a beneficial effect on word learning.[16]

What about sentence learning and mothers' responses to their children's gesture + speech combinations? The children produced gesture + speech combinations in which gesture added to the information conveyed in speech (*nap* + point at bird), as well as gesture + speech combinations in which gesture reinforced the information conveyed in speech (*bird* + point at bird). If you were to respond to these gesture + speech combinations, you'd likely say, "Yes, the bird's taking a nap" in response to the first type of combination, and "Yes, that's a bird" in response to the second type of combination. It turns out that the mothers in our sample did just that, which meant that they produced longer utterances in response to gesture + speech combinations like *nap* + point at bird than to gesture + speech combinations like *bird* + point at bird. And the words they produced were often a combination of the information conveyed in the child's gesture (point at bird) and the information conveyed in the child's speech (*nap*): "The bird's taking a nap."[17]

Did these translations have an impact on when children produced their first two-word sentence? The short answer is yes. We calculated how often each mother responded to her child's gestures by translating the gestures into speech. The children whose mothers were big translators turned out to be the first to produce two-word sentences. So if you respond appropriately to a child's gestures, that child will make more progress toward linguistic milestones than if you ignore the gestures or respond in a non-helpful way.

We've established that children's early gestures reflect two separate abilities—word learning and sentence making—on which later linguistic abilities can be built. Expressing many different meanings in gesture early in development is a sign of the child's corresponding receptivity to and potential for vocabulary development, and expressing many different types of gesture + speech combinations is a sign of the child's corresponding receptivity to and potential for constructing sentences. The early gestures children produce thus reflect their cognitive potential for learning particular aspects of language. But having a parent who responds to your gestures with translations into speech that are targeted to your level will speed up your linguistic trajectory. Parents who take advantage of the teachable moments provided by a child's gestures are playing a role in the child's word and sentence learning.

Parent responses to child gesture on nonlanguage tasks can also propel children forward. Try presenting your child with one of the mathematical equivalence problems we talked about earlier, say, $4 + 3 + 6 = \underline{} + 6$. Your child may add up all of the numbers in the problem and put 19 in the blank. When explaining how she solved the problem, she says she added up all of the numbers in the problem. But, at the same time, she covers the two sixes in the problem with her palms. She has noticed that there is a six on each side of the equation and has told you she noticed through her hands, not through her mouth. Her gestures signal that this would be a good time to start talking about what the equals sign means (the two sides of the equation have to sum to the same amount) and what having the same addends on the left and right sides of the equation licenses (equal addends allow you to group the unique numbers on the left side, $4 + 3$, sum them, and put 7 in the blank). This is a teachable moment visible only in your child's hands. Respond to it!

In fact, even very young children expect you to respond to their gestures, and they expect your responses to be informative. They don't just want to share their appreciation of the object they point at with you. They want you to give them information about the object. At twelve months, children point to objects more often when they interact with a knowledgeable person than when they interact with a poorly informed person, one who has just given the wrong names for familiar objects in the child's presence. At eighteen months, they remember object labels provided in response to their points better than they remember object labels provided in response to their vocalizations. Responses to gestures are compelling. The general rule of thumb is for you to be on the lookout for teachable moments provided by your child's gestures and to respond to those gestures as best you can.[18]

ENCOURAGE YOUR CHILD TO GESTURE

Children's gestures tell you what they need to hear. Paying attention and targeting input to those gestures can propel child learning. But your child's gestures can also propel learning in other ways: gesturing can help children realize their potential. For example, the act of expressing meanings in gesture could be playing an active role in helping children expand their potential vocabulary, or the act of expressing sentence-like meanings in gesture + speech combinations could be playing an active role in helping children become better sentence learners.

We have seen that the number of gestures children spontaneously produce early in development relates to the size of their spoken vocabularies several years later. This is an important result because the size of a child's vocabulary when the child enters school is a good predictor of academic success. Of course, the gestures children spontaneously produce could reflect their interest in communication and play no role at all in determining the size of the child's vocabulary. But we have good evidence that child gesture *does* play a causal role in word learning.[19]

Recall the study described in Chapter 3 in which Eve LeBarton modeled pointing for one group of children and encouraged them to copy her points. Over a period of seven weekly sessions, these children increased the amount of gesturing they did not only with Eve but also with their parents. And—the important result—at the end of the eighth week, the children who had been told to point throughout the study had larger spoken vocabularies than the children who had not been told to point. The more points the children produced, the larger their vocabularies. This means that child pointing can play a role in vocabulary growth.[20]

Encouraging your language-learning child to point can help the child learn words. This phenomenon has provided the impetus for the trend to teach young children *baby signs*. The idea is that children are able to learn "words" produced by the hands more easily than words produced by the mouth. Teaching children these manual words/signs should then give them a leg up on word learning. The baby sign movement is very popular: my grandchildren learned to put their two hands together, fingers touching, to ask for more and to put their hands to their chests to say please. It was useful to me to know what was on their minds and nice for them to have an easy way to tell me. Many babies know how to produce *more* (illustration on the left) and *please* (illustration on the right).[21]

The controversial part of the baby sign movement is the claim that teaching your child manual words for objects and actions speeds up the spoken-language learning process. The evidence for this claim is unfortunately not very solid. Elizabeth Kirk, a gesture researcher in England, undertook a well-designed study testing the impact of teaching children signs before they are able to speak. She randomly assigned families to one of four groups. In one group, the mothers were given British Sign Language signs for a set of objects to teach their children. In another, the mothers were given iconic gestures for the same objects to teach their children. In the third group, the mothers were told to teach their children the words for the same objects. And in the fourth group, the mothers were told to interact with their children as they typically would, with no instructions about particular words or signs. The intervention study followed forty infants, ten in each group, from the ages of eight to twenty months—it was a long study. The experimenters checked in with the mothers to assess how often they presented the words to the children and tested the children's language abilities periodically.

The disappointing news, from one point of view, is that there were no differences between any of the groups. All four groups progressed through language learning at the same rate. From another point of view, however, the news is quite good. Teaching children signs as labels for objects and actions didn't hurt their word acquisition—you can imagine how it might have. Why learn a word for an object if you already have a sign for that object? The other piece of good news is that mothers in the gesture-training conditions ended up being more responsive to their children's nonverbal cues and encouraging more independent action by their children. So there was a benefit, just not one specific to learning spoken language.[22]

But remember we learned earlier that telling children to produce an iconic gesture for an action made it easy for them to remember a novel word for that action. The children could also extend the newly learned word to the same action performed on a different set of objects. This study sounds like it contradicts the Kirk findings. However, the study described earlier compared learning by gesture to learning by action, not to hearing the word with no movement at all. Hearing the word without gesture might have been just as good a teaching tool as hearing the word with gesture—as Kirk and her colleagues found. And remember that the iconic gestures children spontaneously produce do *not* predict their later action words, even though the pointing gestures they spontaneously produce *do* predict their later object words. Iconic gestures seem to be different from pointing gestures in how they support word learning.

The upshot is that we don't really know whether encouraging children to produce iconic gestures or baby signs improves their spoken vocabularies. But we do know that it doesn't hurt their word acquisition and has the potential to improve your interactions with your children. We also know that encouraging your children to produce pointing gestures *does* have an impact on their later vocabularies. So encourage your children to gesture—it won't hurt and it could have at-the-moment as well as future benefits for language learning.

Once children have gotten the basics down with respect to language, they can use gesture to learn other skills. Here we do have good evidence that giving children gestures to produce during a math lesson helps them benefit from that lesson and retain what they have learned. But it's not so easy to figure out which gestures you should teach your child for a particular task. The good news is that you don't have to tell your children *how* to gesture; you merely have to tell them *to* gesture. Even telling adults to gesture any way they want as they describe an event they have seen helps them remember that event better than if they hadn't been told to gesture.[23]

We learned earlier that telling children to gesture (but not telling them how to gesture) on a set of math problems brings out ideas that they had not expressed before in either speech or gesture. Many of the new ideas expressed in these gestures conveyed correct problem-solving strategies, which they produced while putting the wrong answer in the blank and giving an incorrect problem-solving strategy in speech. The children knew something about how to solve the problem, but it was deeply hidden in their hands. When merely told to move their hands the next time they solved a similar problem, they were able to express these blossoming ideas in gesture. And then, when given instruction in the problem, they began to solve the problems correctly. Getting them to gesture made them ready to solve the math problems. You might argue that these children were ready to learn the math problems even before they were told to gesture. That may be true, but gesturing clearly played a role in getting them to learn how to solve the problem: children who were told not to gesture did not improve after the lesson as much as children who were told to gesture.[24]

Gesturing is beneficial not only for math concepts but even for more abstract concepts. As described earlier, telling children to gesture as they explain their reasoning on a moral dilemma brings out new ideas that they had not previously expressed in either gesture or speech. And that gesturing makes them ready to benefit from a subsequent lesson in moral reasoning. We know from the literature that telling learners to give explanations reinforces and cements learning. Maybe it's not the explanations per se that are so beneficial; maybe it's the gestures produced along with those explanations that also enrich and cement learning. In any event, you don't need to tell your children which gestures to make as they describe their take on a problem—just tell them to gesture, and their hands will do the rest.[25]

GESTURE YOURSELF

Children from high-income families have large vocabularies at fifty-four months, a relation that can be explained, at least in part, by the children's gestures at fourteen months. But there's an interesting twist to this phenomenon: the relation between child gesture and family income can be explained by how much the parents gestured when the children were fourteen months old. The path goes from early parent gesture to early child gesture to later child speech. On its own, parent gesture does *not* predict child speech—it's the link to child gesture that does the work. In general, parents who gesture a lot have children who gesture a lot, and these child gestures lead to language.[26]

But parent gesture can have other effects as well. The nonverbal circumstances in which a parent produces a word can have a big effect on how easily the meaning of that word can be guessed—the more cues, including gesture, parents give to an object's identity, the easier it is for everyone, including children, to guess that the parents' word refers to it. The really interesting finding to me is that parents vary a lot in how well they use these nonverbal cues to word meaning. And this variability predicts differences in child language outcomes—the quality of a parent's nonverbal input when a child is fourteen to eighteen months old predicts the size of the child's spoken vocabulary three years later. Interestingly, this measure of parent input *quality* is not related to the economic status of the family—high- and low-income parents alike know how to give their children good-quality input. Note that this is not true of how much parents talk to their children, parent input *quantity*; parents from economically advantaged homes talk more to their children than parents from disadvantaged homes (perhaps not a surprise since it's tough to talk to your kid a lot when you're working several jobs). And the amount of talk parents give their children when they're young also predicts the size of their later spoken vocabularies. Importantly, the effects of parent input *quality* and *quantity* are independent: each has its own effect on later child language.[27]

Parent gesturing can also set up the conditions for child word learning. Parents can use their gestures to get their children to focus on a particular object or scene with them—in other words, to establish what is known as *joint attention*. Joint attention provides a good situation for word learning: children are more likely to remember words parents produce during moments of joint attention than words presented out of joint attention. When your child points at a dog and you respond with the word *dog*, you are focusing your attention on what your child is interested in, which is likely one reason that "translating" pointing gestures into speech helps word learning.[28]

The gestures you produce with your child can do more than affect the size of the child's spoken vocabulary—they can also affect the nature of that vocabulary. Children learn words for objects more deeply when those words are presented along with either a shape gesture or an action gesture. For example, a child hears the nonsense word *pam* and sees a gesture that portrays the shape that a Play-Doh cutter has made on the clay. Or the child hears the word and sees a gesture that mimics how the cutter is pushed down onto the clay. Children who see either of these gestures need fewer reminders when trying to recall the word than children who hear only the word and see no gesture. The gesture in their input has deepened their word learning.[29]

The gestures children see can also influence the meanings they attach to words. Here's an example of how this can work. You place felt pieces on a board so that they form a cloud shape. You then say a novel word and produce one of two gestures. One gesture highlights the *manner* in which the felt-placing action was done: it depicts the vertical hand movements you used to make the cloud. The other gesture highlights the *outcome* of the felt-placing action: it depicts the shape of the cloud. The gesture the children see will influence what they think the word means. If they see the manner gesture, they think the word refers to how the felt was placed and will extend the word to a new situation in which the placing movements are the same but a new shape is made. If they see the outcome gesture, they think the word refers to the cloud shape that the felt took and will extend the word to a new situation in which different movements are used to create the same cloud shape. The type of gesture you use as you describe new events to your child can have an impact on what the child sees in the event. These studies on how gesture influences word meanings were done with experimenters in the lab, not with parents in the home. But there's no reason to think that the findings won't apply to you and your children. Use your gestures wisely to guide your child's interpretation of objects and events.[30]

Your gestures also have the potential to influence your child's attitudes. Suppose you tell your child that boys and girls are equally good at math. But when you talk about the skills boys have, you gesture up around your eyes; when you talk about girls' skills, you gesture down around your chin or lower. Your child will hear one thing but see another. And often the gestures are most powerful. We are currently exploring the impact of these subtle gestures on children's attitudes. I think it's a good bet that children pick up on attitudes that you express only in your hands, whether or not you want them to.

The bottom line is that you should gesture when you talk to your children and be attentive to what you're gesturing. Meredith Rowe, a former postdoc in my lab who did many of the studies highlighting the importance of spontaneous gesture, is developing a program, called Pointing to Success, in which she teaches parents about the importance of gesturing. The brief training program stresses the fact that a child's language development is malleable and that parents can play an important role in that development. It includes a five-minute video that underscores the importance of pointing, gives examples of parents and children pointing in their play with one another, and emphasizes that parents can help their children's language grow by pointing and encouraging their child's pointing.[31]

The intervention is still being tested, but a first pass increased pointing in parents of ten-month-olds. The intervention also increased pointing in the children. Interestingly, the effects were stronger for both parents and children in families who, before the intervention, did not believe that children's language development was malleable. These families learned not only that parents can play a role in their child's language development but also how to play that role—by making ample use of pointing gestures. For these families, children increased their use of pointing gestures and also increased the size of their spoken vocabularies. This was important information for the parents to get, and they made good use of it.

To bring this chapter to a close, as a parent, you can have an impact on your child's language development and acquisition of other skills by using gesture in four simple ways. First, watch what your children are doing with their hands—those hands are likely to hold secrets to their minds that they don't even know they have. Second, respond to your children's gestures by picking up the information conveyed in them and translating it into speech if appropriate or, if not, responding in some other targeted way. Third, encourage your child to gesture. Getting your children to gesture gets them to reveal their unspoken ideas, which has two important effects: it gives you a clear view of those unspoken ideas, and it energizes their learning process. Finally, gesture yourself when interacting with your child. Augment what you say with your hands and, if you can, think about what your hands are telling your child. You'd like the messages that you convey in your hands to be just the messages that you want your child to get.

7

USING HANDS TO
DIAGNOSE AND TREAT

GESTURE CAN BE A VALUABLE TOOL FOR ASSESSING AND TREATING both mental and physical health at all ages. As an example, let's turn to a study done by Eve Sauer, who became Eve LeBarton and did the seminal work described earlier showing that encouraging children to gesture has a positive effect on their vocabulary. Eve compared two groups of children born with brain injury. At eighteen months, both groups were delayed in word production, but they differed from each other in gesture production. One group produced the same number of gestures as a typically developing eighteen-month-old child and showed no delay with respect to gesture. The other group produced fewer gestures and was delayed. A year later we found that the two groups of children still differed with respect to gesture. But now they also differed with respect to words: the children who had gestured like a typically developing child at eighteen months now also looked like the typically developing child with respect to words; at thirty months they were no longer delayed. The other children had not caught up and remained delayed in word production. This result is important because, as a clinician, you can use early gesture to diagnose who is likely to experience language delay in the future and who is not—and you can do it *before* the delay becomes intractable.[1]

Children with pre- or perinatal brain injury exhibit remarkable plasticity in language development and an ability to recover, unlike adults who typically exhibit persistent language difficulties even when their brain injuries are comparable to a child's. But there is also variability among children with early focal brain injury, who often go through a protracted period of language delay. This delay resolves for some children but not for others. The exciting result is that gesture has the potential to help us figure out whose delay will resolve and whose won't. Our goal should be to offer children interventions while their language-learning trajectory is most malleable.[2]

WATCH THE GESTURES THAT CHILDREN WITH LANGUAGE DELAY PRODUCE

We need to watch what children with language delay do with their hands. Our question is whether gesture is characteristically different enough in different disorders to serve as a diagnostic for a particular disorder or, at the least, as a signal that subsequent language problems are likely.

Autism is a neurodevelopmental disorder whose hallmark is impairment in social interaction and communication, along with restricted and repetitive behaviors and interests. But a deficit in gesture is also among the diagnostic indicators of autism and is listed in classic descriptions of the disorder. The absence of pointing, along with the infrequent use of gesture to initiate joint attention, is part of the Autism Diagnostic Observation Schedule, the gold standard for evaluating the disorder. Pointing is a sensitive and useful marker since its absence can be detected *before* language delay becomes apparent. The absence of early pointing, when it occurs along with other behaviors, can serve as an early sign that a child may develop autism, which is of practical significance since many children with autism are not diagnosed until they enter a school setting.[3]

To establish the signal value of pointing as a marker of autism, researchers have retrospectively analyzed home videos of children later diagnosed with the condition. Since nearly everyone records their child's first birthday, one clever study compared home videos of the first birthday party of eleven children later diagnosed with autism to home videos of eleven typically developing children. Compared to typically developing children, children subsequently diagnosed with autism produced fewer gestures overall and almost no instances of pointing. In fact, children later diagnosed as autistic failed to use many social interaction gestures (such as shaking the head *no*, waving, indicating that an object is *so big*) and used their gestures to establish joint attention or to comment on an object much less often than typically developing children.[4]

Another approach has been to study the younger siblings of children diagnosed with autism. Younger siblings of children diagnosed with autism are two to three hundred times more likely to be diagnosed as autistic than children who do not have autistic siblings. There were a couple of striking results. First, before eighteen months, gesture is more informative about a future autism diagnosis than word comprehension or word production. Second, siblings who go on to have a diagnosis of autism do not increase the numbers of gesture + vocalization combinations they produce over time. All other groups—siblings who aren't diagnosed as autistic but do have language delay, siblings who aren't diagnosed as autistic and don't have language delay, and children who have no association with autism—showed an increase in combinations beginning at twelve months. The absence of growth was unique to the children later diagnosed as autistic.[5]

Autism is often difficult to diagnose. Gesture can be helpful in adding another behavior that can serve as a marker. In contrast, Down syndrome and Williams syndrome are both caused by known genetic anomalies and are easy to diagnose. Both are associated with distinct (and different) facial appearances, so it's also not hard to recognize a child with Down or Williams syndrome. We don't need gesture to help in the diagnosis, but perhaps gesture is used differently by these two groups, both of which display difficulties with language. If so, we could look to gesture as a way to improve their language skills.

Children with Down syndrome tend to have expressive language abilities that are not as advanced as their cognitive skills. Perhaps they can use gesture to compensate for these deficiencies. Although studies of spontaneous communication do not find a gesture advantage for children with Down syndrome, lab-based probes do. When asked to fill out a survey about their child's gesture, parents report that their children with Down syndrome have bigger gestural repertoires than the repertoires reported by parents of typically developing children. Laboratory studies on older children with Down syndrome (ages three to eight) also find a gesture boost—their performance on a picture-naming task is much better if their gestures (producing a hammering motion in response to a picture of a hammer) are counted, although their performance still ranks lower than the performance of typically developing children. The children with Down syndrome use gestures to convey correct information that they do not (and maybe cannot) express in speech. Gesture shows us that their ability to get meaning out of a picture exceeds their capacity to link a word to that picture. Ignoring gesture and using speech on its own to assess children with Down syndrome may substantially underestimate what they know.[6]

Children with Williams syndrome have poor visuo-spatial processing skills but relatively intact facial recognition. Although language was, at one point, thought to be spared in these children, researchers now think they do have linguistic deficiencies. Individuals with Williams syndrome have rich vocabularies and fluent speech in everyday conversational interactions, but their performance on laboratory-based tasks that require rapid picture naming is not perfect. They produce comparable numbers of correct and incorrect naming responses, and similar types of errors, as typically developing children; their representations of the meanings of words are not impaired. But they take twice as long to name the pictures as typically developing children. They produce gestures along with their circumlocutions (like typically developing children), but they also produce gestures along with their *correct* responses (which typically developing children do not do). Children with Williams syndrome use gesture when it's *not* essential, perhaps because it's an important vehicle for them or maybe because they can't really tell when gesture is needed. Overall, including gesture in assessments of disordered language systems is a good idea; it gives us a unique window into the children's skills.[7]

We have been looking at children with known physical problems. But some children have no obvious physical issues and still have difficulties with language. Children with specific language impairment have no identifiable intellectual impairments, yet do not acquire age-appropriate language skills. These children comprehend speech better when it is accompanied by gesture, and they gesture themselves, often conveying information in gesture not found in their speech. Preschool children identified as having language impairments produce more gestures per utterance than typically developing children. In fact, the poorer a child's language, the higher the child's gesture rate. Gesture can also compensate for poor oral language in older children with specific language impairment. When asked to solve a conservation task, these older children did not use gesture more often than typically developing children, but they did express information in their explanations that could *only* be found in gesture. For example, when given a liquid conservation task, a child with specific language impairment indicated the height of the container in speech ("it's taller") and its width in gesture (two hands displaying the width of the container). You need to consider both dimensions of a container to understand that a tall, skinny glass can have the same amount of liquid as a short, wide glass. Children with specific language impairment display more knowledge than their peers when we look at both gesture and speech than when we look only at speech.[8]

And then there are late talkers, young children who exhibit delays in expressive language but don't have hearing loss, mental difficulties, behavioral disturbances, or any other known form of neurological impairment. Late talkers at two years of age, by definition, have a vocabulary of fewer than fifty words and/or no two-word combinations. As in the LeBarton study of children with brain injury described at the beginning of this chapter, for some children, this early delay is transient, and they catch up with their peers around age three. For others, the initial delay persists and may be the first sign of an ongoing language impairment. Can gesture help us figure out which are which in this group without brain injury? The short answer is yes. Late talkers were given two tasks involving object-related gestures: imitating an adult performing a single object-related movement (pretending to drink from a cup or making a toy airplane fly) or a series of movements (putting a teddy bear in a high chair, putting on his bib, feeding him an apple, and wiping his mouth). One year later, the children who had done well on this task and on a word-comprehension task had caught up with their peers; these were the "late bloomers." The children who did not do well on these tasks continued to be delayed. Late bloomers use gesture differently from truly delayed children not only in lab-based tests but also in spontaneous production. Late talkers who are eventually identified as late bloomers produce more gestures than late talkers who are later identified as truly delayed.[9]

We learned in Part I of the book that gestures produced along with speech can tell us about a speaker's underlying thought processes. It should come as no surprise then that gesture can provide unique information about challenges, as well as strengths, in children with language disorders. Importantly, the gestures produced with atypical language are not qualitatively different from those produced with typical language. In other words, gestures produced with atypical language do not form a substitute system that replaces speech. These gestures are just like the gestures used by people with typical language abilities, although speakers with language difficulties may use their gestures more often to compensate for their difficulties.

RESPOND TO THE GESTURES THAT CHILDREN WITH LANGUAGE DELAY PRODUCE

Parents of typically developing children respond to their children's gestures by translating those gestures into speech. Do parents of children who have language delay or difficulties do the same? They do, and at the same rates as parents of typically developing children.[10]

Parents of children with Down syndrome translate the gestures their children produce that communicate unique information not conveyed in speech (the child points at a ball without saying the word *ball*). In other words, they provide their child with just the word he or she needs to hear at the moment when the child has displayed an interest in hearing it—at a teachable moment. Their rates of gesture translations are identical to the rates for parents of typically developing children when the children are twenty-two months old. But by sixty-three months, parents of typically developing children begin to decrease their translations; parents of Down syndrome children continue to translate at the same rate. Presumably, the decrease in how often parents of typically developing children translate their children's gestures is in response to the children's increasing vocabularies, which are considerably bigger than Down syndrome children's vocabularies at sixty-three months.

Parents of children with autism also translate (likely without awareness) their children's gestures into words, and at the same rates as parents of typically developing children and children with Down syndrome. A study headed by Şeyda Özçalışkan, a former postdoc in my lab who studies gesture in both typically developing children and children with developmental disorders, illustrates this point. The children were matched for expressive language abilities, so they differed in age. The typically developing children were eighteen months old, and the average age of the children with Down syndrome and the children with autism was thirty months. Parents of children in all three groups responded with verbal responses to almost all of their children's gestures indicating objects not mentioned in speech. And most of those responses were translations of the child's gesture. Importantly, these responses had a positive effect on children's subsequent vocabularies. In each group, words corresponding to gestures that were translated entered the children's vocabularies at greater rates than words corresponding to gestures that were *not* translated. As an example, a child points at a hat, and mother responds by saying, "That's a hat." But after the child points at a ball, she doesn't respond, or she says, "That's a colorful one." The child produces *hat* for the first time before he produces *ball*. This pattern was there in each of the groups. But, overall, children with Down syndrome acquired words at lower rates than the other two groups; they were, in general, less good at learning words even under optimal circumstances.

Jana Iverson, a former graduate student who did the original work on gesture in blind children, and her students studied parent translations in siblings of children with autism and in children who have no association with autism. She found that parents of both groups translated their children's gestures into speech at the same high rates. Both sets of parents were more likely to translate their children's pointing or showing gestures (pointing at a bottle, or holding the bottle up for mother to see) than their children's giving or requesting gestures (extending a bottle out to give to the parent, or extending a hand to request the bottle). Although the parents of the two groups didn't differ in their translations, the children differed in the gestures that elicited these responses. The children without any association with autism produced more pointing/showing gestures than giving/requesting gestures. The children whose siblings had autism did the opposite. As a result, these children ended up receiving *fewer* translations than the children without any association with autism simply because they produced fewer of the types of gestures that their parents translated into words. In other words, they gave their parents fewer opportunities to provide them with input tailored to their needs.

A bit of advice for parents of children with developmental disorders: translate your children's gestures—all of them, not just their pointing gestures—into speech as often as you can.

ENCOURAGE CHILDREN WITH LANGUAGE DELAY TO GESTURE

Baby signs are popular with parents of typically developing children. Teaching children signs for frequently used objects, actions, and states hasn't been shown to increase the size of a typically developing child's vocabulary, but it does have other benefits for parent-child interaction (and it does no harm).

Baby signs have also been taught to children with Down syndrome. What effect does encouraging these children to learn baby signs have? The first thing to note is that children with Down syndrome are able to learn baby signs, which is not to be taken for granted. Children with Down syndrome, whose average age was twenty-seven months (mental age twenty months), completed a workshop on baby signs. Three months later, most of the children did better at producing gestures on a vocabulary test, and some had even improved at understanding spoken words and sentences.[11]

Another group of children with Down syndrome, whose average age was thirty months, had learned baby signs and used them in a seminaturalistic observation session with their parents in the lab. The number of baby signs they produced during this session predicted the size of their spoken vocabularies one year later. In fact, baby signs predicted later spoken language better than the children's spontaneous gestures.

Encouraging children with Down syndrome to learn and use baby signs can have beneficial effects on their language. There isn't much known about the impact of encouraging gesture in children with other developmental disorders. But there is no reason to believe that encouraging them to gesture will have bad effects, and there is the potential for good effects. Even if encouraging children with language disorders to gesture doesn't improve their later spoken language, it could still make interacting with others easier and less frustrating. At the moment, there are no known downsides.

GESTURE TO CHILDREN WITH LANGUAGE DELAY

Parents gesture to their children, and parents of children with developmental disorders are no exception. In fact, in a study of typically developing children, children with Down syndrome, and children with autism, Şeyda Özçalışkan and her colleagues found that the *parents* of these three groups of children produced the same number of gestures overall and the same number of gesture + speech combinations. In contrast, the typically developing *children* produced more gestures overall and more gesture + speech combinations than the children with Down syndrome and the children with autism. The gesture differences across the three child groups are not coming from their parents. But maybe we should be encouraging parents of children with Down syndrome or autism to gesture *even more* than parents of typically developing children gesture. Perhaps children with these conditions need that much more gestural input in order to increase their own gesture rates.[12]

Parents might also want to pay attention to the types of gestures they produce. Jana Iverson and her colleagues found that mothers of children with Down syndrome produce more *showing* gestures than *pointing* gestures (holding up a bottle to call for attention rather than pointing at the bottle). Mothers of typically developing children do the opposite. The mothers of the children with Down syndrome may be adjusting their gesture to the developmental status of their child. But maybe that's not such a good idea. Pointing is a more "distanced" way of indicating an object than holding it up. A gradual increase from hold-ups to points on the part of the mothers might be helpful in getting children with Down syndrome to respond to and use point gestures more than hold-up gestures.[13]

GESTURE IN THERAPY SESSIONS

Gesture isn't just for kids, and it's not just for diagnosing developmental disorders. As we have seen, adult speakers can reveal their hidden beliefs in their hands (often unbeknownst to them). An astute listener can learn things about adults that they can't or won't say. I have long thought that clinical therapists with an eye for gesture could learn important things about their clients, which they could then use to move their therapy sessions forward. And, of course, it's a two-way street: a therapist can convey unintended messages to a client, which might help the therapeutic process—or even hurt it, since the messages are unplanned and not likely to be thought through.

When Sara Broaders joined my lab as a graduate student, she wanted to investigate the implicit messages that adults and children convey either in a clinical setting (e.g., a therapy session) or in a legal setting (e.g., an interview with an eyewitness). She wanted to analyze the gestures and the speech produced in these naturalistic contexts to see if anything unsaid was nevertheless expressed in gesture. It was impossible at the time (and probably still is) to get hold of therapy sessions or legal interviews because of privacy issues. So she did the next best thing: she set up an event for a group of children to witness, videotaped it so she would know exactly what happened, and then interviewed the children individually about what they saw. The event featured a musician who came into the classroom, played a number of instruments, and did some clumsy things. She later asked children open-ended questions ("What else did he do?" accompanied by a pipe-playing gesture) and targeted questions ("Where did he hurt himself?" accompanied by a tap on her hip).[14]

Children incorporated into their verbal reports information that was conveyed uniquely in the interviewer's gestures, even if that information was misleading. Importantly, gesture's misleading effects carried over to subsequent interviews and thus had a long-lasting impact on the child. Misleading verbal information has long been known to have continuing effects on children's testimony. But this study shows that misleading *gesture* can have a long-term impact on the veracity of children's reports. In addition, the gestures that the children produced often revealed knowledge that they had but did not report in speech: 80 percent of the details the children conveyed in their gestures were *never* spoken.[15]

This, of course, was an experiment. Maybe in a less scripted situation, neither interviewer nor interviewee would gesture. To find out, we set up a seminaturalistic setting addressing this concern. We asked undergraduate students to participate in pairs in mock forensic interviews. One participant in each pair was randomly assigned as the interviewer, the other as the witness. The witness watched a video of one of the musician's classroom visits from the child study. While the witness was watching the video, the interviewer was given instructions on how to conduct the investigation. Interviewers were told to proceed as if this were an investigative interview for legal purposes and to discover as much as possible about the event from the witness while avoiding leading questions. No explicit instruction was given about the use or avoidance of gesture.

All of the witnesses and all but one of the interviewers produced gestures just like those Sara had programmed into her study. And their gestures often conveyed information that was not found anywhere in the speaker's talk. But these gestures were really part of the conversation. Partners not only copied each other's gestures but also picked up information conveyed uniquely in the other person's gestures, either by mentioning the information in their speech or by incorporating it into their own gestures. The fact that naive interviewers and witnesses spontaneously produced the gestures Sara used in her study suggests that gestures of this type, and gesture in general, are a robust aspect of investigative interviews.

Do these studies tell us anything about clinical therapy sessions? I think they do. It is easy to imagine clients, who have not admitted certain ideas even to themselves, letting those ideas slip out in their hands. Take, for example, a client who describes the tight relationship she has with her spouse; at the same time, she intertwines the fingers of one hand with the fingers of the other but then separates her two hands abruptly. Her words tell her therapist that all is well, but her gestures suggest otherwise. This information is available to therapists who watch and interpret their clients' gestures. The therapist can then respond to those gestures and ask further questions about the client's relationship with her spouse, explicitly mentioning the client's gestures or not. As a clinician, you can have an impact on your clients' next steps by watching and responding to their gestures.

The third piece of advice I gave parents—to tell their children to gesture——may not be appropriate for clinicians to tell their clients. But getting them to gesture would be a good idea, and you can subtly achieve that goal by gesturing yourself. Gesture begets gesture, and the more gesture there is in a therapy session, the more potential for hidden beliefs to reveal themselves. You do have to be careful to monitor your own gestures though, particularly if you have preconceived notions about what your client is experiencing. Even if interviewers are trying to conduct a nonsuggestive interview, preconceptions often make their way in. An interrogator who thinks that a perpetrator was wearing a scarf may ask an open-ended, nondirective question ("What else was he

wearing?") but, at the same time, produce a leading SCARF gesture (moving as though putting on a scarf), which we now know
people understand and can be misled by. The same is likely to
be true of clinicians. Gesture is one route through which these
preconceptions can be (unintentionally) communicated and reinforced in a therapy session.[16]

In general, gesture gives clinicians another source of input on
and data about a client's mind. But nonverbal behavior is typically
not the focus of clinical interviews, and when it is, it is used to
assess a client's feelings—as a way into their *emotions*. In psychiatry, clinicians are advised not only to pay attention to what their
clients say but also to note how they respond to their questions.
Clinicians are also advised to recognize the two-way street—
that their own nonverbal behavior can facilitate or hinder the
therapist-client interaction. But the focus is always on what nonverbal behavior tells us about the rapport between therapist and
client, not on what nonverbal behavior tells us about the clients'
insights into their own problems and lives. I have argued from the
beginning of this book that gesture is a window into thoughts as
well as feelings. Examining the ideas clients reveal in their gestures during therapy sessions is a wide-open and promising area
of research. Another pressing question, given the current increase
in telecommunications in clinical interviews, is whether gestural
communication is effective in treatment at a distance and, if not,
how the process can be improved. At the least, we need to be able
to see one another and our hands to profit from each other's gestures. Perhaps the boxes on our FaceTime and Zoom applications
need to be enlarged to accommodate our gestures.[17]

8

USING HANDS TO EDUCATE

PAY ATTENTION TO YOUR STUDENTS' GESTURES

It should be clear by now what my first piece of advice to teachers is going to be: pay attention to what your students do with their hands. The gestures that learners produce, both children and adults, reveal what's on their minds, and those gestures can let you know what their breakthrough thoughts are—their newest ways of thinking about a particular problem. And if the information conveyed in a learner's gestures differs from the information in his or her speech, that mismatch tells you the learner is ready to make progress on the problem. Gesture is a useful signal. Why not pay attention to it?

Most studies of gesture and learning have been done in one-on-one tutorials where the teacher—who is often, but not always, the experimenter—presents a lesson. But learning typically takes place in the classroom. Does what we've learned about gesture in tutorials scale up to the classroom?

Teachers do notice the gestures produced in their classrooms. Take the following exchange, which took place in a science class.

The teacher asked the students whether the shadows cast by a streetlight (simulated by a light bulb hung from a ladder in the classroom) on a line of twenty-centimeter sticks would lengthen, shorten, or stay the same as the sticks got farther away from the ladder. In response, Malik, one of the students, said, "I think that the longer one's gonna have a longer shadow and the shorter one's shadow gonna be . . ." At the same time, he pointed to the sticks *farthest* from the ladder. Notice that the student's verbal response doesn't really make any sense—all of the sticks are the same length. But instead of pointing this out, the teacher restated Malik's ideas as follows: "So the ones up here closer to the light bulb are gonna have shorter ones and the ones further away are gonna have longer ones." The teacher focused on distance from the light, picking up on Malik's gesture at the far sticks. In this instance, we know the teacher made good use of her student's gestures, but we can't tell whether the teacher was aware of having used Malik's gestures to make inferences about his thoughts.[1]

There are times when a teacher not only responds to a student's gestures but even asks the student to make those gestures more explicit. For example, Chrystal is taking part in a lesson about the seasons and is struggling. She says, "It turns around," giving the teacher little to go on to figure out what *it* refers to—the Earth or the sun—and whether *around* means spinning or orbiting. But the gestures Chrystal produces make it clear that she is referring to the Earth spinning on its axis. The teacher's next move is to ask Chrystal to make her gestures more explicit. Chrystal translates her gestures into words and talks about the Earth's spin, specifying both of the ambiguous terms in her original statement. Chrystal understood the concept at some level from the beginning but seemed unable to put it into words. The teacher's push toward clarity took Chrystal a step closer to mastering the difference between the Earth's seasonal revolution around the sun and its spin on its axis, which creates night and day.[2]

Of course, teachers don't always notice the contributions displayed uniquely in their students' gestures. When students produce gesture-rich but speech-poor explanations, teachers often go with the speech, overlooking gesture even if its message is key to the discussion. Comments that appear only in gesture are often at the forefront of a student's understanding of the task. If those comments are not ratified by the teacher, they are likely to remain "under the radar" for the student, and to be lost to the group and to subsequent discussion. This is why it's imperative that teachers pay attention to their students' gestures.

But how do we help teachers to become gesture readers? Spencer Kelly, a former student who became the president of the International Society for Gesture Studies, headed a project to find out. We gave adults instruction in how to read the gestures children produce on a conservation task and then tested their ability to glean information conveyed uniquely in gesture. To assess how good a job we did in teaching the adults to attend to gesture, we gave them a gesture-reading test prior to instruction, then gave them instruction, and finally tested them again after instruction. The gesture-reading test asked them to check off aspects of the problem-solving task that they thought the child understood, with no mention of how the child expressed those thoughts.[3]

Here's the important part: we varied how much we taught the adults about gesture. One group got no instruction at all about gesture. Another group got a hint: "Pay close attention not only to what the children on the videotape say with their words, but also to what they express with their hands."

A third group saw a five-minute instructional videotape on how to interpret hand gestures. The tape highlighted the three components of hand gestures—shape, motion, and placement of the hand—and gave an example of each component in three novel contexts. For instance, the person on the tape described an object's size in speech—"It was a really big one"—and indicated its shape in gesture, making a two-handed gesture shaped like a sphere. This example highlights the potential for conveying meaning via handshape. Examples were selected from tasks other than conservation so that the adults were forced to learn general principles of gesture interpretation and apply them to a novel task.

A fourth group also saw a five-minute instructional videotape on the three components of gesture but in the context of conservation. The instruction focused on three conservation examples that the adults had seen once already in the pretest and would be seeing again on the posttest. Let's take the water conservation problem as an example. The person on the tape demonstrated how children sometimes represent multiple pieces of information when explaining their misguided belief that a tall, thin glass contains a different amount of water than a short, wide dish. The experimenter explained that a child will sometimes say that the amount of water in the two containers is different because "one is short and one is tall," while producing a wide C-shape gesture near the dish and a narrow C-shape gesture near the glass. In speech, the child was comparing the heights of the containers, but in gesture the child focused on their widths. In this way, the child's handshapes conveyed information not found in the child's speech.

The good news is that adults who got instruction about gesture were able to interpret the children's gestures better after instruction than before; the group that got no instruction didn't change at all. Did it matter what type of instruction the adults got? The group that got specific instruction in the conservation gestures picked up 50 percent more explanations expressed uniquely in gesture after instruction than before. But the group that got a general introduction to gesture, and even the group that only got a hint, picked up 30 percent more explanations expressed uniquely in gesture after instruction than before. All of the adults were able to generalize the instruction they had received to new gestures they had not seen during instruction. And improvement in reading gesture did *not* damage the adults' ability to glean information from speech—they identified the child's spoken conservation explanations perfectly before and after instruction.

This is a very encouraging study. Just giving adults a hint to pay attention to what learners say with their hands is enough to turn them into better gesture readers. And becoming a better gesture reader means that you will then be privy to the information learners hide in their hands. Our natural ability to interpret gesture just needs to be honed; we need to make sure that all teachers know this.

But we still have the classroom problem. Teachers can't pay attention to the gestures that all of the students in their classes produce, just as they can't pay attention to everything all of their students *say*. But you need to be looking at gesture in order to understand it; you don't need to be looking at speakers in order to understand their words. So let's be creative about setting up situations where teachers can watch their students' hands.

If students in the classroom are working at their seats, teachers can visit the children individually, ask them to explain what they're doing, and watch their hands during the explanations. Teachers just have to make sure they're positioned so that they can see the child's hands.

Teachers can also invite students up to the board to solve a problem in front of the class. Asking them to explain their responses will likely elicit gesturing. This situation also gives the teacher the opportunity to explicitly talk about the gestures the student produces, particularly if those gestures convey ideas that the student isn't expressing in speech. Take a sixth-grade student's response to a question about how plate movements create earthquakes. The student, Kerry, says, "When the plates are moving in the same direction . . ." But does she mean vertical, horizontal, or circular motion? Her hands clarify: both hands are flat with palms facing down and move toward each other; when the fingertips meet, the palms move vertically, creating a mountain shape. Her hands tell the teacher, and all of the other students, that she is talking about two plates converging, colliding, and rising, a nice description of *buckling*. Encouraging children to explain their thinking is good for their learning. Asking them to explain their thinking at the board where everyone can see their gestures is good for everyone's learning.[4]

Teachers can also put children into groups where they can be both teacher and learner. Kerry produced the BUCKLING gesture but didn't talk about buckling. In the next few turns, Eliana and Leo, two other students in the class, talked about buckling in speech. Kerry responded, "That's what I said," and the others agreed that she had been the first to introduce buckling, even though she said it only in her hands. This interchange is an instance of multimodal coconstruction, with gesture playing a pivotal role. The information expressed uniquely in gesture was picked up, put into speech, and discussed by all, which served to deepen the students' shared understanding of buckling. Gesture offers a second medium (in addition to speech) that students can use to make teachers and fellow classmates aware of their fledgling ideas, and provides a shared space in which those ideas can be negotiated and debated.

RESPOND TO YOUR STUDENTS' GESTURES

You can already see where I'm going next: respond to your students' gestures. If the ideas they express in their hands are incorrect, you can correct them. If they are correct, you can reinforce them. In order to have control over the instruction children get, in lab studies we systematically vary the instruction we give to different groups of children. Importantly, this instruction is *not* conditioned on what each child does. In this way, we make sure that all of the children within a group are receiving the same input. But teachers are likely to adjust their instruction to the child they are teaching. To find out if they do, and if they respond specifically to child gesture, we brought teachers into the lab individually, asked them to watch the responses given by a nine- to ten-year-old child on a mathematical equivalence test, and then asked them to teach that child mathematical equivalence. This procedure gave the teacher some idea of what the child was thinking about mathematical equivalence before beginning the lesson. The teacher taught the child at the blackboard using whatever techniques he or she wanted to use. At the end, the child took another mathematical equivalence test.

We were interested in how "ready" the child was to learn this math concept and whether the teacher recognized this readiness. We classified children according to their gesture-speech mismatches: some produced mismatches during instruction and some didn't. Did the teachers notice these differences? If so, they might teach children whose gestures suggested they were particularly ready to learn mathematical equivalence differently from children whose gestures suggested that they were not yet ready.

We calculated how many different types of problem-solving strategies each teacher produced when instructing children in these two groups. This measure gives us a sense of how diversified the teacher's lesson was and whether that diversity varied as a function of the children's gestures. It did. Teachers spontaneously used more different types of strategies when teaching children who produced mismatches during instruction than when teaching children who produced no mismatches. Importantly, the teachers didn't differ in the total number of strategies they used to teach the two groups, only in the *variety* of different strategies.[5]

Sometimes the teachers produced their own gesture-speech mismatches during instruction, which is another index of variety. Typically, both strategies were correct but differed from one another—for example, the *grouping* strategy (i.e., group the numbers that do not appear on both sides) in gesture, paired with the *equalizer* strategy (i.e., make both sides sum to the same amount) in speech. Teachers produced more of their own mismatches when teaching children who produced mismatches than when teaching children who produced no mismatches. But they weren't just copying the children's mismatches. The teachers' mismatches rarely contained incorrect strategies; the children's mismatches contained at least one, and often two, incorrect strategies.

We know, however, that teachers were responding to the children's gesture-speech mismatches and not to other characteristics about them. The two groups were identical on many other measures—they produced the same number and proportion of correct and incorrect problem-solving strategies and differed only in how many mismatches they produced. The teachers were sensitive not only to the presence of mismatch, but also to how often it happened: the more mismatches a child produced during instruction, the more different types of strategies and the more mismatches the teacher produced.

To give you a sense of what a teacher's response to a child's mismatch looks like, take the following example. Working on the problem $7 + 6 + 5 = \_\_ + 5$, one child added up all of the numbers in the problem and put 23 in the blank. The teacher asked the child to explain his incorrect solution, and he produced this mismatch:

Child speech: "I added 13 plus 10 equals 23" (adding all numbers, an incorrect strategy).

Child gesture: Holds hand under 7 and 6, points at blank, points at 7 and 6 (grouping, a correct strategy).

In response to the child's mismatch, the teacher said, while obscuring the 7 and 6 with her hand, "I am going to cover this up. Now what do you see on both sides? Five and five, right?" The teacher ignored the child's incorrect solution *and* spoken explanation. She focused on the child's gestures and used them as the basis for her next instructional step. She covered the two numbers that the child had indicated in gesture (the two numbers which, if added together, give the correct answer), which forced the child to notice that there was a 5 on each side of the problem (equal addends). The gestures that the child produced in the mismatch gave the teacher insight into what this child was thinking—the teacher noticed and responded accordingly by turning the mismatch into a teachable moment.

We now know that teachers spontaneously respond to their students' gestures, although they may have no idea that they are targeting mismatches. They can comment on the information produced uniquely in gesture, which brings it into full focus. They can even comment on the fact that the student expressed the information uniquely in gesture. We don't know whether bringing attention to the gesture (as opposed to just highlighting the information conveyed by gesture) helps or hinders learning. This would be a good topic for future research.

As a teacher, you can respond to your students' gestures when they are produced in an individual tutorial, at the board, or in small groups of interacting students. In other words, a learner's gestures offer insight into their learning process, and it's fair game to bring those insights to bear upon their education, no matter the context or setting in which that information is produced.

ENCOURAGE YOUR STUDENTS TO GESTURE

You can use the gestures your students produce on a task to figure out who is ready to make progress on that task and who is not. But students have to gesture in order for you to be able to use gesture as a diagnostic. How can you get your students to gesture?

We have reviewed many studies in which gestures were modeled for one group of children who were then told to produce those gestures during a math lesson. Importantly, telling children to move their hands in a particular way increased how much the children learned from a lesson. But it's not always easy to know which gestures are the best ones to teach to children to promote learning a particular task. Are there other ways of getting your students to gesture?

In some studies described earlier, children were merely told to move their hands the next time they explained how they either solved a math problem or reasoned about a moral dilemma—they were not told what to do with their hands. All of the children followed the instructions they were given and gestured. And being encouraged to gesture brought out new ways of thinking about the problem or dilemma that the child hadn't expressed before the encouragement. It also increased learning after a lesson. So you can just tell students to move their hands as they explain their responses to a problem, and they will know what you mean.

Another possibility is for you to gesture yourself. The gestures you produce will encourage your students to gesture. We gave one group of children instruction containing the equalizer strategy in speech and another group instruction containing the equalizer strategy in both speech and gesture. We found that children who didn't gesture much on the pretest increased how much they gestured *if* they saw the experimenter gesture but not if they did *not* see gesture. Not only did the children gesture, but they conveyed the equalizer strategy found in the experimenter's gesture, and they did so even if they gestured a lot from the very beginning. In other words, children who saw gesture gestured, and they gestured the particular strategy they saw.[6]

Encouraging your students to gesture has two effects. First, it makes your students into gesturers, which gives you a window into their thoughts and allows you to target instruction to those thoughts—you can correct misconceptions and ratify correct ideas. Second, it gives your students a way to express new ideas and concepts on the frontier of their knowledge, and expressing those thoughts in gesture heightens the students' readiness to learn.

GESTURE WHEN YOU TEACH AND ATTEND TO WHAT YOUR GESTURES REVEAL ABOUT THE LESSON

Current recommendations for math curricula encourage teachers to present ideas through a variety of representations: diagrams, physical models, written text. The idea is to translate among alternative symbolic representations of a problem—for example, a math symbol and a number line—rather than working within a single symbolic form. Gesture is an ideal candidate for one of these representational formats, particularly since it has such a strong visual component. Gesture is often better suited to conveying certain types of information than speech. Gesture can therefore work with speech to convey a richer message than the message conveyed in speech alone. Consider a teacher who describes in speech where a set of trenches were dug during World War I but indicates in gesture the zigzagging course the trenches took. Gesture can provide students with a second, vivid representation, and multiple representations can enhance learning.[7]

Gesture is different from other representational formats, such as a map or a diagram. It is transitory, disappearing in the air just as quickly as speech, which may be an advantage or a disadvantage. But gesture does have one clear advantage over other representations: it can—indeed *must*—be integrated temporally with the speech it accompanies. Visual information is more effective when timed appropriately with spoken information, which gives gesture its advantage. Gesture and speech present a more naturally unified picture to students than a diagram and speech.[8]

We know that teachers spontaneously gesture when instructing children in one-on-one tutorials. To learn more about this process, we again brought teachers into the lab and asked them to individually instruct nine- and ten-year-old children in mathematical equivalence. All of the teachers gestured during their lessons. And the children noticed the teachers' gestures. We know that they noticed because the children treated the teachers' instructions differently as a function of the gesture that accompanied those instructions. The children were *more* likely to repeat the teacher's speech if it was accompanied by a matching gesture, as opposed no gesture at all; they were *less* likely to repeat teacher speech if it was accompanied by mismatching gesture, as opposed to no gesture at all. For example, children repeated their teacher's equalizer strategy in speech *more* often when it was produced with an equalizer strategy in gesture than if it was produced on its own; they did so *less* often when it was produced with a grouping strategy in gesture than if it was produced on its own. In other words, they were sensitive to the information conveyed in gesture and whether it matched the information conveyed in speech. The children were also able to glean problem-solving strategies from the teacher's gesture and recast them in their own words. As an example, children produced a grouping strategy in speech after seeing their teacher produce it only in gesture.[9]

In one-on-one math tutorials, teachers express 40 percent of the problem-solving strategies they give their students in gesture—that's quite a lot. Do teachers gesture when instructing a roomful of children? Gesture occurs frequently in talk about topics that are taught in schools—counting, addition, control of variables, gears, rate of change. It should come as no surprise then that gesture is also frequent in classrooms, particularly classrooms of experienced teachers. First-grade teachers use from five to seven nonspoken representations of mathematical ideas per minute, almost one every ten seconds, in their classrooms. And gesture is by far the most frequent nonspoken form for teachers; the others are pictures, objects, and writing. For example, a teacher points (gesture) to a frame that has room for ten beans but contains only two beans (object). The teacher then points to another partially filled ten frame (gesture, object), while explaining that one ten frame must be completely filled before putting beans into another. When teachers combine their nonspoken representations, gesture is almost always part of the combination. In other words, gesture is the glue that links different forms of unspoken information to one another and to speech. And gesture grounds speech in the world of objects and actions, which means that adding gesture ensures that the entire communicative act will be grounded.[10]

Teachers don't just use their gestures haphazardly. They use them strategically, often responding to a student's confusion with a gesture. Teachers will repeat their own speech while clarifying the meaning of the utterance with gesture. And it works: children frequently come up with the correct answer. In the following instance, the teacher uses gesture initially, but her gesture becomes more explicit when the student fails to understand. The teacher asks, "How many leftovers?" pointing quickly toward the eight leftover beans. The student doesn't respond. The teacher asks again but this time points more slowly, one by one, to the leftover beans. The student correctly responds, "Eight."[11]

Teachers, like all speakers, can also use their gestures to add new information to their speech. When teaching mathematical equivalence to nine- and ten-year-olds, a teacher wrote the problem $3 + 7 + 9 = \_\_ + 9$ on the board. She described the equalizer strategy in speech and, at the same time, displayed the grouping strategy in gesture. In other words, she produced a gesture-speech mismatch.[12]

> Teacher speech: "We're going to do it like before. We're going to make this side equal to this side" (equalizer, a correct strategy).

> Teacher gesture: Holds hand under 3 and 7 (grouping, a correct strategy).

In response, the child exclaimed, "Oh!" and solved the problem correctly. When asked to explain her solution, the child produced the following response, containing matching speech and gesture:

Child speech: "We have the 9s so we need the same (equal addends), and we can't put two numbers, so I just added these two and put it here, and it equaled 10" (grouping).

Child gesture: Points at left 9, points at right 9 (equal addends), points between 3 and 7 twice, points at blank, points at 3, points at 7 (grouping).

Despite the lack of overlap between the correct strategy in speech and the different, but also correct, strategy in gesture, the child picked up on grouping found only in gesture. Children can clearly glean information from teacher gesture in a mismatch. In fact, the gestural modality might be particularly accessible to a child who hasn't yet mastered the math task. But then, why not present the gestured strategy in a gesture-speech match instead of a gesture-speech mismatch? A match would give the child an opportunity to see the strategy in *both* the spoken and gestural modalities. But gesture-speech mismatches have one possible advantage over matches: they make the contrast between strategies salient by placing two different strategies side by side within a single utterance. This contrast underscores the fact that different approaches to the same problem are possible, an important concept for anyone grappling with how to solve math problems. I think it's highly unlikely that teachers consciously produce gesture-speech mismatches. Teacher mismatch may come about because teachers are uncertain about how to teach a child who expresses one idea in speech and another idea in gesture. But presenting children with mismatches does not seem to confuse them—in fact, it seems to catalyze learning.

Teachers use gesture in the classroom—at least in math classrooms and probably all classrooms—to good effect to reinforce promising ideas and to clarify and correct misconceptions. But do teachers get all that they can out of gesture? In fact, teachers in the United States do *not* use gesture in their eighth-grade math classes as effectively as teachers in Hong Kong and Japan. It's not clear why—it could be the result of training in gesture that teachers in Hong Kong and Japan get, or it could reflect cultural differences in attitudes toward gesture. In 1999, a group of researchers conducted the Trends in International Mathematics and Science Study, a large-scale international video study of classroom mathematics instruction. Looking at the video portion of the data collected, Lindsey Richland, my former colleague, found that teachers in the United States introduce the same number of analogies in their math lessons as teachers in Hong Kong and Japan. Analogy allows students to see commonalities between mathematical representations, which can then help them understand new problems and concepts. But teachers in Hong Kong or Japan use gestures to signal an intended comparison (for example, pointing back and forth between a scale and an equation) much more often than teachers in the United States. Without gestural cues to guide the comparisons they make, US students may fail to learn a concept, or they may learn an entirely different concept from the one the teacher has in mind. Students in Hong Kong and Japan are more advanced in mathematics than comparably aged US students, hinting that nonverbal supports to analogy can play an important role in math learning. So there is room for improvement in how teachers in the United States use gesture in math classrooms.[13]

Including gesture in a lesson is helpful to all learners. But interesting new findings suggest that gesture may be particularly helpful to children who come from less advantaged homes. Breckie Church and her colleagues gave two groups of students a videotaped lesson on mathematical equivalence. One group got a lesson containing the equalizer strategy in speech; the other got a lesson containing the equalizer strategy in both speech and gesture. As we have now come to expect, overall, the group that saw the speech and gesture lesson did better on a test afterward than the group that saw the speech-only lesson. The new finding is that this difference was particularly pronounced in children from families in which neither parent had gone to college. Children from families in which one or both parents had gone to college profited equally from both types of lessons. But children from families in which neither parent went to college profited more from the speech + gesture lesson than from the speech-alone lesson. The exciting finding is that, when given the speech + gesture lesson, children from families in which neither parent had gone college did almost as well as children from families in which parents had gone to college. In other words, the disparity between children was most apparent when they received the speech-alone lesson—children whose parents had gone to college did much better than children whose parents had not. But this difference disappeared when the children were given the speech + gesture lesson. What's surprising—and hopeful in terms of closing the gap between learners from less and more advantaged homes—is that adding gesture to a lesson is particularly helpful to children from homes with more limited resources: it can raise their learning levels to those achieved by children from more advantaged homes.[14]

Gesture is a powerful teaching tool that can and should be used in the classroom. However, gesture isn't always a positive force—it can be used for evil as well as good. A teacher's well-chosen gesture can clarify and deepen a learner's understanding of a task. But a teacher's inadvertent gesture highlighting the wrong part of a task might also lead the learner astray. So it's best to pay attention to the gestures that you produce in your classroom and make sure they say what you want them to say—your students will be watching.

9

WHAT IF GESTURE WERE CONSIDERED AS IMPORTANT AS LANGUAGE?

OUR HANDS REVEAL OUR THOUGHTS TO THOSE WHO KNOW WHERE to look. If you don't have access to the established language of your community and can't share your thoughts that way, your hands take over. You recreate the fundamental structures of human language and use those structures to express your thoughts in homesign.

Even if you do learn the established language of your community, your hands are not idle. They express ideas that can echo ideas conveyed in language. But they can also express ideas not found anywhere in your language. You may not know you have these ideas, but others have access to them and may act on them. They can become part of the conversation without anyone intending them to.

Your hands don't just reflect your mind; they can also change it. Seeing other people's hand movements and producing your own can change how you think. Just being asked to move your hands as you explain your ideas can bring out thoughts you didn't know you had. And producing these new thoughts in your hands, in turn, makes you more receptive to instruction.

How extensive is this phenomenon? Are there ideas that your hands *cannot* express? Let's first think about homesign and whether there are limits to the ideas that can be expressed in the homemade gesture systems that a deaf child creates without help from the linguistic community. Homesigners express many of the ideas that children convey in the languages they learn from language models. The fact that homesigners can do this means that these ideas are *not* shaped by language. If anything, it's the ideas that are shaping language.

But there are some ideas that homesigners don't express. It could be that they have no interest in expressing these ideas. But it also could be that they don't have the tools to express them. If so, these ideas require a language model in order to be developed. Let's consider an example. Dedre Gentner, my colleague and friend at Northwestern University, led a team including me and Asli Özyürek, a former student now one of the directors of the Max Planck Institute for Psycholinguistics in Nijmegen in the Netherlands, to determine whether Turkish homesigners can do a nonlinguistic task requiring understanding of spatial relations. We suspected that the homesigners might fail at this task simply because they didn't encode spatial relations in their gestures. They used their homesigns to describe objects moving toward other objects (a directional relation) but not the end-state relation between the two objects (a spatial relation). For instance, after a toy pig moves toward a fence, a good way of capturing the pig's end state is to describe the pig as *next to* the fence. The homesigners didn't create sentences with this message, even though it would be easy to produce a gesture for the pig next to a gesture for the fence.[1]

If we were to assess the deaf children's understanding of spatial relations on the basis of their homesign, we might guess that they would have trouble with these relations in general. And this guess would be correct. We gave the homesigners a spatial-mapping task containing a box that had three levels: top, middle, bottom. Each level had a different picture on it, and there was a star on the back of one of the pictures. The children were given their own box, which had the same three pictures on the same levels. We showed the children where the star was on our box and asked them to point to the place in their box where the star should be. This task was easy for hearing children, all of whom had mastered the linguistic devices needed to express spatial relations in Turkish. But the Turkish homesigners didn't do so well, even though we matched them to the hearing children on a cognitive task that didn't involve understanding spatial relations. The homesigners failed at spatial relations in both their gestures and on a non-linguistic task.

The fact that homesign has no linguistic construction that captures a spatial relation suggests that expressing spatial relations is not easy—it doesn't come naturally, even if you're communicating in a manual language that should (in principle) make expressing spatial relations easy. The fact that homesigners fail on the spatial-mapping task suggests that they haven't developed the cognitive skills to do a spatial-relations task. Teaching them signs and linguistic constructions that convey spatial relations might help them develop these skills, an important hypothesis that needs to be tested. In fact, this hypothesis has a good chance of being correct. Dedre Gentner and her colleagues have found, in other work, that teaching English-speaking hearing children words that capture the spatial relations of the box—*top*, which refers to the highest level of the box; *bottom*, which refers to the lowest level; and *middle*, which refers to the level in between—improves their performance on the spatial-mapping task. The bottom line is that some ideas may require language in order to be developed. Notions that are *not* conveyed in homesign are good candidates for these ideas.[2]

Not all ideas will be developed in homesign. How about in the gestures that accompany language? Are some ideas impossible, or at least very difficult, to express in gesture? If so, these would be ideas that we cannot use our hands to convey and that require language (or some other form of representation) to express. Ideas that are imagistic and can be displayed in space are particularly amenable to expression in the manual modality. But, of course, any idea can be laid out in space. As I have mentioned throughout the book, if you're talking about a power relation, which is not inherently spatial, it is still natural to express your ideas along a vertical continuum, with the most powerful on top of the continuum and the least powerful on the bottom. Gesture spatializes ideas. But some ideas may resist spatializing, particularly if we don't have a spatial metaphor handy to capture these ideas. Think about *kindness*—it's hard to come up with the perfect gesture for this idea. You could use your hands to express more or less kindness, but along which dimension? The vertical dimension doesn't seem right. There may well be ideas that just don't lend themselves to gesture. If you're going to reveal these ideas, you'll need to find another vehicle besides the hands.

I began this book by saying that I would talk about what happens when we make people aware of their gestures. We've seen that what we say and what we hear is shaped by gesture when we're not paying attention to it. What would happen if we encouraged people to be aware of and to focus on the gestures they and others produce? Would gesture lose its power to reflect and change our thinking?

I used to think that if we attended to our gestures, those gestures would no longer reveal our natural, subconscious thoughts. But I was wrong. When we tell children to gesture as they explain their solutions to a math problem or their thoughts about a moral dilemma, their gestures still display ideas not found in their speech—they still produce gesture-speech mismatches. In fact, telling children to gesture leads to an increase in mismatches.

Intentionally produced gesture can reveal ideas not found in speech. These mismatches, in turn, make the children who produce them more likely to improve when later given a lesson in math or morality. Intentionally produced gesture can also set the stage for changing ideas.[3]

The important finding is that consciously attending to your own or others' gestures does *not* prevent those gestures from reflecting your hidden ideas or changing how you think. But it might slow things down. I can imagine that some controversial or threatening ideas would be easier to accept if you didn't acknowledge and focus on them. If so, *not* bringing gesture into focus could be important in fostering these ideas. Even if keeping gesture below consciousness only improves learning a little bit, it would be good to know about this property of gesture so that we can exploit it when necessary. This is an interesting and important area for future research. It's not so easy to figure out how to manipulate peoples' conscious access to their own gestures, but it's worth thinking about how this can be accomplished.

Since bringing gesture into focus does not seem to destroy its ability to either inspire or tap into underlying cognition, I argue that we should elevate gesture so that it is recognized as central to language. Language is still the bedrock of human communication. Spontaneous gestures can, chameleonlike, change their meaning as a function of the speech they accompany; speech changes its meaning as a function of gesture much less often. But gesture nonetheless completes our thoughts. To ignore gesture is to see only the tip of the iceberg in a conversation and to miss the information beneath the surface.

Encouraging a focus on gesture will have its biggest impact in situations where speakers are not currently aware that they are conveying messages in gesture. In classrooms, students convey unintended messages through their gestures, and teachers use those gestures to assess students' skills. Conversely, teachers convey unintended messages through their gestures, and students react to those gestures. Legal interviews are another space where unintended messages can loom large. Legal interactions are "structured through talk." This means that the interaction can be understood without reference to the nonverbal environment. Facial expressions, gaze direction, and gestures can offer relevant information. But when nonverbal cues are missing—as in an audio recording or a transcript of the session—the conversation remains more or less comprehensible. If, as is likely, participants in a legal interview use gesture to reveal knowledge not found in their speech, this information will not be included in the legal transcript of the event. But, as we have seen, it will not go undetected by participants in the interview. The information will be incorporated into the individual's assessment of the situation, even if it is not incorporated into the written record. That's a problem for legal transactions.[4]

Let's take a hypothetical case. Imagine an interviewer who suspects that a child has been mistreated by someone with a mustache. Although interviewers are careful not to mention their suspicions in their words (they are aware of the swaying effects that leading questions can have on young children), they might inadvertently produce a MUSTACHE gesture while questioning the child. The child may then describe a person with a mustache, not because the person really had a mustache but in response to the interviewer's (unintended) gestural suggestion. In other words, as we now know is very likely, suggestions can be introduced into an interview through gesture as well as talk. Interviewers are, however, less aware of their gestures and don't monitor them as well as they monitor their speech. They might then let them slip in unacknowledged. We need to get legal interviewers—in fact, all interviewers—to acknowledge their gestures.[5]

Now let's consider a child interviewee who produces a gesture for a mustache when describing the person who hurt them but doesn't mention the mustache in speech. The interviewer picks up on the gesture and asks, "Did he have a mustache?" To someone reading the transcript of the exchange, the interviewer has produced a leading question—in reality, the lead came from the child. In this case, information that has spontaneously come from the child is wrongly interpreted as having been introduced by the adult interviewer—all because gesture is not considered part of the legal world. There is a sub rosa conversation taking place in gesture that will not make it onto the transcripts that become the legal documents. Given that the way an interviewer poses a question frequently influences the way both adults and children remember an event, this issue has important implications.

In all of these situations and many others, knowledge conveyed in gesture is there for the taking. As listeners, we often do take it, although we rarely acknowledge its source. Particularly in domains where it is important to keep track of who says what—the legal world is a prime example—we may want to begin tracking gesture as well as speech.

Deaf education is another realm from which nonverbal behavior, and gesture in particular, has been banned. As discussed earlier, most deaf children are born to hearing parents who want their children to learn to speak. The oralist tradition grew up as a response to this parental desire. But oralism has many different profiles. Some traditions insist that developing whatever hearing a deaf child has and augmenting that hearing with aids or cochlear implants is the best way to teach a deaf child to talk. These educators cover their mouths and often have the child face the other way so that they can fine-tune their hearing. But *hearing children* are not prevented from seeing the lips or gestures of their communication partners, and, indeed, hearing listeners rely on those cues. So why do we make the task harder for a deaf child than it is for a hearing child? The rationale is that deaf children won't make use of auditory cues if they have access to visual cues. But I've not seen any good evidence to support this claim. An alternative approach is to capitalize on *all* of the cues available to a deaf child, auditory and visual. Using all cues has the potential to better integrate deaf children into the social world around them and facilitate their communication with that world. If we're going to widen the window for hearing children learning language, we should be widening it for deaf children as well. Speech leaves out parts of the conversation. Why should deaf children be excluded from those parts?[6]

How can we raise consciousness about gesture? One way is to tell people to pay attention to the gestures they see. Another is to tell them to pay attention to the gestures they produce. But what should we tell them about planning their own gestures? An example of how it can be done well comes from Amanda Gorman, the first National Youth Poet Laureate, who presented her poem "The Hill We Climb" at the Joe Biden–Kamala Harris inauguration on January 20, 2021. Her words were inspirational, but so were her gestures. Gorman moved her hands in ways that brought her thoughts to life, allowing us to know her, see her, and feel her unique experience as a Black woman. She *designed* her gestures to underscore her words. As she said, "In a time where a skinny Black girl, descended from slaves and raised by a single mother . . . ," she pointed her two thumbs toward her shoulders; then, moving her two hands gracefully away from her head, she continued, ". . . can dream of becoming president," making it clear that the dreams are hers.

Gorman consciously choreographed her gestures for the inauguration. But she patterned those gestures after the gestures she uses spontaneously. Following the inauguration, Gorman was interviewed on *The Late Late Show with James Corden*. She described how she and her sister used to peek in as they passed the studio where Corden was shooting his show when they were little girls—we "put our faces to the iron gate," she said holding her palms at the sides of her face, simulating her small face peering through that gate. Gorman said that being interviewed by Corden was "a full-circle moment" for her, and she personalized the moment by crossing her two palms over her heart. Gorman, like everyone else, at times lets ideas sneak out in gesture that are not there in her speech. Such a moment occurred when she told Corden about getting the invitation to present at the inauguration. "I get this Zoom call," she said, while making a TELEPHONE gesture (thumb and pinky held to the ear). She showed us with her gesture that Zoom, a distanced and relatively inactive medium, has not replaced collaborative and more traditional forms of communication for her. Gorman's spontaneous gestures supply her with material for the gestures she interleaves into her poetry. She has learned the art of using her hands to augment her words and employs it to dramatic effect.

It's time to acknowledge that a complete picture of human communication contains *both* speech and gesture. Doing so might lead to fewer misunderstandings—if you recognize that you've expressed inequality between women and men with your hands, you won't be surprised when your listener accuses you of bias. It might also make you less willing to indiscriminately accept technological advances that eliminate gesture from your conversations. The printed word and the telephone were the first steps in this direction. FaceTime and Zoom concentrate on the face, not the hands, and thus eliminate the messages you convey in gesture. They also frequently make it more difficult to gesture even when we do see people's faces—for example, when we FaceTime

someone while holding our phone in our hands, we lose the benefits found in our hands. These developments could decrease the
role hands play in communication and have a profound effect on
what communication and learning may look like in the future.

What can you do to slow the loss of gesture in your conversations? You can make yourself aware of how important your and
others' hands are to the messages people transmit. And you can
begin advocating for technology that brings back our hands. When
I have recorded my talks on Zoom, I have had to consciously raise
my hands to make sure that my gestures are visible in the box so
that my audience can see them. I know how important my hands
are to my message. But most people don't, and they don't make
this extra effort. It shouldn't be that hard for programmers to let
our hands reach out to the virtual world.

Another arena in which gesture should receive particular attention is online teaching. Often an online lesson is shown without a
teacher—in Khan Academy courses, you simply hear a voice along
with examples or just see examples on the screen. In addition to
not being able to see the teacher's gaze and facial expressions,
learners can't see their gestures. This omission may be particularly harmful for children from disadvantaged homes. Adding
gesture to a lesson can boost performance in children from less
advantaged homes so that it equals performance in children from
advantaged homes. In other words, gesture has the potential to
level the playing field in education, a very exciting and promising application of the power of gesture to bridge long-standing
divides. One step toward this leveled playing field is to make sure
that teachers' hands are visible in the online lessons students see.[7]

We can all learn to punctuate our conversations with gestures
that deepen the meaning and intent of our words—in fact, we do
this naturally. We just have to learn to do it thoughtfully and with
intention. And we need to pay attention to the gestures that others
produce and take the thoughts that our hands express as seriously

as the words we speak. Paying attention to what we say with our hands has the potential to minimize threats to others and to help us understand why others feel threatened. Gesture can't solve the problems we have in understanding each other. But recognizing that our thoughts run through our hands as a vital, electric current is an important first step.

ACKNOWLEDGMENTS

This book is a labor of love. It is dedicated to my husband, Bill Meadow, who passed away on September 14, 2019. Bill is responsible for this book in more ways than I can count. He supported my goal of doing psychology when, during my junior year abroad, I discovered that that's what I wanted to do. He had confidence in me, even when I didn't. But Bill did more than just cheer me on. He read every word I wrote (except, of course, this book) and made the words better with his flair for language and his astute scientific eye. We'd argue over ideas and how best to express them. No one has taken me more seriously than my husband did.

Bill was the best at hearing a convoluted idea and saying it back simply and engagingly. I have tried to channel that talent of his, a talent that made him the best teacher I have ever known. He also knew how to give students the next step in a lesson (tennis, windsurfing, chemistry, math, really anything) that was just what the student needed to move forward. I was fortunate to be one of those students with respect to teaching and writing.

Bill was an enthusiast. I love my work and always have. He appreciated that love and supported it with his own enthusiasm. If I have made you excited about any of the ideas in this book, he and I will both have succeeded.

Bill respected science. He loved data, as do I. We are people who like to look at the world and try to figure out how it works.

This is not to say that I didn't have theories or intuitions about how my studies might come out, but when the data didn't support my theories, the data won. I have tried to highlight the respect for science that we shared by telling you when my intuitions were wrong and how doing science got me back on the right (or righter) track.

Bill and I were a team. We managed to create a root system that supported our team of two for fifty years, longer if we had had more time. At the same time, our intertwined roots allowed each of us to branch out (so to speak) and follow our own paths. Meeting and marrying Bill changed my life for the better—as he (being a lover of sports metaphors) might have put it, it was a game changer for both of us.

Now to the science itself, which was all done in collaboration with colleagues, postdocs, and students. I am fortunate to have many, many people to thank. For help on the homesign studies, I first thank Lila Gleitman, one of my graduate school advisors who inspired me to study homesign for deep theoretical reasons. She remained my collaborator (and friend) for forty years—we wrote our first paper together in 1978 and our last in 2019. Although she too has passed on, I am forever grateful to her for being there after Bill died. She loved him too. I thank Heidi Feldman, my fellow graduate student, who began the homesign work with me and then went on to put her knowledge to practical use as a pediatrician; she became a respected clinician and researcher. I thank Carolyn Mylander, my lab manager and collaborator for forty years officially, and then another ten when she helped out after she retired. She is a meticulous coder—when Carolyn transcribed a videotape, I knew it captured what was there, a very comforting feeling.

Many others have been instrumental in my homesign studies— Molly Flaherty, Lillia Rissman, Dea Hunsicker, Amy Franklin, Sarah van Deusen Phillips, Jill Morford, Şeyda Özçalışkan, Laura Horton, Asli Özyürek, and my friend of many years,

Dedre Gentner. Others have helped extend the homesign work to Nicaragua—Natasha Abner, Liesje Spaepen, Marie Coppola, and Annie Senghas. I thank them and my colleague Diane Brentari, who helped establish fruitful connections between the homesign work, cross-linguistic studies of sign, and emerging language, and who has been a joy to work with (both intellectually and personally). I am grateful to all of these collaborators for setting the stage for the new work that Ruthe Foushee and Michelle Madlansacay are doing on how homesign is used in communicative interaction.

The silent gesture studies (studies in which we asked hearing people to describe scenes using their hands and not their voices) were a theoretical offshoot of the homesign studies. I began this work with my colleague, David McNeill, and my postdoc at the time, Jenny Singleton, and continued it with Lisa Gershkoff-Stowe, Wing-Chee So, and Şeyda Özçalışkan (who extended the work to blind speakers). I thank them for the firm foundation that they put this work on, which has led to new work with Monica Do and Simon Kirby exploring the forces that have led to modern-day language.

The homesign work also led me to study language learning in hearing children, with a focus on how gesture helps them do it. I thank my colleague Janellen Huttenlocher (who has also passed on) for getting me to spearhead what turned out to be a series of three five-year program project grants to study longitudinally sixty typically developing children and forty children with brain injury, interacting naturally with their parents at home. With my colleagues (and friends) Susan Levine, Steve Raudenbush, and Steve Small, I am still following these children twenty years later, and we have added Lindsey Richland and Marisa Casillas to the team. The longitudinal videotapes of the children have provided data for projects and dissertations for countless students and will hopefully continue to do so for many years. I thank Cindy Butcher, Jana Iverson (who also began the work on gesture in blind children), Meredith Rowe, Şeyda Özçalışkan, Erica Cartmill, and Eve

Sauer LeBarton, for help with the studies of gesture in typically developing children and in children with brain injury, and Ece Demir-Lira, Anthony Dick, and Steve Small, for taking me into the world of brain imaging to explore gesture-speech integration in children and adults. They set the stage for my current work with Mandy Seccia, Hannah Guo, and my colleague Marc Berman, in which we are exploring how gesture differs from action-on-objects in its impact on learning, generalization, and retention.

This brings us to the work on co-speech gesture, which was inspired by a videotape that Rochel Gelman, my other advisor in graduate school and a giant in cognitive development, gave me of hearing children participating in Piagetian conservation tasks and, of course, gesturing. I thank Breckie Church, Michelle Perry, Martha Alibali, Melissa Singer, Philip Garber, Susan Cook, Spencer Kelly, and my colleague Howard Nusbaum for helping me see how important gesture is to thinking and talking. I thank Miriam Novack, Elisa Congdon, Liz Wakefield, Cristina Carrazza, Alyssa Kersey, Raedy Ping, Kensy Cooperrider, Sara Broaders, and my former colleague Sian Beilock for taking the phenomenon to the next level to probe the mechanisms underlying gesture's role in learning. I thank Carol Padden and Aaron Shield for helping me extend this work to co-sign gesture in deaf signers; Sandy Waxman, Diane Brentari, and Miriam Novack for helping me think about the cognitive impact of gesture and sign on young language learners, deaf or hearing; Casey Ferrara and Jenny Lu for their help in figuring out where the boundary between gesture and sign is; and Nina Semushina, Breckie Church, and Zena Levan for their help in asking whether including gesture in instruction promotes learning in deaf signers.

This book has also benefited from the many, many conversations that I have had with colleagues over the years about language, thought, and gesture. I thank them for sharing their ideas, their enthusiasm, and, most of all, their friendship with me—Diane Brentari, Heidi Feldman, Dedre Gentner, Lila Gleitman, Barbara

Landau, Susan Levine, Martha McClintock, David McNeill, Elissa Newport, Howard Nusbaum, Steve Raudenbush, Lindsey Richland, Steve Small, Liz Spelke, Barbara Tversky, Sandy Waxman, Bill Wimsatt, and Amanda Woodward.

I thank my funders. Over the years, I have been fortunate to have support from many organizations—NSF (BNS-7705990; BNS-8004313; BCS-1654154), NIDCD (R01 DC00491 1-24), and the Spencer Foundation for the homesign studies; NICHD (P01 HD040605) and IES (R305A190467) for the longitudinal studies of typically developing children and brain-injured children; and NICHD (R01 HD18617; R01 HD31185; R01 HD47450) and NSF (BCS-09255595; BCS-142224; DRL-1561405; SMA-1640893) for the studies of gesture's role in learning. I have also been fortunate to have the best administrative support possible. I thank Kristi Schonwald, Jodi Khan, Carolyn Mylander, Markie Theophile, and Jessica Breeze for their help in keeping the trains running smoothly. I thank Linda Huff, who created the drawings for the book—her beautiful renditions have brought the phenomena I describe to life.

And now for the writing itself. I have recruited colleagues, students, friends, and children to be my readers—Nathaniel (Shmug) Meadow, Jacqueline (Beanie) Meadow, Meredith Rowe, Martha Alibali, Sandy Waxman, Robert Seyfarth, Kathy and Kevin Clougherty, Katie Kinzler, Jim Chandler, Donna Schatt, Harriet Horwitz, and Deborah Epstein. I am grateful for their input at many levels—theoretical, conceptual, empirical, stylistic, even typographical. I thank Eric Henney, who was at Basic Books when I began this project. He convinced me that there was a book there and helped me put together a compelling prospectus. I thank Emma Berry and Marissa Koors, my editors at Basic Books, for the many readings they gave the book and their help in finding the right organization for it, and Kelly Lenkevich for her thoughtful copy editing. I greatly appreciate the care each reader took with the book. It is a much better book for their input.

I started writing the book on Washington Island, Wisconsin, at the Gibsons' on the west side of the island in 2021 and finished it the next summer. My family has spent the month of August on the island for the last forty-two years. It is the perfect place to think hard (and to windsurf), and I thank the Gibson family for their friendship and support, particularly during Bill's illness. Washington Island is an idyllic place in which to think and write about gesture (and anything else).

I thank my children—Alexander (Xander), Nathaniel (Shmug), and Jacqueline (Beanie) Meadow—and their spouses—Jessica Kumar, Lucy Jacobson Meadow, and Drew Weirman—for stepping in to cheer me on as Bill would have. And I thank Xander, Shmug, and Beanie for learning language so effortlessly when they were young and for gesturing as they did it. I thank my grandchildren—Cody, Zia, and Will—for giving me the opportunity to see the process all over again, this time through a grandmother's eye. Finally, I thank Bill, my life partner, for always being there for me and for us. In an essential way, he still is.

NOTES

Introduction: My Journey into Gesture

1. *The Crown*, Season 4, written by Peter Morgan and produced by Left Bank Pictures and Sony Pictures Television for Netflix.

2. Haviland, J. (1993). Anchoring, iconicity and orientation in Guugu Yimithirr pointing gestures. *Linguistic Anthropology*, *1*, 3–45. Haviland, J. (2000). Pointing, gesture spaces, and mental maps. In D. McNeill (ed.), *Language and gesture* (pp. 13–46). Cambridge: Cambridge University Press.

3. "The Good Conversationalist: The Basics," Emily Post Institute, https://emilypost.com/advice/the-good-conversationalist-the-basics.

4. On communication in all species, see Hauser, M. D. (1996). *The evolution of communication*. Cambridge, MA: MIT Press.

5. The Nixon White House tapes are audio recordings of conversations between President Richard Nixon and his administration officials, family members, and White House staff, held between 1971 and 1973. The Nixon/Kennedy debates were held prior to the presidential election in 1960. Most *radio* listeners called the first debate a draw or pronounced Nixon the victor, but Kennedy was proclaimed the winner by a broad margin of the seventy million *television* viewers. History.com Editors, "The Kennedy-Nixon Debates," updated June 10, 2019, History.com, https://www.history.com/topics/us-presidents/kennedy-nixon-debates.

6. Franklin, A. (2007). Liar, liar hands on fire: What gesture-speech asynchrony reveals about thinking. Unpublished doctoral dissertation, University of Chicago.

Chapter 1: Why Do We Use Our Hands When We Talk?

1. On mechanism and function in alligators, see Lang, J. W. (1976). Amphibious behavior of *Alligator mississippiensis*: Roles of a circadian rhythm and light. *Science, 191,* 575–577.

2. Cook, S. W., & Tanenhaus, M. K. (2009). Embodied communication: Speakers' gestures affect listeners' actions. *Cognition, 113*(1), 98–104.

3. Hostetter, A. B., & Alibali, M. W. (2008). Visible embodiment: Gestures as simulated action. *Psychonomic Bulletin & Review, 15,* 495–514. On theories of embodied cognition, see Pulvermüller, F. (2005). Brain mechanisms linking language and action. *Nature Reviews Neuroscience,* 6(7), 576–582. doi: 10.1038/nrn1706. PMID: 15959465. Chambers, C. G., Tanenhaus, M. K., Eberhard, K. M., Filip, H., & Carlson, G. N. (2002). Circumscribing referential domains during real-time language comprehension. *Journal of Memory and Language, 47,* 30–49. Wilson, M. (2002). Six views of embodied cognition. *Psychonomic Bulletin & Review, 9,* 625–636. Wilson, M., & Knoblich, G. (2005). The case for motor involvement in perceiving conspecifics. *Psychological Bulletin, 131,* 460–473.

4. Aglioti, S., DeSouza, J. F. X., & Goodale, M. A. (1995). Size-contrast illusions deceive the eye but not the hand. *Current Biology, 5*(6), 679–685. doi: 10.1016/S0960-9822(95)00133-3. Bruno, N., & Franz, V. H. (2009). When is grasping affected by the Müller-Lyer illusion? A quantitative review. *Neuropsychologia, 47*(6), 1421–1433. doi: 10.1016/j.neuropsychologia.2008.10.031.

5. Brown, A. R., Pouw, W., Brentari, D., & Goldin-Meadow, S. (2021). People are less susceptible to illusion when they use their hands to communicate rather than estimate. *Psychological Science, 32*(8), 1227–1237. doi: 10.1177/0956772199552.

6. Wakefield, E., Congdon, E. L., Novack, M. A., Goldin-Meadow, S., & James, K. H. (2019). Learning math by hand: The neural effects of gesture-based instruction in 8-year-old children. *Attention, Perception & Psychophysics, 81,* 2343–2353. doi: 10.3758/s13414-019-01755-y. James, K. H., & Atwood, T. P. (2009). The role of sensorimotor learning in the perception of letter-like forms: Tracking the causes of neural specialization for letters. *Cognitive Neuropsychology, 26,* 91–110.

7. Cole, J. (1991). *Pride and a daily marathon.* London: Duckworth. Gallagher, S., Cole, J., & McNeill, D. (2001). The language-thought-hand system. In C. Cave, I. Guaitella, & S. Santi (eds.), *Oralite et gestualite:*

Interactions et comportements multimodaux dans la communication (pp. 420–424). Paris: L'Harmattan.

8. Ramachandran, V. S., & Blakeslee, S. (1998). *Phantoms in the brain: Probing the mysteries of the human mind*. New York: William Morrow & Co., 41.

9. Graham, J. A., & Argyle, M. (1975). A cross-cultural study of the communication of extra-verbal meaning by gestures. *International Journal of Psychology, 10,* 57–67. McNeil, N., Alibali, M. W., & Evans, J. L. (2000). The role of gesture in children's comprehension of spoken language: Now they need it, now they don't. *Journal of Nonverbal Behavior, 24,* 131–150. Hostetter, A. B. (2011). When do gestures communicate? A meta-analysis. *Psychological Bulletin, 137*(2), 297.

10. Trujillo, J., Özyürek, A., Holler, J., & Drijvers, L. (2021). Speakers exhibit a multimodal Lombard effect in noise. *Scientific Reports,* 11, 16721. doi: 10.1038/s41598-021–95791-0.

11. On gesture facilitating lexical retrieval when you talk, see Butterworth, B., & Hadar, U. (1989). Gesture, speech, and computational stages: A reply to McNeill. *Psychological Review, 96,* 168–174. Krauss, R. M. (1998). Why do we gesture when we speak? *Current Directions in Psychological Science, 7,* 54–60. Rauscher, F. H., Krauss, R. M., & Chen, Y. (1996). Gesture, speech, and lexical access: The role of lexical movements in speech production. *Psychological Science, 7,* 226–231. On gesture *not* facilitating lexical retrieval when you talk, see Alibali, M. W., Kita, S., & Young, A. J. (2000). Gesture and the process of speech production: We think, therefore we gesture. *Language and Cognitive Processes, 15*(6), 593–613. Kisa, Y. D., Goldin-Meadow, S., & Casasanto, D. (2021). Do gestures really facilitate speech production? *Journal of Experimental Psychology: General,* Advance online publication. doi: 10.1037/xge0001135.

12. Wakefield, E., Novack, M. A., Congdon, E. L., Franconeri, S., & Goldin-Meadow, S. (2018). Gesture helps learners learn, but not merely by guiding their visual attention. *Developmental Science, 21*(6). doi: 10.1111/desc.12664.

13. Alibali, M. W., & DiRusso, A. A. (1999). The function of gesture in learning to count: More than keeping track. *Cognitive Development, 14,* 37–56.

14. Cook, S. W., Yip, T. K-Y., & Goldin-Meadow, S. (2010). Gesturing makes memories that last. *Journal of Memory and Language, 63*(4), 465–475.

15. Cowan, N., & Morey, C. C. (2007). How can dual-task working memory retention limits be investigated? *Psychological Science*, *18*(8), 686–688. doi: 10.1111/j.1467-9280.2007.01960.x.

16. Goldin-Meadow, S., Nusbaum, H., Kelly, S., & Wagner, S. (2001). Explaining math: Gesturing lightens the load. *Psychological Science*, *12*, 516–522. Wagner, S., Nusbaum, H., & Goldin-Meadow, S. (2004). Probing the mental representation of gesture: Is handwaving spatial? *Journal of Memory and Language*, *50*, 395–407.

17. Ping, R., & Goldin-Meadow, S. (2010). Gesturing saves cognitive resources when talking about non-present objects. *Cognitive Science*, *34*(4), 602–619.

18. Beaudoin-Ryan, L., & Goldin-Meadow, S. (2014). Teaching moral reasoning through gesture. *Developmental Science*, *17*(6), 984–990. doi: 10.1111/desc.12180.

19. Tversky, B. (2019). *Mind in motion: How action shapes thought.* New York: Basic Books.

20. Newcombe, N. S. (2017). Harnessing spatial thinking to support STEM learning. *Organisation for Economic Co-operation and Development (OECD) Reports.* doi: 10.1787/7d5cae6-en. On the method of loci, see O'Keefe, J., & Nadel, L. (1978). *The hippocampus as a cognitive map.* Oxford: Oxford University Press.

21. Mayer, R. (2009). *Multimedia learning, 2nd edition.* New York: Cambridge University Press.

22. Goldin-Meadow, S., & Brentari, D. (2017). Gesture, sign and language: The coming of age of sign language and gesture studies. *Behavioral and Brain Sciences*, *40*, e46. doi: 10.1017/S0140525X15001247. Emmorey, K. (1999). Do signers gesture? In L. S. Messing & R. Campbell (eds.), *Gesture, speech, and sign* (pp. 133–159). Oxford: Oxford University Press.

23. Perry, M., Church, R. B., & Goldin-Meadow, S. (1988). Transitional knowledge in the acquisition of concepts. *Cognitive Development*, *3*, 359–400.

24. Goldin-Meadow, S., Shield, A., Lenzen, D., Herzig, M., & Padden, C. (2012). The gestures ASL signers use tell us when they are ready to learn math, *Cognition*, *123*, 448–453.

25. On actions impacting how you see the world, see Barsalou, L. W. (1999). Perceptual symbol systems. *Behavioral and Brain Sciences*, *22*, 577–660. Beilock, S. L., Lyons, I. M., Mattarella-Micke, A., Nusbaum, H. C., & Small, S. L. (2008). Sports experience changes the

neural processing of action language. *Proceedings of the National Academy of Sciences of the United States of America, 105,* 13269–13273. Casile, A., & Giese, M. A. (2006). Nonvisual motor training influences biological motion perception. *Current Biology, 16,* 69–74. Glenberg, A. M., & Robertson, D. A. (2000). Symbol grounding and meaning: A comparison of high-dimensional and embodied theories of meaning. *Journal of Memory and Language, 43,* 379–401. Niedenthal, P. M. (2007). Embodying emotion. *Science, 316,* 1002–1005. Zwaan, R. A. (1999). Embodied cognition, perceptual symbols, and situation models. *Discourse Processes, 28,* 81–88.

26. Beilock, S. L., & Goldin-Meadow, S. (2010). Gesture grounds thought in action. *Psychological Science, 21,* 1605–1610. Goldin-Meadow, S., & Beilock, S. L. (2010). Action's influence on thought: The case of gesture. *Perspectives on Psychological Science, 5,* 664–674.

27. Maimon-Mor, R. O., Obasi, E., Lu, J., Odeh, N., Kirker, S., MacSweeney, M., Goldin-Meadow, S., & Makin, T. R. (2020). Talking with your (artificial) hands: Communicative hand gestures as an implicit measure of embodiment, *iScience, 23*(11). doi: 10.1016/j.isci.2020 .101650.

28. On watching action that activates your own motor system, see Buccino, G., Binkofski, F., Fink, G. R., Fadiga, L., Fogassi, L., Gallese, V., Seitz, R. J., Zilles, K., Rizzolatti, G., & Freund, H. J. (2001). Action observation activates premotor and parietal areas in a somatotopic manner: An fMRI study. *European Journal of Neuroscience, 13*(2), 400–404. Hamilton, A., Wolpert, D. M., & Frith, U. (2004). Your own action influences how you perceive another person's action. *Current Biology, 14,* 493–498. Wilson, A. D., Collins, D. R., & Bingham, G. P. (2005). Perceptual coupling in rhythmic movement coordination: Stable perception leads to stable action. *Experimental Brain Research, 164,* 517–528. Sebanz, N., Bekkering, H., & Knoblich, G. (2006). Joint action: Bodies and minds moving together. *Trends in Cognitive Sciences, 10*(2), 70–76. On the overlap between neural circuitry activated when seeing someone act and planning/producing that same action yourself, see Buccino, G., Binkofski, F., Fink, G. R., Fadiga, L., Fogassi, L., Gallese, V., Seitz, R. J., Zilles, K., Rizzolatti, G., & Freund, H. J. (2001). Action observation activates premotor and parietal areas in a somatotopic manner: An fMRI study. *European Journal of Neuroscience, 13*(2), 400–404. Calvo-Merino, G., Glaser, D. E., Grezes, J., Passingham, R. E., & Haggard, P. (2005). Action observation

and acquired motor skills: An fMRI study with expert dancers. *Cerebral Cortex, 15*(8), 1243–1249. Jacobs, A., & Shiffrar, M. (2005). Walking perception by walking observers. *Journal of Experimental Psychology: Human Perception and Performance, 31,* 157–169. Hamilton, A., Wolpert, D. M., & Frith, U. (2004). Your own action influences how you perceive another person's action. *Current Biology, 14,* 493–498. Maeda, F., Mazziotta, J., & Iacoboni, M. (2002). Transcranial magnetic stimulation studies of the human mirror neuron system. *International Congress Series, 1232,* 889–894. On reducing motor resources and its effect on understanding a task, see Beilock, S. L., & Holt, L. E. (2007). Embodied preference judgments: Can likeability be driven by the motor system? *Psychological Science, 18,* 51–57.

29. Ping, R., Goldin-Meadow, S., & Beilock, S. (2014). Understanding gesture: Is the listener's motor system involved? *Journal of Experimental Psychology: General, 143*(1), 195–204. doi: 10.1037/a0032246.

30. Novack, M. A., Congdon, E. L., Hemani-Lopez, N., & Goldin-Meadow, S. (2014). From action to abstraction: Using the hands to learn math. *Psychological Science, 25*(4), 903–910. doi: 10.1177/0956797613518351.

31. Wakefield, E. M., Hall, C., James, K. H., & Goldin-Meadow, S. (2018). Gesture for generalization: Gesture facilitates flexible learning of words for actions on objects. *Developmental Science, 21*(5), e12656. doi: 10.1111/desc.12656.

32. Hegarty, M., Mayer, S., Perez-Kriz, S., & Keehner, M. (2005). The role of gestures in mental animation. *Spatial Cognition and Computation, 5,* 333–356. doi: 10.1207/s15427633scc0504_3.

33. Lakoff, G., & Núñez, R. (2000). *Where mathematics comes from: How the embodied mind brings mathematics into being.* New York: Basic Books.

34. Marghetis, T., & Núñez, R. (2013). The motion behind the symbols: A vital role for dynamism in the conceptualization of limits and continuity in expert mathematics. *Topics in Cognitive Science, 5,* 299–316. doi: 10.1111/tops.12013.

Chapter 2: Our Hands Reflect Our Minds

1. Darwin, C. (2009). *The expression of the emotions in man and animals.* New York: Oxford University Press (original work published 1872). de Waal, F. (1998). *Chimpanzee politics: Power and sex among*

apes. Baltimore: Johns Hopkins University Press. Mayr, E. (1974). Behavior programs and evolutionary strategies. *American Scientist, 62,* 650–659.

2. Carney, D. R., Cuddy, A. J. C., & Yap, A. J. (2010). Power posing: Brief nonverbal displays affect neuroendocrine levels and risk tolerance. *Psychological Science, 21*(10), 1363–1368. doi: 10.1177 /0956797610383437. Ranehill, E., Dreber, A., Johannesson, M., Leiberg, S., Sul, S., & Weber, R. A. (2015). Assessing the robustness of power posing: No effect on hormones and risk tolerance in a large sample of men and women. *Psychological Science, 26*(5), 653–656. Cuddy, A. J. C., Schultz, J., & Fosse, N. E. (2018). *P*-curving a more comprehensive body of research on postural feedback reveals clear evidential value for power-posing effects: Reply to Simmons and Simonsohn. *Psychological Science, 29*(4), 656–666. doi: 10.1177/0956797617746749.

3. Ekman, P., & Friesen, W. (1969). The repertoire of nonverbal behavior: Categories, origins, usage, and coding. *Semiotica, 1,* 49–98.

4. Iverson, J. M., & Goldin-Meadow, S. (1998). Why people gesture as they speak. *Nature, 396,* 228.

5. Özçalışkan, Ş., Lucero, C., & Goldin-Meadow, S. (2016). Is seeing gesture necessary to gesture like a native speaker? *Psychological Science, 27*(5), 737–747. doi: 10.1177/0956797616629931.

6. Kendon, A. (1980). Gesticulation and speech: Two aspects of the process of utterance. In M. R. Key (ed.), *Relationship of verbal and nonverbal communication* (pp. 207–228). The Hague: Mouton. McNeill, D. (1992). *Hand and mind.* Chicago: University of Chicago Press. Kita, S. (1993). Language and thought interface: A study of spontaneous gestures and Japanese mimetics. Unpublished doctoral dissertation, University of Chicago. Nobe, S. (2000). Where do *most* spontaneous representational gestures actually occur with respect to speech? In D. McNeill (ed.), *Language and gesture* (pp. 186–198). New York: Cambridge University Press. Graziano, M., & Gullberg, M. (2018). When speech stops, gesture stops: Evidence from developmental and crosslinguistic comparisons. *Frontiers in Psychology,* June. doi: 10.3389/fpsyg.2018.00879. Mayberry, R. I., & Jaques, J. (2000). Gesture production during stuttered speech: Insights into the nature of speech-gesture integration. In D. McNeill (ed.), *Language and gesture* (pp. 199–214). Cambridge: Cambridge University Press.

7. Argyle, M. (1975). *Bodily communication.* New York: International Universities Press.

8. On gesture identifying us as liars, see Ekman, P., & Friesen, W. V. (1972). Hand movements. *Journal of Communication, 22,* 353–374. On facial expressions telling us about others' minds, see Wu, Y., Schulz, L., Frank, M., & Gweon, H. (2021). Emotion as information in early social learning. *Current Directions in Psychological Science, 30*(6), 468–475. doi: 10.1177/09637214211040779.

9. Kendon, A. (1980). Gesticulation and speech: Two aspects of the process of utterance. In M. R. Key (ed.), *Relationship of verbal and non-verbal communication* (pp. 207–228). The Hague: Mouton. McNeill, D. (1992). *Hand and mind.* Chicago: University of Chicago Press.

10. Beattie, G., & Shovelton, H. (1999). Do iconic hand gestures really contribute anything to the semantic information conveyed by speech? An experimental investigation. *Semiotica, 123,* 1–30 (quote is on p. 5). Kendon, A. (1985). Some uses of gesture. In D. Tannen & M. Saville-Troike (eds.), *Perspectives on silence* (pp. 215–234, quote is on p. 225). Norwood, NJ: Ablex.

11. Piaget, J. (1965). *The child's conception of number.* New York: W. W. Norton and Company.

12. Church, R. B., & Goldin-Meadow, S. (1986). The mismatch between gesture and speech as an index of transitional knowledge. *Cognition, 23,* 43–71.

13. Perry, M., Church, R. B., & Goldin-Meadow, S. (1988). Transitional knowledge in the acquisition of concepts. *Cognitive Development, 3,* 359–400. Perry, M., Church, R. B., & Goldin-Meadow, S. (1992). Is gesture-speech mismatch a general index of transitional knowledge? *Cognitive Development, 7*(1), 109–122. Pine, K. J., Lufkin, N., & Messer, D. (2004). More gestures than answers: Children learning about balance. *Developmental Psychology, 40,* 1059–1106. Gibson, D., Gunderson, E. A., Spaepen, E., Levine, S. C., & Goldin-Meadow, S. (2018). Number gestures predict learning of number words. *Developmental Science, 22*(3). doi: 10.1111/desc.12791.

14. Gershkoff-Stowe, L., & Smith, L. B. (1997). A curvilinear trend in naming errors as a function of early vocabulary growth. *Cognitive Psychology, 34,* 37–71. Evans, M. A., & Rubin, K. H. (1979). Hand gestures as a communicative mode in school-aged children. *Journal of Genetic Psychology, 135,* 189–196. Alibali, M. W., & DiRusso, A. A. (1999). The function of gesture in learning to count: More than keeping track. *Cognitive Development, 14,* 37–56. Graham, T. A. (1999). The role of gesture in children's learning to count. *Journal of Experimental Child*

Psychology, 74, 333–355. Gunderson, E. A., Spaepen, E., Gibson, D., Goldin-Meadow, S., & Levine, S. C. (2015). Gesture as a window onto children's number knowledge. *Cognition*, *144*, 14–28. doi: 10.1016/j. cognition.2015.07.008. Crowder, E. M., & Newman, D. (1993). Telling what they know: The role of gesture and language in children's science explanations. *Pragmatics and Cognition*, *1*, 341–376. Church, R. B., Schonert-Reichl, K., Goodman, N., Kelly, S. D., & Ayman-Nolley, S. (1995). The role of gesture and speech communication as reflections of cognitive understanding. *Journal of Contemporary Legal Issues*, 6, 123–154. Garber, P., & Goldin-Meadow, S. (2002). Gesture offers insight into problem-solving in children and adults. *Cognitive Science*, 26, 817–831. Stone, A., Webb, R., & Mahootian, S. (1992). The generality of gesture-speech mismatch as an index of transitional knowledge: Evidence from a control-of-variables task. *Cognitive Development*, 6, 301–313. Schwartz, D. L., & Black, J. B. (1996). Shuttling between depictive models and abstract rules: Induction and fallback. *Cognitive Science*, 20, 457–497. Morrell-Samuels, P., & Krauss, R. M. (1992). Word familiarity predicts temporal asynchrony of hand gestures and speech. *Journal of Experimental Psychology: Learning, Memory, and Cognition*, 18, 615–622. Alibali, M. W., Bassok, M., Solomon, K. O., Syc, S. E., & Goldin-Meadow, S. (1999). Illuminating mental representations through speech and gesture. *Psychological Sciences*, *10*, 327–333. Beattie, G., & Shovelton, H. (1999). Do iconic hand gestures really contribute anything to the semantic information conveyed by speech? An experimental investigation. *Semiotica*, *123*, 1–30. McNeill, D. (1992). *Hand and mind*. Chicago: University of Chicago Press. Rauscher, F. H., Krauss, R. M., & Chen, Y. (1996). Gesture, speech, and lexical access: The role of lexical movements in speech production. *Psychological Science*, 7, 226–231.

15. Lakshmi, A., Fiske, S. T., & Goldin-Meadow, S. (July 20, 2020). The communication of stereotype content through gestures. https:// aspredicted.org/gt4ff.pdf.

16. Iverson, J. M., & Goldin-Meadow, S. (2005). Gesture paves the way for language development. *Psychological Science*, *16*, 368–371.

17. Ping, R., Church, R. B., Decatur, M-A., Larson, S. W., Zinchenko, E., & Goldin-Meadow, S. (2021). Unpacking the gestures of chemistry learners: What the hands tell us about correct and incorrect conceptions of stereochemistry. *Discourse Processes*, *58*(2), 213–232. doi: 10.1080/0163853X.2020.1839343.

18. On seamlessly integrating gesture and speech, see McNeill, D. (1992). *Hand and mind*. Chicago: University of Chicago Press. Kelly, S. D., Özyürek, A., & Maris, E. (2009). Two sides of the same coin: Speech and gesture mutually interact to enhance comprehension. *Psychological Science, 21*(2), 260–267. doi: 10.1177/0956797609357327.

19. McNeill, D., Cassell, J., & McCullough, K.-E. (1994). Communicative effects of speech-mismatched gestures. *Research on Language and Social Interaction, 27*, 223–237.

20. Goldin-Meadow, S., Wein, D., & Chang, C. (1992). Assessing knowledge through gesture: Using children's hands to read their minds. *Cognition and Instruction, 9*, 201–219. Alibali, M. W., Flevares, L., & Goldin-Meadow, S. (1997). Assessing knowledge conveyed in gesture: Do teachers have the upper hand? *Journal of Educational Psychology, 89*, 183–193.

21. Geary, D. C. (1995). Reflections of evolution and culture in children's cognition: Implications for mathematical development and instruction. *American Psychologist, 50*, 24–37.

22. Goldin-Meadow, S., & Sandhofer, C. M. (1999). Gesture conveys substantive information about a child's thoughts to ordinary listeners. *Developmental Science, 2*, 67–74. Morford, M., & Goldin-Meadow, S. (1992). Comprehension and production of gesture in combination with speech in one-word speakers. *Journal of Child Language, 19*, 559–580. Kelly, S. D. (2001). Broadening the units of analysis in communication: Speech and nonverbal behaviours in pragmatic comprehension. *Journal of Child Language, 28*, 325–349. Kelly, S. D., & Church, R. B. (1997). Can children detect conceptual information conveyed through other children's nonverbal behaviors? *Cognition and Instruction, 15*, 107–134. Kelly, S. D., & Church, R. B. (1998). A comparison between children's and adults' ability to detect conceptual information conveyed through representational gestures. *Child Development, 69*, 85–93.

23. Goldin-Meadow, S., & Singer, M. A. (2003). From children's hands to adults' ears: Gesture's role in teaching and learning. *Developmental Psychology, 39*(3), 509–520. Goldin-Meadow, S., Kim, S., & Singer, M. (1999). What the teacher's hands tell the student's mind about math. *Journal of Educational Psychology, 91*, 720–730.

24. Singer, M. A., & Goldin-Meadow, S. (2005). Children learn when their teachers' gestures and speech differ. *Psychological Science, 16*, 85–89.

Chapter 3: Our Hands Can Change Our Minds

1. McNeil, N. M., Alibali, M. W., & Evans, J. L. (2000). The role of gesture in children's comprehension of spoken language: Now they need it, now they don't. *Journal of Nonverbal Behavior*, 24(2), 131–150. https://doi.org/10.1023/A:1006657929803; see also Perry, M., Berch, D., & Singleton, J. (1995). Constructing shared understanding: The role of nonverbal input in learning contexts. *Journal of Contemporary Legal Issues*, 6, 213–235. Valenzeno, L., Alibali, M. W., & Klatzky, R. (2003). Teachers' gestures facilitate students' learning: A lesson in symmetry. *Contemporary Educational Psychology*, 28(2), 187–204.

2. Church, R. B., Ayman-Nolley, S., & Mahootian, S. (2004). The role of gesture in bilingual education: Does gesture enhance learning? *International Journal of Bilingual Education and Bilingualism*, 7(4), 303–319. doi: 10.1080/13670050408667815.

3. Singer, M. A., & Goldin-Meadow, S. (2005). Children learn when their teachers' gestures and speech differ. *Psychological Science*, 16, 85–89.

4. Congdon, E. L., Novack, M. A., Brooks, N., Hemani-Lopez, N., O'Keefe, L., & Goldin-Meadow, S. (2017). Better together: Simultaneous presentation of speech and gesture in math instruction supports generalization and retention. *Learning and Instruction*, 50, 65–74. doi: 10.1016/j.learninstruc.2017.03.005.

5. On the benefits of providing more than one problem-solving strategy, see Woodward, J., Beckman, S., Driscoll, M., Franke, M., Herzig, P., Jitendra, A., Koedinger, K. R., & Ogbuehi, P. (2018). *Improving mathematical problem solving in grades 4 through 8* (NCEE 2012–4055). US Department of Education, Institute of Education Sciences, National Center for Education Evaluation and Regional Assistance. https://ies.ed.gov/ncee/wwc/PracticeGuide/16. On teachers adjusting their input to student gesture, which helps them learn, see Goldin-Meadow, S., & Singer, M. A. (2003). From children's hands to adults' ears: Gesture's role in teaching and learning. *Developmental Psychology*, 39(3), 509–520. Singer, M. A., & Goldin-Meadow, S. (2005). Children learn when their teachers' gestures and speech differ. *Psychological Science*, 16, 85–89.

6. Iverson, J. M., & Goldin-Meadow, S. (2005). Gesture paves the way for language development. *Psychological Science*, 16, 367–371. Goldin-Meadow, S., Goodrich, W., Sauer, E., & Iverson, J. (2007). Young children use their hands to tell their mothers what to say. *Developmental Science*, 10, 778–785.

7. Newell, A., & Simon, H. A. (1972). *Human problem-solving.* Englewood Cliffs, NJ: Prentice Hall.

8. Beilock, S. L., & Goldin-Meadow, S. (2010). Gesture grounds thought in action. *Psychological Science, 21,* 1605–1610. Goldin-Meadow, S., & Beilock, S. L. (2010). Action's influence on thought: The case of gesture. *Perspectives on Psychological Science, 5,* 664–674. Trofatter, C., Kontra, C., Beilock, S., & Goldin-Meadow, S. (2015). Gesturing has a larger impact on problem-solving than action, even when action is accompanied by words. *Language, Cognition and Neuroscience, 30*(3), 251–260. doi: 10.1080/23273798.2014.905692.

9. Pine, K. J., Lufkin, N., & Messer, D. (2004). More gestures than answers: Children learning about balance. *Developmental Psychology, 40,* 1059–1106. Schwartz, D. L., & Black, J. B. (1996). Shuttling between depictive models and abstract rules: Induction and fallback. *Cognitive Science, 20,* 457–497. Cook, S. W., & Tanenhaus, M. K. (2009). Embodied communication: Speakers' gestures affect listeners' actions. *Cognition, 113*(1), 98–104. doi: 10.1016/j.cognition.2009.06.006. Stevanoni, E., & Salmon, K. (2005). Giving memory a hand: Instructing children to gesture enhances their event recall. *Journal of Nonverbal Behavior, 29*(4), 217–233.

10. Alibali, M., Spencer, R. S., Knox, L., & Kita, S. (2011). Spontaneous gestures influence strategy choices in problem solving. *Psychological Science, 22*(9), 1138–1144. doi: 10.1177/0956797611417722.

11. Bates, E., Benigni, L., Bretherton, I., Camaioni, L., & Volterra, V. (1979). *The emergence of symbols: Cognition and communication in infancy.* New York: Academic Press. Acredolo, L. P., & Goodwyn, S. W. (1988). Symbolic gesturing in normal infants. *Child Development, 59,* 450–466. Iverson, J. M., & Goldin-Meadow, S. (2005). Gesture paves the way for language development. *Psychological Science, 16,* 368–371. Rowe, M. L., & Goldin-Meadow, S. (2009). Differences in early gesture explain SES disparities in child vocabulary size at school entry. *Science, 323,* 951–953. Rowe, M. L., & Goldin-Meadow, S. (2009). Early gesture selectively predicts later language learning. *Developmental Science, 12,* 182–187.

12. LeBarton, E. S., Raudenbush, S., & Goldin-Meadow, S. (2015). Experimentally-induced increases in early gesture lead to increases in spoken vocabulary. *Journal of Cognition and Development, 16*(2), 199–220. doi 10.1080/15248372.2013.858041.

13. Wakefield, E. M., Hall, C., James, K. H., & Goldin-Meadow, S. (2018). Gesture for generalization: Gesture facilitates flexible learning

of words for actions on objects, *Developmental Science, 21*(5), e12656. doi 10.1111/desc.12656.

14. Cook, S. W., Mitchell, Z., & Goldin-Meadow, S. (2008). Gesturing makes learning last. *Cognition, 106*, 1047–1058. Goldin-Meadow, S., Cook, S. W., & Mitchell, Z. A. (2009). Gesturing gives children new ideas about math. *Psychological Science, 20*(3), 267–272.

15. Broaders, S., Cook, S. W., Mitchell, Z., & Goldin-Meadow, S. (2007). Making children gesture brings out implicit knowledge and leads to learning. *Journal of Experimental Psychology: General, 136*(4), 539–550.

16. Nunez, R., & Sweetser, E. (2006). With the future behind them: Convergent evidence from Aymara language and gesture in the cross-linguistic comparison of spatial construals of time. *Cognitive Science, 30*, 401–450.

17. Jamalian, A., & Tversky, B. (2012). Gestures alter thinking about time. In N. Miyake, D. Peebles, & R. P. Cooper (eds.), *Proceedings of the 34th Annual Conference of the Cognitive Science Society* (pp. 551–557). Austin, TX: Cognitive Science Society.

18. On training moral reasoning, see Walker, L., & Taylor, J. (1991). Stage transitions in moral reasoning: A longitudinal study of developmental processes. *Developmental Psychology, 27*, 330–337. On using gesture to teach moral reasoning, see Beaudoin-Ryan, L., & Goldin-Meadow, S. (2014). Teaching moral reasoning through gesture. *Developmental Science, 17*(6), 984–990. doi: 10.1111/desc.12180.

19. Carrazza, C., Wakefield, E. M., Hemani-Lopez, N., Plath, K., & Goldin-Meadow, S. (2021). Children integrate speech and gesture across a wider temporal window than speech and action: A case for why gesture helps learning. *Cognition, 210*, 104604. doi: 10.1016/j.cognition.2021.104604.

Chapter 4: As Long as There Are Humans, There Will Be Language

1. Edwards, T., & Brentari, D. (2020). Feeling phonology: The conventionalization of phonology in protactile communities in the United States. *Language, 96*(4), 819–840.

2. Klima, E., & Bellugi, U. (1979). *The signs of language.* Cambridge, MA: Harvard University Press. Perniss, P. M., Pfau, R., & Steinbach, M. (eds). (2007). *Visible variation: Comparative studies on sign language*

structure. New York: Mouton De Gruyter. Brentari, D. (ed.). (2012). *Sign languages.* New York: Cambridge University Press.

3. Novack, M. A., Brentari, D., Goldin-Meadow, S., & Waxman, S. (2021). *Cognition, 215.* doi: 10.1016/j.cognition.2021.104845.

4. Goldin-Meadow, S., & Brentari, D. (2017). Gesture, sign and language: The coming of age of sign language and gesture studies. *Behavioral and Brain Sciences, 40,* e46. doi: 10.1017/S0140525X15001247.

5. On deaf children acquiring sign language naturally, see Lillo-Martin, D. (2009). Sign language acquisition studies. In E. Bavin (ed.). *The Cambridge handbook of child language* (pp. 399–415). Cambridge: Cambridge University Press. Newport, E. L., & Meier, R. P. (1985). *The acquisition of American Sign Language.* In D. I. Slobin (ed.), *The cross-linguistic study of language acquisition,* Vol. 1: *The data* (pp. 881–938). Mahwah, NJ: Lawrence Erlbaum Associates. Petitto, L. A., & Marentette, P. F. (1991). Babbling in the manual mode: Evidence for the ontogeny of language. *Science, 251,* 1493–1496. Petitto, L. (2000). The acquisition of natural signed languages: Lessons in the nature of human language and its biological foundations. In C. Chamberlain, J. P. Morford, & R. Mayberry (eds.), *Language Acquisition by Eye* (pp. 41–50). Mahwah, NJ: Lawrence Erlbaum Associates.

6. Mitchell, R. E., & Karchmer, M. A. (2004). Chasing the mythical ten percent: Parental hearing status of deaf and hard of hearing students in the United States. *Sign Language Studies, 4*(2), 138–163. doi: 10.1353/sls.2004.0005. Summerfield, A. Q. (1983). Audio-visual speech perception, lipreading and artificial stimulation. In M. E. Lutman & M. P. Haggard (eds.), *Hearing science and hearing disorders* (pp. 132–179). New York: Academic Press.

7. Goldin-Meadow, S. (2020). Discovering the biases children bring to language learning. *Child Development Perspectives, 14*(4), 195–201.

8. Goldin-Meadow, S., & Feldman, H. (1977). The development of language-like communication without a language model. *Science, 197,* 401–403. Feldman, H., Goldin-Meadow, S., & Gleitman, L. (1978). Beyond Herodotus: The creation of a language by linguistically deprived deaf children. In A. Lock (ed.), *Action, symbol, and gesture: The emergence of language,* 351–414. New York: Academic Press. Goldin-Meadow, S. (1979). Structure in a manual communication system developed without a conventional language model: Language without a helping hand. In H. Whitaker & H. A. Whitaker (eds.), *Studies in Neurolinguistics,* Vol. 4 (pp. 125–207). New York: Academic Press. Goldin-Meadow, S.,

& Mylander, C. (1984). Gestural communication in deaf children: The effects and non-effects of parental input on early language development. *Monographs of the Society for Research in Child Development, 49* (3–4), 1–151, chaps. 2 and 3. Goldin-Meadow, S., Mylander, C., & Butcher, C. (1995). The resilience of combinatorial structure at the word level: Morphology in self-styled gesture systems. *Cognition, 56,* 195–262. Goldin-Meadow, S. (2003). *The resilience of language: What gesture creation in deaf children can tell us about how all children learn language.* New York: Psychology Press.

9. Goldin-Meadow, S., Butcher, C., Mylander, C., & Dodge, M. (1994). Nouns and verbs in a self-styled gesture system: What's in a name? *Cognitive Psychology, 27,* 259–319.

10. Hunsicker, D., & Goldin-Meadow, S. (2012). Hierarchical structure in a self-created communication system: Building nominal constituents in homesign. *Language, 88*(4), 732–763.

11. Greenfield, P. M., & Savage-Rumbaugh, E. S. (1991). Imitation, grammatical development, and the invention of protogrammar by an ape. In N. A. Krasnegor, D. M. Rumbaugh, R. L. Schiefelbusch, & M. Studdert-Kennedy (eds.), *Biological and behavioral determinants of language development* (pp. 235–262). Hillsdale, NJ: Lawrence Erlbaum Associates.

12. Franklin, A., Giannakidou, A., & Goldin-Meadow, S. (2011). Negation, questions, and structure building in a homesign system. *Cognition, 118*(3), 398–416.

13. Phillips, S. B. V. D., Goldin-Meadow, S., & Miller, P. J. (2001). Enacting stories, seeing worlds: Similarities and differences in the cross-cultural narrative development of linguistically isolated deaf children. *Human Development, 44,* 311–336.

14. On Chinese hearing parents interacting differently with their children than American hearing parents, see Wu, D. Y. H. (1985). Child training in Chinese culture. In W.-S. Tseng, & D. Y. H. Wu (eds.), *Chinese culture and mental health* (pp. 113–134). New York: Academic Press. Chen, C., & Uttal, D. H. (1988). Cultural values, parents' beliefs, and children's achievement in the United States and China. *Human Development, 31,* 351–358. Lin, C.-Y. C., & Fu, V. R. (1990). A comparison of child-rearing practices among Chinese, immigrant Chinese, and Caucasian-American parents. *Child Development, 61,* 429–433. On Chinese hearing mothers gesturing more than American hearing mothers, see Goldin-Meadow, S., & Saltzman, J. (2000). The cultural

bounds of maternal accommodation: How Chinese and American mothers communicate with deaf and hearing children. *Psychological Science*, *11*, 311–318. On similarities in homesign in the United States, Turkey, and Nicaragua, see Goldin-Meadow, S., Özyürek, A., Sancar, B., & Mylander, C. (2009). Making language around the globe: A cross-linguistic study of homesign in the United States, China, and Turkey. In J. Guo, E. Lieven, N. Budwig & S. Ervin-Tripp (eds.), *Crosslinguistic approaches to the psychology of language: Research in the tradition of Dan Isaac Slobin* (pp. 27–39). New York: Taylor & Francis. Goldin-Meadow, S., Namboodiripad, S., Mylander, C., Özyürek, A., & Sancar, B. (2015). The resilience of structure built around the predicate: Homesign gesture systems in Turkish and American deaf children. *Journal of Cognition and Development*, *16*, 55–88. doi: 10.1080/15248372.2013.803970. Flaherty, M., Hunsicker, D., & Goldin-Meadow, S. (2021). Structural biases that children bring to language-learning: A cross-cultural look at gestural input to homesign. *Cognition*, *211*, 104608. doi: 10.1016/j.cognition.2021.104608.

15. On similarities in homesign in the United States and China, see Zheng, M., & Goldin-Meadow, S. (2002). Thought before language: How deaf and hearing children express motion events across cultures. *Cognition*, *85*, 145–175. Goldin-Meadow, S., & Mylander, C. (1998). Spontaneous sign systems created by deaf children in two cultures. *Nature*, *391*, 279–281. Goldin-Meadow, S., Mylander, C., & Franklin, A. (2007). How children make language out of gesture: Morphological structure in gesture systems developed by American and Chinese deaf children. *Cognitive Psychology*, *55*, 87–135. Goldin-Meadow, S., Gelman, S., & Mylander, C. (2005). Expressing generic concepts with and without a language model. *Cognition*, *96*, 109–126.

16. Miller, P. J., Fung, H., & Mintz, J. (1996). Self-construction through narrative practices: A Chinese and American comparison of early socialization. *Ethos*, *24*(2), 237–280.

17. Phillips, S. B. V. D., Goldin-Meadow, S., & Miller, P. J. (2001). Enacting stories, seeing worlds: Similarities and differences in the cross-cultural narrative development of linguistically isolated deaf children. *Human Development*, *44*, 311–336.

18. On the prevalence of gesturing in speakers, see Kendon, A. (1980). Gesticulation and speech: Two aspects of the process of utterance. In M. R. Key (ed.), *Relationship of verbal and nonverbal communication* (pp. 207–228). The Hague: Mouton. McNeill, D. (1992). *Hand and*

mind. Chicago: University of Chicago Press. Feyereisen, P., & de Lannoy, J.-D. (1991). *Gestures and speech: Psychological investigations*. Cambridge: Cambridge University Press. Goldin-Meadow, S. (2003). *Hearing gesture: How our hands help us think*. Cambridge, MA: Harvard University Press.

19. On emblems, see Ekman, P., & Friesen, W. (1969). The repertoire of nonverbal behavior: Categories, origins, usage, and coding. *Semiotica*, *1*, 49–98.

20. On iconic gestures, see Wang, X.-L., Mylander, C., & Goldin-Meadow, S. (1993). Language and environment: A cross-cultural study of the gestural communication systems of Chinese and American deaf children. *Belgian Journal of Linguistics*, *8*, 167–185. Wang, X.-L., Mylander, C., & Goldin-Meadow, S. (1995). The resilience of language: Mother-child interaction and its effect on the gesture systems of Chinese and American deaf children. In K. Emmorey & J. Reilly (eds.), *Language, gesture, and space* (pp. 411–433). Hillsdale, NJ: Lawrence Erlbaum Associates.

21. On hearing English speakers producing one gesture per clause, see McNeill, D. (1992). *Hand and mind*. Chicago: University of Chicago Press. On the differences between homesign and hearing parents' gestures, see Goldin-Meadow, S., & Mylander, C. (1983). Gestural communication in deaf children: Non-effect of parental input on language development. *Science*, *221*(4608), 372–374. Goldin-Meadow, S., & Mylander, C. (1984). Gestural communication in deaf children: The effects and non-effects of parental input on early language development. *Monographs of the Society for Research in Child Development*, *49*(3–4), 1–151, chaps. 4 and 5. Goldin-Meadow, S., Mylander, C., & Butcher, C. (1995). The resilience of combinatorial structure at the word level: Morphology in self-styled gesture systems. *Cognition*, *56*, 195–262. Zheng, M., & Goldin-Meadow, S. (2002). Thought before language: How deaf and hearing children express motion events across cultures. *Cognition*, *85*, 145–175.

22. On how hearing parents respond to their hearing children, see Brown, R., & Hanlon, C. (1970). Derivational complexity and order of acquisition in child speech. In J. R. Hayes (ed.), *Cognition and the development of language* (pp. 11–53). New York: Wiley.

23. On similarities in how hearing parents respond to deaf versus hearing children's communications, see Goldin-Meadow, S., & Mylander, C. (1984). Gestural communication in deaf children: The effects

and non-effects of parental input on early language development. *Monographs of the Society for Research in Child Development*, 49(3–4), 1–151, chap. 6.

24. Pica, P., Lemer, C., Izard, V., & Dehaene, S. (2004). Exact and approximate arithmetic in an Amazonian indigene group. *Science*, *306*, 499–503. Gordon, P. (2004). Numerical cognition without words: Evidence from Amazonia. *Science*, *306*, 496–499. Frank, M. C., Everett, D. L., Fedorenko, E., & Gibson, E. (2008). Number as a cognitive technology: Evidence from Pirahã language and cognition. *Cognition*, *108*, 819–824.

25. Gelman, R., & Butterworth, B. (2005). Number and language: How are they related? *Trends in Cognitive Science*, *9*, 6–10.

26. On the absence of large exact numbers in homesigning adults, see Spaepen, E., Coppola, M., Spelke, E., Carey, S., & Goldin-Meadow, S. (2011). Number without a language model. *Proceedings of the National Academy of Sciences of the United States of America*, *108*(8), 3163–3168. Spaepen, E., Coppola, M., Flaherty, M., Spelke, E., & Goldin-Meadow, S. (2013). Generating a lexicon without a language model: Do words for number count? *Journal of Memory and Language*, *69*(4), 496–505. doi: 10.1016/j.jml.2013.05.004. On the absence of large exact numbers in homesigning children, see Abner, N., Namboodiripad, S., Spaepen, E., & Goldin-Meadow, S. (2021). Emergent morphology in child homesign: Evidence from number language. *Language Learning and Development*, *18*(1), 16–40. doi: 10.1080/15475441.2021.1922281. Coppola, M., Spaepen, E., & Goldin-Meadow, S. (2013). Communicating about quantity without a language model: Number devices in homesign grammar. *Cognitive Psychology*, *67*, 1–25. doi: 10.1016/j.cogpsych.2013.05.003.

Chapter 5: Watching Language
Grow Naturally and in the Lab

1. Brentari, D., & Goldin-Meadow, S. (2017). Language emergence. *Annual Review of Linguistics*, *3*, 363–388. doi: 10.1146/annurev-linguistics-011415-040743. Fusellier-Souza, I. (2006). Emergence and development of sign languages: From a semiogenetic point of view. *Sign Language Studies*, *7*(1), 3–56. Kegl, J. (1994). The Nicaraguan Sign Language project: An overview. *Signpost*, *7*, 24–31. Kegl, J., Senghas, A., & Coppola, M. (1999). Creation through contact: Sign language

emergence and sign language change in Nicaragua. In M. DeGraff (ed.), *Language creation and language change: Creolization, diachrony, and development* (pp. 179–237). Cambridge, MA: MIT.

2. Polich, L. (2005). *The emergence of the deaf community in Nicaragua: "With sign language you can learn so much."* Washington, DC: Gallaudet University Press.

3. Gleitman, L. R., Senghas, A., Flaherty, M., Coppola, M., & Goldin-Meadow, S. (2019). The emergence of a formal category "symmetry" in a new sign language. *Proceedings of the National Academy of Sciences of the United States of America, 116*(24), 11705–11711. doi: 10.1073/pnas.1819872116.

4. Goldin-Meadow, S., Brentari, D., Coppola, M., Horton, L., & Senghas, A. (2015). Watching language grow in the manual modality: Nominals, predicates, and handshapes. *Cognition, 135*, 381–395. doi: 10.1016/j.cognition.2014.11.029.

5. Rissman, L., Horton, L., Flaherty, M., Senghas, A., Coppola, M., Brentari, D., & Goldin-Meadow, S. (2020). The communicative importance of agent-backgrounding: Evidence from homesign and Nicaraguan Sign Language. *Cognition, 203*. doi: 10.1016/j.cognition.2020.104332.

6. Kirby, S., Tamariz, M., Cornish, H., & Smith, K. (2015). Compression and communication in the cultural evolution of linguistic structure. *Cognition, 141*, 87–102.

7. Fay, N., Lister, C., Ellison, T. M., & Goldin-Meadow, S. (2014). Creating a communication system from scratch: Gesture beats vocalization hands down. *Frontiers in Psychology (Language Sciences), 5*, 354. doi: 10.3389/fpsyg.2014.00354.

8. Goldin-Meadow, S., McNeill, D., & Singleton, J. (1996). Silence is liberating: Removing the handcuffs on grammatical expression in the manual modality. *Psychological Review, 103*, 34–55.

9. Gershkoff-Stowe, L., & Goldin-Meadow, S. (2002). Is there a natural order for expressing semantic relations? *Cognitive Psychology, 45*(3), 375–412.

10. On silent gesturers using the same gesture orders and the same transparency orders, no matter what language they speak, see Goldin-Meadow, S., So, W.-C., Özyürek, A., & Mylander, C. (2008). The natural order of events: How speakers of different languages represent events nonverbally. *Proceedings of the National Academy of Sciences of the United States of America, 105*(27), 9163–9168. On the replicability of the silent gesture effect across languages, see Langus, A., & Nespor, M.

(2010). Cognitive systems struggling for word order. *Cognitive Psychology*, *60*(4), 291–318. doi: 10.1016/j.cogpsych.2010.01.004. Gibson, E., Piantadosi, S. T., Brink, K., Bergen, L., Lim, E., & Saxe, R. (2013). A noisy-channel account of crosslinguistic word order variation. *Psychological Science*, *24*(7), 1079–1088. Hall, M. L., Mayberry, R. I., & Ferreira, V. S. (2013). Cognitive constraints on constituent order: Evidence from elicited pantomime. *Cognition*, *129*(1), 1–17. Hall, M. L., Ferreira, V. S., & Mayberry, R. I. (2014). Investigating constituent order change with elicited pantomime: A functional account of SVO emergence. *Cognitive Science*, *38*(5), 943–972. Meir, I., Aronoff, M., Börstell, C., Hwang, S. O., Ilkbasaran, D., Kastner, I., Lepic, R., Ben-Basat, A., Padden, C., & Sandler, W. (2017). The effect of being human and the basis of grammatical word order: Insights from novel communication systems and young sign languages. *Cognition*, *158*, 189–207.

11. Özçalışkan, Ş., Lucero, C., & Goldin-Meadow, S. (2016). Does language shape silent gesture? *Cognition*, *148*, 10–18. doi: 10.1016/j.cognition.2015.12.001.

12. Bohn, M., Kachel, G., & Tomasello, M. (2019). Young children spontaneously recreate core properties of language in a new modality. *Proceedings of the National Academy of Sciences of the United States of America*, *116*(51), 26072–26077. doi: 10.1073/pnas.1904871116.

13. Schouwstra, M., & de Swart, H. (2014). The semantic origins of word order. *Cognition*, *131*(3), 431–436.

14. On moving from the lab to a natural situation of language emergence, see Flaherty, M., & Schouwstra, M. (2023). Validating lab studies of silent gesture with a naturally emerging sign language: How order is used to describe intensional vs. extensional events. *Topics in Cognitive Science*, in press.

15. Abner, N., Flaherty, M., Stangl, K., Coppola, M., Brentari, D., & Goldin-Meadow, S. (2019). The noun-verb distinction in established and emergent sign systems. *Language*, *95*(2), 230–267. doi: 10.1353/lan.2019.0030.

16. On moving from language emergence in a natural situation to the lab, see Motamedi, Y., Montemurro, K., Abner, N., Flaherty, M., Kirby, S., & Goldin-Meadow, S. (2022). The seeds of the noun-verb distinction in the manual modality: Improvisation and interaction in the emergence of grammatical categories. *Languages*, *7*, 95. doi: 10.3390/languages7020095.

Chapter 6: Using Hands to Parent

1. On hearing children's gestures, see Bates, E. (1976). *Language and context: The acquisition of pragmatics.* New York: Academic Press. Bates, E., Benigni, L., Bretherton, I., Camaioni, L., & Volterra, V. (1979). *The emergence of symbols: Cognition and communication in infancy.* New York: Academic Press. Iverson, J. M., Capirci, O., & Caselli, M. S. (1994). From communication to language in two modalities. *Cognitive Development,* 9, 23–43. Özçalışkan, Ş., & Goldin-Meadow, S. (2011). Is there an iconic gesture spurt at 26 months? In G. Stam & M. Ishino (eds.), *Integrating gestures: The interdisciplinary nature of gesture* (pp. 163–174). Amsterdam: John Benjamins.

2. On early gestures predicting later vocabulary, see Acredolo, L. P., & Goodwyn, S. W. (1988). Symbolic gesturing in normal infants. *Child Development,* 59, 450–466. Rowe, M. L., & Goldin-Meadow, S. (2009). Differences in early gesture explain SES disparities in child vocabulary size at school entry. *Science,* 323, 951–953. Özçalışkan, Ş., Gentner, D., & Goldin-Meadow, S. (2014). Do iconic gestures pave the way for children's early verbs? *Applied Psycholinguistics,* 35(6), 1143–1162. doi: 10.1017/S0142716412000720. Rowe, M., Özçalışkan, Ş., & Goldin-Meadow, S. (2008). Learning words by hand: Gesture's role in predicting vocabulary development. *First Language,* 28, 185–203.

3. On hearing children not combining gestures, see Goldin-Meadow, S., & Morford, M. (1985). Gesture in early child language: Studies of deaf and hearing children. *Merrill-Palmer Quarterly,* 31(2), 145–176. On the gestures in children's earliest gesture + speech combinations complementing speech, see Capirci, O., Iverson, J. M., Pizzuto, E., & Volterra, V. (1996). Communicative gestures during the transition to two-word speech. *Journal of Child Language,* 23, 645–673. de Laguna, G. (1927). *Speech: Its function and development.* Bloomington: Indiana University Press. Greenfield, P., & Smith, J. (1976). *The structure of communication in early language development.* New York: Academic Press. Guillaume, P. (1927). Les debuts de la phrase dans le langage de l'enfant. *Journal de Psychologie,* 24, 1–25. On the onset of complementary gesture + speech combinations predicting the onset of determiner + noun combinations, see Cartmill, E. A., Hunsicker, D., & Goldin-Meadow, S. (2014). Pointing and naming are not redundant: Children use gesture to modify nouns before they modify nouns in speech. *Developmental Psychology,* 50(6), 1660–1666. doi: 10.1037/a0036003.

4. On gesture + speech combinations that supplement speech, see Goldin-Meadow, S., & Morford, M. (1985). Gesture in early child language: Studies of deaf and hearing children. *Merrill-Palmer Quarterly*, 31(2), 145–176. Greenfield, P., & Smith, J. (1976). *The structure of communication in early language development*. New York: Academic Press. Masur, E. F. (1982). Mothers' responses to infants' object-related gestures: Influences on lexical development. *Journal of Child Language*, 9, 23–30. Masur, E. F. (1983). Gestural development, dual-directional signaling, and the transition to words. *Journal of Psycholinguistic Research* 12: 93–109. Morford, M., & Goldin-Meadow, S. (1992). Comprehension and production of gesture in combination with speech in one-word speakers. *Journal of Child Language*, 19, 559–580. On the onset of supplementary gesture + speech combinations predicting the onset of sentences, see Goldin-Meadow, S., & Butcher, C. (2003). Pointing toward two-word speech in young children. In S. Kita (ed.), *Pointing: Where language, culture, and cognition meet* (pp. 85–107). Mahwah, NJ: Lawrence Erlbaum Associates. Iverson, J. M., Capirci, O., Volterra, V., & Goldin-Meadow, S. (2008). Learning to talk in a gesture-rich world: Early communication of Italian vs. American children. *First Language*, 28, 164–181. Iverson, J. M., & Goldin-Meadow, S. (2005). Gesture paves the way for language development. *Psychological Science*, 16, 367–371.

5. Rowe, M. L., & Goldin-Meadow, S. (2009). Early gesture selectively predicts later language learning. *Developmental Science*, 12, 182–187.

6. Özçalışkan, Ş., & Goldin-Meadow, S. (2005). Gesture is at the cutting edge of early language development. *Cognition*, 96, B01–113.

7. On gesture taking a character's perspective and predicting the structure of later stories, see McNeill, D. (1992). *Hand and mind*. Chicago: University of Chicago Press. Demir, O. E., Levine, S., & Goldin-Meadow, S. (2015). A tale of two hands: Children's gesture use in narrative production predicts later narrative structure in speech. *Journal of Child Language*, 42(3), 662–681.

8. On integrating gesture and speech in comprehension, see Morford, M., & Goldin-Meadow, S. (1992). Comprehension and production of gesture in combination with speech in one-word speakers. *Journal of Child Language*, 19, 559–580.

9. On integrating gesture and speech in comprehension, see Morford, M., & Goldin-Meadow, S. (1992). Comprehension and production of gesture in combination with speech in one-word speakers. *Journal of Child Language*, 19, 559–580.

10. On brain structures underlying gesture-speech integration, see Dick, A. S., Goldin-Meadow, S., Hasson, U., Skipper, J., & Small, S. L. (2009). Co-speech gestures influence neural activity in brain regions associated with processing semantic information. *Human Brain Mapping*, *30*(11), 3509–3526. doi: 10.1002/hbm.20774.

11. Demir-Lira, Ö. E., Asaridou, S. S., Beharelle, A. R., Holt, A. E., Goldin-Meadow, S., & Small, S. L. (2018). Functional neuroanatomy of gesture-speech integration in children varies with individual differences in gesture processing. *Developmental Science*, *21*(5), e12648. doi: 10.1111/desc.12648.

12. On teachable moments, see Havighurst, R. J. (1953). *Human development and education*. New York: Longmans, Green.

13. Golinkoff, R. M. (1986). "I beg your pardon?": The preverbal negotiation of failed messages. *Journal of Child Language*, *13*, 455–476. Shwe, H. I., & Markman, E. M. (1997). Young children's appreciation of the mental impact of their communicative signals. *Developmental Psychology*, *33*, 630–636.

14. On adults reacting to others' gestures and recasting them into speech, see Beattie, G., & Shovelton, H. (1999). Mapping the range of information contained in the iconic hand gestures that accompany spontaneous speech. *Journal of Language and Social Psychology*, *18*, 438–462. Driskell, J. E., & Radtke, P. H. (2003). The effect of gesture on speech production and comprehension. *Human Factors*, *45*, 445–454. Goldin-Meadow, S., Kim, S., & Singer, M. (1999). What the teacher's hands tell the student's mind about math. *Journal of Educational Psychology*, *91*, 720–730. Goldin-Meadow, S., & Sandhofer, C. M. (1999). Gesture conveys substantive information about a child's thoughts to ordinary listeners. *Developmental Science*, *2*, 67–74. Goldin-Meadow, S., & Singer, M. A. (2003). From children's hands to adults' ears: Gesture's role in teaching and learning. *Developmental Psychology*, *39*(3), 509–520. McNeill, D., Cassell, J., & McCullough, K.-E. (1994). Communicative effects of speech-mismatched gestures. *Research on Language and Social Interaction*, *27*, 223–237. Thompson, L. A., & Massaro, D. W. (1986). Evaluation and integration of speech and pointing gestures during referential understanding. *Journal of Experimental Child Psychology*, *42*, 144–168. On mothers responding to their children's gestures and translating them into words, see Golinkoff, R. M. (1986). "I beg your pardon?": The preverbal negotiation of failed messages. *Journal of Child Language*, *13*, 455–476.

15. On mothers' responses to children's points without speech, see Goldin-Meadow, S., Goodrich, W., Sauer, E., & Iverson, J. (2007). Young children use their hands to tell their mothers what to say. *Developmental Science*, 10, 778–785.

16. Olson, J., & Masur, E. (2015). Mothers' labeling responses to infants' gestures predict vocabulary outcomes. *Journal of Child Language*, 1(6), 1–23. doi: 10.1017/S0305000914000828.

17. On mothers' responses to children's gesture + speech combinations, see Goldin-Meadow, S., Goodrich, W., Sauer, E., & Iverson, J. (2007). Young children use their hands to tell their mothers what to say. *Developmental Science*, 10, 778–785.

18. Kovacs, A. M., Tauzin, T., Teglas, E., György, G., & Csibra, G. (2014). Pointing as epistemic request: 12-month-olds point to receive new information. *Infancy*, 19(6), 534–557. doi: 10.1111/infa.12060. Begus, K., & Southgate, V. (2012). Infant pointing serves an interrogative function. *Developmental Science*, 15(5), 611–617. Lucca, K., & Wilbourn, M. P. (2016). Communicating to learn: Infants' pointing gestures result in optimal learning. *Child Development*, 89(3), 941–960.

19. On the size of a child's vocabulary on entering school predicting school success, see Anderson, R. C., & Freebody, P. (1981). Vocabulary knowledge. In J. Guthrie (ed.), *Comprehension and teaching: Research reviews* (pp. 77–117). Newark, DE: International Reading Association. On early gesture predicting later vocabulary, see Rowe, M. L., & Goldin-Meadow, S. (2009). Differences in early gesture explain SES disparities in child vocabulary size at school entry. *Science*, 323, 951–953.

20. LeBarton, E. S., Raudenbush, S., & Goldin-Meadow, S. (2015). Experimentally-induced increases in early gesture lead to increases in spoken vocabulary. *Journal of Cognition and Development*, 16(2), 199–220. doi 10.1080/15248372.2013.858041.

21. Goodwyn, S., Acredolo, L., & Brown, C. (2000). Impact of symbolic gesturing on early language development. *Journal of Nonverbal Behavior*, 24(2), 81–103. doi: 10.1023/A:1006653828895. Acredolo, L., & Goodwyn, S. (2002). *Baby signs: How to talk with your baby before your baby can talk*. New York: McGraw-Hill.

22. Johnston, J. C., Durieux-Smith, A., & Bloom, K. (2005). Teaching gestural signs to infants to advance child development: A review of the evidence. *First Language*, 25(2), 235–251. doi: 10.1177/0142723705050340. Kirk, E., Howlett, N., Pine, K. J., &

Fletcher, B. (2013). To sign or not to sign? The impact of encouraging infants to gesture on infant language and maternal mind-mindedness. *Child Development, 84*, 574–590. doi: 10.1111/j.1467-8624.2012.01874.x.

23. On teaching learners gesture to help them get more out of a lesson, see Carrazza, C., Wakefield, E. M., Hemani-Lopez, N., Plath, K., & Goldin-Meadow, S. (2021). Children integrate speech and gesture across a wider temporal window than speech and action: A case for why gesture helps learning. *Cognition, 210*, 104604. doi: 10.1016/j. cognition.2021.104604. Cook, S. W., Mitchell, Z., & Goldin-Meadow, S. (2008). Gesturing makes learning last. *Cognition, 106*, 1047–1058. Goldin-Meadow, S., Cook, S. W., & Mitchell, Z. A. (2009). Gesturing gives children new ideas about math. *Psychological Science, 20*(3), 267–272. Novack, M. A., Congdon, E. L., Hemani-Lopez, N., & Goldin-Meadow, S. (2014). From action to abstraction: Using the hands to learn math. *Psychological Science, 25*(4), 903–910. doi: 10.1177/0956797613518351. Cook, S. W., Yip, T. K-Y., & Goldin-Meadow, S. (2010). Gesturing makes memories that last. *Journal of Memory and Language, 63*(4), 465–475.

24. Broaders, S., Cook, S. W., Mitchell, Z., & Goldin-Meadow, S. (2007). Making children gesture brings out implicit knowledge and leads to learning. *Journal of Experimental Psychology: General, 136*(4), 539–550.

25. On telling children to gesture any way they want and its positive effect on learning an abstract concept, see Beaudoin-Ryan, L., & Goldin-Meadow, S. (2014). Teaching moral reasoning through gesture. *Developmental Science, 17*(6), 984–990. doi: 10.1111/desc.12180. On explanations helping children learn, see Chi, M. T. H., Bassok, M., Lewis, M. W., Reimann, P., & Glaser, R. (1989). Self-explanations: How students study and use examples in learning to solve problems. *Cognitive Science, 13*, 145–182.

26. Iverson, J. M., Capirci, O., Longobardi, E., & Caselli, M. C. (1999). Gesturing in mother-child interactions. *Cognitive Development, 14*, 57–75. Namy, L. L., Acredolo, L., & Goodwyn, S. (2000). Verbal labels and gestural routines in parental communication with young children. *Journal of Nonverbal Behavior, 24*, 63–79. doi: 10.1023/A:1006601812056. Özçalışkan, Ş., & Dimitrova, N. (2013). How gesture input provides a helping hand to language development. *Seminars in Speech and Language, 34*(4), 227–236. doi: 10.1055/s-0033–1353447. Rowe, M. L., &

Goldin-Meadow, S. (2009). Differences in early gesture explain SES disparities in child vocabulary size at school entry. *Science, 323,* 951–953. Salomo, D., & Liszkowski, U. (2013). Sociocultural settings influence the emergence of prelinguistic deictic gestures. *Child Development, 84*(4), 1296–1307.

27. Cartmill, E. A., Armstrong, B. F., III, Gleitman, L. R., Goldin-Meadow, S., Medina, T. N., & Trueswell, J. C. (2013). Quality of early parent input predicts child vocabulary 3 years later. *Proceedings of the National Academy of Sciences of the United States of America, 110*(28), 11278–11283. doi: 10.1073/pnas.1309518110.

28. On using gesture to create joint attention and its impact on language learning, see Yu, C., & Smith, L. B. (2013). Joint attention without gaze following: Human infants and their parents coordinate visual attention to objects through eye-hand coordination. *PLOS ONE 8*(11), e79659. doi: 10.1371/journal.pone.0079659. Tomasello, M., & Farrar, M. (1986). Joint attention and early language. *Child Development, 57,* 1454–1463. Tomasello, M., & Todd, J. (1983). Joint attention and lexical acquisition style. *First Language, 4*(12), 197–211. doi: 10.1177/014272378300401202.

29. On learning words more deeply when the words are presented with gesture, see Capone, N. C., & McGregor, K. K. (2005). The effect of semantic representation on toddlers' word retrieval. *Journal of Speech, Language, and Hearing Research, 48*(6), 1468–1480. doi: 10.1044/1092–4388(2005/102).

30. Mumford, K. H., & Kita, S. (2014). Children use gesture to interpret novel verb meanings. *Child Development, 85*(3), 1181–1189. doi: 10.1111/cdev.12188.

31. Rowe, M. L., & Leech, K. A. (2018). A parent intervention with a growth mindset approach improves children's early gesture and vocabulary development. *Developmental Science, 22*(4), e12792. doi: 10.1111/desc.12792.

Chapter 7: Using Hands to Diagnose and Treat

1. Sauer, E., Levine, S. C., & Goldin-Meadow, S. (2010). Early gesture predicts language delay in children with pre- and perinatal brain lesions. *Child Development, 81,* 528–539.

2. On case studies of children with brain injury and gesture, see Dall'Oglio, A. M., Bates, E., Volterra, V., Di Capua, M., & Pezzini, G.

(1994). Early cognition, communication and language in children with focal brain injury. *Developmental Medicine and Child Neurology, 36,* 1076–1098. On children with brain injury displaying plasticity that adults don't, see Bates, E., & Dick, F. (2002). Language, gesture, and the developing brain. *Developmental Psychobiology, 40,* 293–310. Feldman, H. M. (2005). Language learning with an injured brain. *Language Learning and Development, 1*(3–4), 265–288. Levine, S. C., Kraus, R., Alexander, E., Suriyakham, L., & Huttenlocher, P. (2005). IQ decline following early unilateral brain injury: A longitudinal study. *Brain and Cognition, 59,* 114–123. Reilly, J., Levine, S. C., Nass, R., & Stiles, J. (2008). Brain plasticity: Evidence from children with prenatal brain injury. In J. Reed & J. Warner (eds.), *Child neuropsychology* (pp. 58–91). Oxford, UK: Blackwell. Stiles, J., Reilly, J., Paul, B., & Moses, P. (2005). Cognitive development following early brain injury: Evidence for neural adaptation. *Trends in Cognitive Sciences, 9*(3), 136–143.

3. On gesture as an indicator for autism, see American Psychiatric Association. (2000). *Diagnostic and statistical manual of mental disorders, 4th edition, text revision.* Washington, DC: American Psychiatric Association. Asperger, H. (1944/1991). "Autistic psychopathy" in childhood. In U. Frith (ed.), *Autism and Asperger syndrome* (pp. 37–92). Cambridge: Cambridge University Press (originally published as Die "autistichen psychopathen" im kindesalter. *Archive für Psychiatrie und Nervenkrankheiten, 117,* 76–136). Wing, L. (1981). Language, social, and cognitive impairments in autism and severe mental retardation. *Journal of Autism and Developmental Disorders, 11,* 31–44. On late diagnosis of autism, see Mandell, D., Novak, M. M., & Zubritsky, C. D. (2005). Factors associated with age of diagnosis among children with autism spectrum disorders. *Pediatrics, 116,* 1480–1486. On the Autism Diagnostic Observation Schedule as the gold standard for evaluating autism, see Lord, C., Risi, S., Lambrecht, L., Cook, E. H., Jr., Leventhal, B. L., DiLavore, P. C., Pickles, A., & Rutter, M. (2000). The Autism Diagnostic Observation Schedule—Generic: A standard measure of social and communication deficits associated with the spectrum of autism. *Journal of Autism and Developmental Disorders, 30,* 205–223. On failure to point by 12 months as a red flag for autism, see Filipek, P., Accardo, P., Ashwal, S., Baranek, G., Cook, E., Dawson, G., Gordon, B., Gravel, J., Johnson, C., Kallen, R., Levy, S., Minshew, N., Ozonoff, S., Prizant, B., Rapin, I., Rogers, S., Stone, W., Teplin, S., Tuchman, R., & Volkmar, F. (2000). Practice parameter: Screening and diagnosis of autism. *Neurology, 55,* 468–479.

4. Osterling, J., & Dawson, G. (1994). Early recognition of children with autism: A study of first birthday home videotapes. *Journal of Autism and Developmental Disorders*, 24, 247–257. Crais, E. R., Watson, L. R., Baranek, G. T., & Reznick, J. S. (2006). Early identification of autism: How early can we go? *Seminars in Speech and Language*, 27, 143–160. Colgan, S. E., Lanter, E., McComish, C., Watson, L. R., Crais, E. R., & Baranek, G. T. (2006). Analysis of social interaction gestures in infants with autism. *Child Neuropsychology*, 12, 307–319. Clifford, S. M., & Dissanayake, C. (2008). The early development of joint attention in infants with autistic disorder using home video observations and parental interview. *Journal of Autism and Developmental Disorders*, 38(5), 791–805. Buitelaar, J. K., van Engeland, H., de Kogel, K. H., de Vries, H., & van Hooff, J. A. R. A. M. (1991). Differences in the structure of social behavior of autistic children and non-autistic controls. *Journal of Child Psychology and Psychiatry*, 32(6), 995–1015. Wetherby, A. Yonclas, D. G., & Bryan, A. A. (1989). Communicative profiles of preschool children with handicaps: Implications for early identification. *Journal of Speech and Hearing Disorders*, 54, 148–158.

5. On younger siblings of children with autism being very likely to be diagnosed as autistic, see Iverson, J. M., Poulos-Hopkins, S., Winder, B., & Wozniak, R. H. (May 2008). Gestures and words in the early communication of infant siblings of children with autism. Poster presented at the International Meeting for Autism Research, London, United Kingdom. On gesture being more informative about diagnosis of autism than words, see Iverson, J. M., Poulos-Hopkins, S., Winder, B., & Wozniak, R. H. (May 2008). Gestures and words in the early communication of infant siblings of children with autism. Poster presented at the International Meeting for Autism Research, London, United Kingdom. Parlade, M. V., & Iverson, J. M. (2015). The development of coordinated communication in infants at heightened risk for autism spectrum disorder. *Journal of Autism and Developmental Disorders*, 45, 2218–2234.

6. On spontaneous communication not showing a gesture advantage for children with Down syndrome, see Chan, J., & Iacono, T. (2001). Gesture and word production in children with Down syndrome. *AAC: Alternative and Augmentative Communication*, 17, 73–87. Iverson, J. M., Longobardi, E., & Caselli, M. C. (2003). Relationship between gestures and words in children with Down's syndrome and typically developing children in the early stages of communicative development.

International Journal of Language & Communication Disorders, 38, 179–197. On lab studies showing a gesture advantage for children with Down syndrome, see Caselli, M. C., Vicari, S., Longobardi, E., Lami, L., Pizzoli, C., & Stella, G. (1998). Gestures and words in early development of children with Down syndrome. *Journal of Speech, Language, and Hearing Research*, 41, 1125–1135. Singer Harris, N., Bellugi, U., Bates, E., Jones, W., & Rossen, M. (1997). Contrasting profiles of language development in children with Williams and Down syndromes. *Developmental Neuropsychology*, 13, 345–370. Stefanini, S., Caselli, M. C., & Volterra, V. (2007). Spoken and gestural production in a naming task by young children with Down syndrome. *Brain and Language*, 101, 208–221.

7. On children with Williams syndrome having poor visuo-spatial processing skills but relatively intact facial recognition and some deficiencies in language, see Bellugi, U., Lichtenberger, L., Jones, W., Lai, Z., & St. George, M. (2000). The neurocognitive profile of Williams syndrome: A complex pattern of strengths and weaknesses. *Journal of Cognitive Neuroscience*, 12, 7–30. Karmiloff-Smith, A., Grant, J., Berthoud, I., Davies, M., Howlin, P., & Udwin, O. (1997). Language and Williams syndrome: How intact is "intact"? *Child Development*, 68, 274–290. Rossen, M., Klima, E., Bellugi, U., Bihrle, A., & Jones, W. (1997). Interaction between language and cognition: Evidence from Williams syndrome. In J. H. Beitchman, N. Cohen, M. Konstantareas, & R. Tannock (eds.), *Language, learning and behaviour disorders: Developmental, biological and clinical prospectives* (pp. 367–392). New York: Cambridge University Press. Vicari, S., Carlesimo, G., Brizzolara, D., & Pezzini, G. (1996). Short-term memory in children with Williams syndrome: A reduced contribution of lexical-semantic knowledge to word span. *Neuropsychologia*, 34, 919–925. Stevens, T., & Karmiloff-Smith, A. (1997). Word learning in a special population: Do individuals with Williams syndrome obey lexical constraints? *Journal of Child Language*, 24, 737–765. On children with Williams syndrome using gesture differently from typically developing children on a naming task, see Bello, A., Capirci, O., & Volterra, V. (2004). Lexical production in children with Williams syndrome: Spontaneous use of gesture in a naming task. *Neuropsychologia*, 42, 201–213.

8. On children with specific language impairment having no identifiable intellectual impairments yet not acquiring age-appropriate

language skill, see Leonard, L. B. (1998). *Children with Specific Language Impairment*. Cambridge, MA: MIT Press. On children with specific language impairment compensating for their language deficiencies with gesture, see Evans, J. L., Alibali, M. W., & McNeil, N. M. (2001). Divergence of embodied knowledge and verbal expression: Evidence from gesture and speech in children with specific language impairment. *Language and Cognitive Processes*, 16, 309–331. Kirk, E., Pine, K. J., & Ryder, N. (2010). I hear what you say but I see what you mean: The role of gestures in children's pragmatic comprehension. *Language and Cognitive Processes*, 26(2), 149–170. doi: 10.1080/01690961003752348. Mainela Arnold, E., Evans, J. L., & Alibali, M. W. (2006). Understanding conservation delays in children with specific language impairment: Task representations revealed in speech and gesture. *Journal of Speech, Language, and Hearing Research*, 49, 1267–1279. Iverson, J. M., & Braddock, B. A. (2011). Gesture and motor skill in relation to language in children with language impairment. *Journal of Speech, Language, and Hearing Research*, 54(1), 72–86. doi: 10.1044/1092-4388(2010/08-0197).

9. On late talkers and gesture, see Klee, T., Pearce, K., & Carson, D. K. (2000). Improving the positive predictive value of screening for developmental language disorder. *Journal of Speech, Language, and Hearing Research*, 43, 821–833. Rescorla, L. A. (1989). The Language Development Survey: A screening tool for delayed language in toddlers. *Journal of Speech and Hearing Disorders*, 54, 587–599. Thal, D. J., & Tobias, S. (1992). Communicative gestures in children with delayed onset of oral expressive vocabulary. *Journal of Speech and Hearing Research*, 35, 1281–1289. Thal, D., Tobias, S., & Morrison, D. (1991). Language and gesture in late talkers: A 1-year follow-up. *Journal of Speech and Hearing Research*, 34, 604–612.

10. Dimitrova, N., Özçalışkan, Ş., & Adamson, L. B. (2016). Parents' translations of child gesture facilitate word learning in children with autism, Down syndrome and typical development. *Journal of Autism and Developmental Disorders*, 46(1), 221–231. doi: 10.1007/s10803-015-2566-7. Lorang, W., Sterling, A., & Schroeder, B. (2018). Maternal responsiveness to gesture in children with Down syndrome. *American Journal of Speech Language Pathology*, 27(3), 1018–1029. doi: 10.1044/2018_AJSLP-17-0138. Leezenbaum, N. B., Campbell, S. B., Butler, D., & Iverson, J. M. (2014). Maternal verbal responses to

communication of infants at low and heightened risk of autism. *Autism*, *18*(6), 694–703. doi: 10.1177/1362361313491327.

11. Linn, K., Cifuentes, F. S. V., Eugenin, M. I., Rio, B., Cerda, J., & Lizama, M. (2019). Development of communicative abilities in infants with Down syndrome after systematized training in gestural communication. *Revista Chilena de Pediatria*, *90*(2):175–185. doi: 10.32641/ rchped.v90i2.670. Özçalışkan, S., Adamson, L. B., Dimitrova, N., Bailey, J., & Schmuck, L. (2016). Baby sign but not spontaneous gesture predicts later vocabulary in children with Down syndrome. *Journal of Child Language*, *43*(4), 948–963. doi: 10.1017/S030500091500029X.

12. Özçalışkan, Ş., Adamson, L. B., Dimitrova, N., & Baumann, S. (2018). Do parents model gestures differently when children's gestures differ? *Journal of Autism and Developmental Disorders*, *48*, 1492–1507. doi: 10.1007/s10803-017-3411-y.

13. Iverson, J. M., Longobardi, E., Spampinato, K., & Caselli, M. C. (2006). Gesture and speech in maternal input to children with Down's syndrome. *International Journal of Language & Communication Disorders*, *41*(3), 235–251. doi: 10.1080/13682820500312151.

14. On simulating interviews in the lab, see Broaders, S., & Goldin-Meadow, S. (2010). Truth is at hand: How gesture adds information during investigative interviews. *Psychological Science*, *21*(5), 623–628.

15. On misleading verbal information having continuous effects on children's testimony, see Fivush, R., Hamond, N. R., Harsch, N., & Singer, N. (1991). Content and consistency in young children's autobiographical recall. *Discourse Processes*, *14*, 373–388. Loftus, E. F. (2003). Our changeable memories: Legal and practical implications. *Nature Reviews Neuroscience*, *4*, 231–234.

16. On an interviewer's preconceptions making their way into the interview, see Ceci, S. J., Hembrooke, H., & Bruck, M. (1997). Children's reports of personal events. In D. Cicchetti & S. L. Toth (eds.), *Developmental perspectives on trauma: Theory, research, and intervention* (pp. 515–534). Rochester Symposium on Developmental Psychopathology 8. Rochester, NY: University of Rochester Press.

17. Philippot, P., Feldman, R., & Coats, E. (2003). The role of nonverbal behavior in clinical settings (pp. 3–13). In Pierre Philippot, Robert S. Feldman, Erik J. Coats, *Nonverbal behavior in clinical settings* (pp. 3–13). New York: Oxford University Press. Foley, G. N., & Gentile, J. P. (2010). Nonverbal communication in psychotherapy. *Psychiatry*, *7*(6), 38–44.

Chapter 8: Using Hands to Educate

1. Crowder, E. M. (1996). Gestures at work in sense-making science talk. *Journal of the Learning Sciences*, 5, 173–208, p. 196.

2. Crowder, E. M., & Newman, D. (1993). Telling what they know: The role of gesture and language in children's science explanations. *Pragmatics and Cognition*, 1, 341–376, p. 370.

3. Kelly, S. D., Singer, M., Hicks, J., & Goldin-Meadow, S. (2002). A helping hand in assessing children's knowledge: Instructing adults to attend to gesture. *Cognition and Instruction*, 20, 1–26.

4. Singer, M., Radinsky, J., & Goldman, S. R. (2008). The role of gesture in meaning construction. *Discourse Processes*, 45(4), 365–386, pp. 366–367, p. 377.

5. Goldin-Meadow, S., & Singer, M. A. (2003). From children's hands to adults' ears: Gesture's role in the learning process. *Developmental Psychology*, 39(3), 509–520, p. 516.

6. Cook, S. W., & Goldin-Meadow, S. (2006). The role of gesture in learning: Do children use their hands to change their minds? *Journal of Cognition and Development*, 7, 211–232.

7. On encouraging mathematics teachers to present ideas through a variety of representations, see National Council of Teachers of Mathematics (NCTM). (1989). *Curriculum and evaluation standards for school mathematics*. Reston, VA: NCTM. Shavelson, R. J., Webb, N. M., Stasz, C., & McArthur, D. (1988). Teaching mathematical problem solving: Insights from teachers and tutors. In R. I. Charles & E. A. Silver (eds.), *The teaching and assessing of mathematical problem solving* (pp. 203–231). Reston, VA: NCTM. On teachers in nonmath classrooms using gesture to augment their speech, see Neill, S., & Caswell, C. (1993). *Body language for competent teachers*. London: Routledge., p. 113.

8. On the effectiveness of visual information when it's timed with spoken information, see Baggett, P. (1984). Role of temporal overlap of visual and auditory material in forming dual media associations. *Journal of Educational Psychology*, 76, 408–417. Mayer, R. E., & Anderson, R. B. (1991). Animations need narrations: An experimental test of a dual-coding hypothesis. *Journal of Educational Psychology*, 83, 484–490.

9. Goldin-Meadow, S., Kim, S., & Singer, M. (1999). What the teacher's hands tell the student's mind about math. *Journal of Educational Psychology*, 91, 720–730.

10. On gesture being used in talk about a variety of topics taught in schools, see Graham, T. A. (1999). The role of gesture in children's learning to count. *Journal of Experimental Child Psychology, 74,* 333–355. Alibali, M. W., & Goldin-Meadow, S. (1993). Gesture-speech mismatch and mechanisms of learning: What the hands reveal about a child's state of mind. *Cognitive Psychology, 25,* 468–523. Perry, M., Church, R. B., & Goldin-Meadow, S. (1988). Transitional knowledge in the acquisition of concepts. *Cognitive Development, 3,* 359–400. Stone, A., Webb, R., & Mahootian, S. (1992). The generality of gesture-speech mismatch as an index of transitional knowledge: Evidence from a control-of-variables task. *Cognitive Development, 6,* 301–313. Perry, M., & Elder, A. D. (1997). Knowledge in transition: Adults' developing understanding of a principle of physical causality. *Cognitive Development, 12,* 131–157. Alibali, M. W., Bassok, M., Solomon, K. O., Syc, S. E., & Goldin-Meadow, S. (1999). Illuminating mental representations through speech and gesture. *Psychological Sciences, 10,* 327–333. On gesture grounding speech in the world of objects and actions, see Glenberg, A. M., & Robertson, D. A. (2000). Symbol grounding and meaning: A comparison of high-dimensional and embodied theories of meaning. *Journal of Memory and Language, 43,* 379–401. On gesture being used in classrooms, see Crowder, E. M., & Newman, D. (1993). Telling what they know: The role of gesture and language in children's science explanations. *Pragmatics and Cognition, 1,* 341–376. Flevares, L. M., & Perry, M. (2001). How many do you see? The use of nonspoken representations in first-grade mathematics lessons. *Journal of Educational Psychology, 93,* 330–345. Neill, S. (1991). *Classroom nonverbal communication.* London: Routledge. Roth, W.-M., & Welzel, M. (2001). From activity to gestures and scientific language. *Journal of Research in Science Teaching, 38,* 103–136. Zukow-Goldring, P., Romo, L., & Duncan, K. R. (1994). Gestures speak louder than words: Achieving consensus in Latino classrooms. In A. Alvarez & P. del Rio (eds.), *Education as cultural construction: Exploration in socio-cultural studies,* Vol. 4 (pp. 227–239). Madrid: Fundacio Infancia y Aprendizage. On experienced teachers being likely to use gesture, see Neill, S., & Caswell, C. (1993). *Body language for competent teachers.* London: Routledge.

11. Flevares, L. M., & Perry, M. (2001). How many do you see? The use of nonspoken representations in first-grade mathematics lessons. *Journal of Educational Psychology, 93,* 330–345, p. 340.

12. Goldin-Meadow, S., & Singer, M. A. (2003). From children's hands to adults' ears: Gesture's role in the learning process. *Developmental Psychology, 39*(3), 509–520, p. 517.

13. On the Trends in International Mathematics and Science Study, see Hiebert, J., Gallimore, R., Garnier, H., Givvin, K. B., Hollingsworth, H., Jacobs, J., Chui, A. M.-Y., Wearne, D., Smith, M., Kersting, N., Manaster, A., Tseng, E., Etterbeek, W., Manaster, C., Gonzales, P., & Stigler, J. (2003). Teaching mathematics in seven countries: Results from the TIMSS 1999 Video Study (NCES 2003-013). Washington, DC: US Department of Education, NCES. On teachers in the United States not using gesture as effectively as teachers in Hong Kong and Japan, see Richland, L. E., Zur, O., & Holyoak, K. (2007). Cognitive supports for analogies in the mathematics classroom. *Science, 316,* 1128–1129.

14. On helping children from disadvantaged homes with gesture, see Tank, S., Pantelic, J., Sansone, J., Yun, Y. E., Alonzo, Y., Koumoutsakis, T., & Church, R. B. (March 2019). The effect of gesture on math learning in conjunction with effects of parental education level on math learning. Poster presented as part of the 2019 Biennial Meeting Society for Research in Child Development (SRCD) Conference, Baltimore, Maryland.

Chapter 9: What If Gesture
Were Considered as Important as Language?

1. Gentner, D., Özyürek, A., Gurcanli, O., & Goldin-Meadow, S. (2013). Spatial language facilitates spatial cognition: Evidence from children who lack language input. *Cognition, 127*(3), 318–330.

2. Loewenstein, J., & Gentner, D. (2005). Relational language and the development of relational mapping. *Cognitive Psychology, 50,* 315–353.

3. Broaders, S., Cook, S. W., Mitchell, Z., & Goldin-Meadow, S. (2007). Making children gesture brings out implicit knowledge and leads to learning. *Journal of Experimental Psychology: General, 136*(4), 539–550. Beaudoin-Ryan, L., & Goldin-Meadow, S. (2014). Teaching moral reasoning through gesture. *Developmental Science, 17*(6), 984–990. doi: 10.1111/desc.12180.

4. On legal interactions structured through talk, see Philips, S. U. (1985). Interaction structured through talk and interaction structured through "silence." In D. Tannen & M. Saville-Troike (eds.), *Perspectives*

on silence (pp. 205–213). Norwood, NJ: Ablex Publishing Corporation, p. 206.

5. On interviewers and leading questions, see Ceci, S. J. (1995). False beliefs: Some developmental and clinical considerations. In D. L. Schacter (ed.), *Memory distortion: How minds, brains, and societies reconstruct the past* (pp. 91–125). Cambridge, MA: Harvard University Press.

6. On listeners relying on cues from the lips and the hands to process language, see Skipper, J. I., Nusbaum, H. C., & Small, S. L. (2005). Listening to talking faces: Motor cortical activation during speech perception. *Neuroimage*, *25*(1), 76–89. doi: 10.1016/j.neuroimage.2004.11.006. Skipper, J. I., Goldin-Meadow, S., Nusbaum, H., & Small, S. (2009). Gestures orchestrate brain networks for language understanding. *Current Biology*, *19*(8), 661–667. doi: 10.1016/j.cub.2009.02.051. On using all cues available to deaf children, see Friedner, M. (2021). *Sensory futures: Deafness and cochlear implant infrastructures in India*. Minneapolis: University of Minnesota Press.

7. On gesture leveling the playing field for children from disadvantaged homes, see Tank, S., Pantelic, J., Sansone, J., Yun, Y. E., Alonzo, Y., Sansone, J., Pantelic, J., Koumoutsakis, T., & Church, R. B. (March 2019). The effect of gesture on math learning in conjunction with effects of parental education level on math learning. Poster presented as part of the 2019 Biennial Meeting Society for Research in Child Development (SRCD) Conference, Baltimore, Maryland. On Khan Academy, and online learning platform, see "Khan Academy," Wikipedia, https://en.wikipedia.org/wiki/Khan_Academy.

INDEX

Rob Kozloff

SUSAN GOLDIN-MEADOW is the Beardsley Ruml Distinguished Service Professor in the department of psychology, the department of comparative human development, and the committee on education at the University of Chicago. She has made pioneering contributions to the study of how language is created and learned, and how the gestures that go along with speech facilitate learning and communication. Goldin-Meadow is a member of the National Academy of Sciences, the American Academy of Arts and Sciences, and the American Association for the Advancement of Science. She's received a Guggenheim Fellowship, a James McKeen Cattell Fund Fellowship, and the David E. Rumelhart Prize. She lives in Chicago with her charming dog, Latke.